O9-BTZ-016

RANDALL J. LUND

Linguistics for Non-Linguists

LINGUISTICS
FOR NON-LINGUISTS

Frank Parker, Ph.D.

Department of English
Louisiana State University

Austin, Texas

© 1986 by PRO-ED, Inc.

All rights reserved. No part of this book may be reproduced in any form or by any means without the prior written permission of the publisher.

Printed in the United States of America

Library of Congress Cataloging in Publication Data
Main entry under:

Parker, Frank, 1946–
    Linguistics for non-linguists.

    Includes bibliographies and index.
    1. Linguistics   I. Title.
P121.P334   1986   410   90-52767

ISBN 0-89079-275-5

8700 Shoal Creek Boulevard
Austin, Texas 78758

1 2 3 4 5 6 7 8 9 10   95 94 93 92 91 90

CONTENTS

ACKNOWLEDGMENTS

I am indebted to Dan Foster, Jane Koenecke, Sarah Liggett, Alan Manning, Chuck Meyer, Tony O'Keeffe, and Jo Powell for reading and commenting on parts of this book. Most of all, however, I want to express my appreciation to Tom Walsh and Kathryn Riley, who have given me their insights on virtually every page. I also owe a debt of gratitude to the hundreds of students I have taught at Purdue University, the University of British Columbia, and Louisiana State University over the past ten years, for showing me exactly where I have failed to make linguistics clear for them.

Chapter 1

Introduction

The title of this book, *Linguistics for Non-Linguists*, delimits both its scope and audience. Let me say something about each one. The primary audience for which this book is intended are people who are not linguists, but who feel they need some familiarity with the fundamentals of linguistic theory in order to help them practice their profession.This includes specialists in such fields as speech-language pathology, experimental phonetics, communication, education, English as a second language (ESL), composition, reading, anthropology, folklore, foreign languages, and literature. The common thread among these disciplines is that, in one form or another and at one time or another, they all deal with language. For example, a researcher in business communication might try to characterize how different managerial styles are reflected in the way that managers give directions to their employees, noting that some managers give instructions like *Type this memo* while others say *Could you type this memo?* A kindergarten teacher might observe that students give more correct responses to questions like *Which of these girls is taller?* than to questions like *Which of these girls is shorter?* A composition instructor might encounter a student who writes *I wanted to know what could I do* rather than *I wanted to know what I could do.* An ESL teacher might have a student who writes *I will taking physics next semester*, rather than *I will take* or *I will be taking physics next semester.* A speech-language pathologist might attempt to evaluate a child who says *tay* for *stay*, but never *say* for *stay*. In each case, these specialists have encountered phenomena that cannot be thoroughly understood without some familiarity with concepts and principles from linguistic theory.

Realistically speaking, however, there are several practical reasons that may have prevented these specialists from acquiring a background in basic linguistic theory. First, courses in linguistics are relatively rare in colleges and universities, and are virtually nonexistent in high schools. Even universities that have such courses generally do not require them of all students. Second, each university curriculum (especially a professional curriculum) quite naturally tends to focus its students' attention on the central concerns of its discipline. Of course, the more courses required of students within their discipline, the fewer they can take from fields outside of their major. Such factors often prevent students in allied areas from being exposed to linguistics. Third, once people complete their formal education, it is often difficult, if not impossible, for them to supplement their knowledge with formal coursework, especially in an unfamiliar area. Finally, linguistics, at least at first glance, appears to be incredibly complicated. Articles and books on the subject are often filled with charts, tables, diagrams, and notation that seem to be uninterpretable, and many people react by running in the opposite direction. In short, there are a number of practical reasons for this gap in the flow of information between linguistics and other fields that deal with language. This book is an attempt to solve this problem, at least in part. It is specifically designed to convey a basic understanding of linguistic theory to specialists in neighboring fields, whether students or practicing professionals.

As for its scope, this book is essentially a primer in linguistics: a short work covering the basic elements of the subject. As such, it is not meant to substitute for an exhaustive linguistics text or for an introductory course in linguistics. Rather, this book is best viewed as a sort of "pre-text"—a work that might be read before taking up a more comprehensive text or before taking a basic course in linguistics. Alternatively, it might be used as supplementary reading in an introductory course.

The book is organized as follows. Chapters 2 through 6 cover the theoretical areas of pragmatics, semantics, syntax, morphology, and phonology, respectively. Chapters 7 through 9 cover the applied areas of language variation, language acquisition, and the neurology of language. Each chapter is divided into four parts: text, exercises, answers to the exercises, and supplementary readings. The text of each chapter focuses on a handful of the basic ideas in that area of linguistics; I have not tried to cover each subject in breadth or in detail. Also, I have made an effort to make explicit the reasoning that lies behind each area discussed. Each chapter begins with a set of observations that can be made about that subject, and the rest of the chapter constructs a partial theory to account for the original observations. Throughout the text, I have tried to emphasize the fact that linguistic theory is a set of categories, rules, and principles devised by linguists in order to explain observations about language. (More on this subject later.)

The exercises and answers at the end of each chapter are included as a means for you to check your understanding of the discussion in the text. Consequently, the questions are in most cases discrete rather than open-ended. That is, each question has a specific answer or range of answers within the framework of the chapter (for example, "Would a child exposed to English be more likely to acquire the meaning of *long* or *short* first? What principle accounts for this?"). The supplementary readings at the end of each chapter consist of an annotated list of several articles and books that I have found useful in introducing others to the field. I have made no attempt to cover each field exhaustively or to restrict the readings to the latest findings, since each of the eight areas covered here has numerous textbooks and primary works devoted to it. However, anyone interested in pursuing one of these areas can at least begin by consulting the supplementary readings at the end of that chapter.

Obviously, an introductory book such as this has several potential limitations. First, there are entire subdomains of linguistics that are not included—language change, writing systems, animal communication, and psycholinguistics, to name just a few. My reason for omitting these areas is that my primary purpose is to focus on the central concepts of linguistic theory in the simplest and most straightforward way possible. The experience of having taught linguistics for 10 years convinces me that students and professionals from neighboring fields are most often in need of a solid grounding in the core areas of pragmatics, semantics, syntax, morphology, and phonology. Once they have a basic understanding of these areas, they have little trouble in mastering the applied areas that overlap with their own field of specialization. I have included chapters on language variation, language acquisition, and the neurology of language, three applied areas which seem to me to be of the most importance to the greatest number of neighboring fields.

Second, this book is limited by my own understanding and interpretation of the field of linguistics. This is a factor that should not be underestimated. No one can study an academic field without incorporating some of his or her own prejudices into a view of that field, and certainly I am no exception. For example, my own views of the field of linguistics are biased toward the work of Noam Chomsky, who is undoubtedly the most influential linguist alive today. Consequently, most of this book is written from the perspective of **generative grammar**, a view of language which Chomsky began developing 30 years ago. (Some of the properties of this theory are discussed in detail in Chapter 10.) In short, it is wise to keep these limitations in mind as you read this book. It represents neither all there is to know about linguistics nor the only way of looking at the field.

Having discussed the audience and scope of this book, let's now turn to its primary subject matter—linguistic theory. There are two questions central to an understanding of this field. First, what do linguists study? And second, how do they go about studying it? Let's take these questions one at a time. First, one common understanding of linguistic theory is that it is the study of the psychological system of unconscious knowledge that underlies our ability to produce and interpret utterances in our native language. It is not the study of how human beings actually produce speech with their vocal mechanism, nor is it the study of speech itself. Thus, we need to distinguish three different domains: (1) the psychological system of language; (2) the means of implementing this system (the vocal tract); and (3) the product (speech).

An analogy may help clarify the distinction among these three areas. In talking about computers, specialists differentiate at least three domains: software, hardware, and output. The software (or program) is essentially the mind of the machine; it is the set of instructions that tells the machine what to do. The hardware is the machine itself; it is the physical mechanism that carries out the instructions contained in the software. The output is the final product that comes out of the hardware; it is the tangible result of the software having told the hardware what to do. Thus, in a very loose sense the psychological system of language is like the software; it is essentially the mind of the system; it provides the instructions. The vocal mechanism is like the hardware; it is the physical system that implements the language. Speech is like the output; it is the final product of the vocal tract, the tangible result of the language faculty having told the vocal tract what to do. This analogy is illustrated in Figure 1-1. Thus, linguistic theory is the study of the psychological system of language. Consequently, the vocal tract and speech are of interest to linguists to the extent that they shed light on this psychological system: the internalized, unconscious knowledge that enables a speaker to produce and understand utterances in his or her native language.

Now that we have some idea of what theoretical linguists study, let's consider how they study it. At this point, our computer analogy breaks down. If a computer specialist wants to study the software of a particular

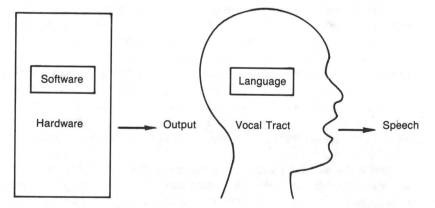

Figure 1-1. Analogy between computer system and linguistic system.

computer system, he or she can access it and examine it directly (by requesting the hardware to produce the software as output) or question the person who designed it. In other words, an understanding of how the software works is part of the conscious knowledge of the person who designed it, and consequently it is directly accessible to anyone who wants to examine it. Language, on the other hand, is not so easily accessible. First, knowledge of language is unconscious in the sense that speakers of a language cannot articulate the rules of that language. Moreover, although linguists can examine the vocal tract and the sounds it produces, they cannot examine language directly. Rather, they must approach the properties of this psychological system *indirectly*.

There are a number of methods that linguists use to infer properties of the system. Some linguists look at language change; they compare different historical stages in the development of a language and try to infer what properties of the system would account for changes. Other linguists look at language pathology; that is, they compare normal language output to that of aphasic patients (people with brain damage that has disrupted normal linguistic functioning) and try to infer what properties of the system would account for such abnormalities. Still others look at language universals—features that all human languages seem to have in common— and try to infer what properties of the system would account for these similarities. The list of approaches goes on and on.

Here, however, we will discuss in some detail another common method that theoretical linguists use to infer properties of language: investigating speakers' judgments about sentences. Under this method, the linguist asks informants (native speakers of the language under investigation) questions such as the following: Is utterance X an acceptable sentence in your language? Does utterance X have the same meaning as utterance Y? In utterance X, can word A refer to word B? And so on and so forth. Consider, for example, the following sentences.

(1)   John thinks that Bill hates him.
(2)   John thinks that Bill hates himself.

The linguist might present (1) and (2) to some informants and ask them to judge the two sentences for acceptability. In response, the informants would undoubtedly say that both (1) and (2) are perfectly acceptable. That is, both are completely unremarkable; people say such things day in and day out, and they go completely unnoticed. (In contrast, note that sentences such as *Him thinks that Bill hates John* and *John thinks that himself hates Bill* are remarkable; that is, speakers of English do not typically produce such sentences.) After having determined that both (1) and (2) are acceptable, the linguist might ask the informants the following questions. (The expected answers appear in parentheses.) In (1), can *him* refer to *John*? (Yes.) Can *him* refer to *Bill*? (No.) In (2), can *himself* refer to *John*?

(No.) Can *himself* refer to Bill? (Yes.) Do sentences (1) and (2) have the same meaning? (No.)

Having gathered these data, the linguist would then try to infer the properties of the internal linguistic system of the informants that would account for these judgments. For example, the linguist might hypothesize that English contains at least two kinds of pronouns: personal pronouns (e.g., *him*) and reflexive pronouns (e.g., *himself*). Moreover, the linguist might hypothesize that a pronoun may have an **antecedent** (i.e., a preceding word or phrase to which the pronoun refers). Finally, the linguist might infer that the antecedents of these two types of pronoun have different distributional properties; that is, the antecedent for a personal pronoun and the antecedent for a reflexive pronoun cannot occupy the same position within a sentence. In order to determine exactly what the distributional limitations are on these antecedents, the linguist might construct some related sentences (e.g., *John hates him, John hates himself*, and so on) and present them to informants for different types of judgments. This process would continue until the linguist had formed a picture of what the psychological system of the informants looks like, at least with respect to the distribution of antecedents for personal and reflexive pronouns.

There are several points to note about this method of inquiry. First, if the linguist is a native speaker of the language being studied, the linguist himself can, and often does, serve as both informant and analyst. In the previous example, any native speaker of English would be able to determine that (1) and (2) are both acceptable, but that they have entirely different meanings. Moreover, any native speaker of English would be able to trace these differences in meaning to the fact that in (1) *him* can refer to *John* but not to *Bill*, and in (2) *himself* can refer to *Bill* but not to *John*. In a clear-cut example like this, there is no need to present these sentences to thousands, hundreds, dozens, or even two speakers of English. The linguist can be reasonably certain in advance that they would all judge the sentences in the same way. Second, the linguist, in forming a picture of the internal linguistic system of the informant, is in essence constructing a **theory** of that system. That is, concepts such as personal pronoun, reflexive pronoun, antecedent, and distribution are not directly observable in the utterances themselves. Rather, the linguist *hypothesizes* such concepts to account for the observable fact that speakers of English can make such clear-cut judgments about sentences like (1) and (2). In short, the linguist uses the directly observable judgments of the informant (i.e., the data) to draw inferences about the unobservable internal system that governs such judgments (i.e., to construct a theory). This procedure can be schematized as follows.

OBSERVABLE DATA→LINGUIST————————→ THEORY

Speaker's judgments of acceptability, sameness of meaning, reference, and so forth.	Makes hypotheses about internal structure of speaker's psychological linguistic system.	English has two kinds of pronouns, whose antecedents have different distributions.

This, of course, is not a complete theory of English; it is not even a complete theory of the distribution of antecedents for personal and reflexive pronouns in English. After all, the linguist in this hypothetical example has not determined where the antecedent for each type of pronoun can occur, but simply that they cannot occur in exactly the same positions within a sentence. The point of this example has been to illustrate one central goal of linguistics: constructing a theory about the unobservable, based upon observable data. And one type of data that linguists commonly use is the judgments of informants.

Having drawn a distinction between data and theory, let's pursue our example further and try to construct a more precise theory of the distribution of antecedents for personal and reflexive pronouns. The sentences in (1) and (2) are repeated in (1a-b) and (2a-b), but here I have incorporated the judgments of our hypothetical informants. (An arrow indicates the antecedent of a pronoun, and an asterisk indicates an unacceptable sentence.)

(1a) *John* thinks that Bill hates *him*.

(1b) *John thinks that *Bill* hates *him*.

(2a) **John* thinks that Bill hates *himself*.

(2b) John thinks that *Bill* hates *himself*.

Each of these structures is to be interpreted as follows.

(1a) is acceptable, if *John* is the antecedent of *him*.
(1b) is unacceptable, if *Bill* is the antecedent of *him*.

(2a) is unacceptable, if *John* is the antecedent of *himself*.

(2b) is acceptable, if *Bill* is the antecedent of *himself*.

How can we explain these observations? That is, what principle accounts for the distribution of antecedents for personal and reflexive pronouns? There is no foolproof method for knowing where to begin. We simply have to start with an educated guess and see how accurately it accounts for our observations. We can begin by noting that each of our sample sentences is complex; that is, it contains more than one clause. In fact, each of our sample sentences has exactly two clauses. Moreover, within each sentence, the dividing line between the two clauses comes precisely between *thinks* and *that*. The sentences in (1) and (2) are repeated once more, with a vertical line separating the clauses in each sentence.

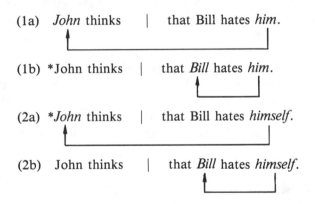

Now, if we consider just the examples in (1), it is clear that the personal pronoun *him* requires an antecedent *outside* of its clause. Note that in (1a), which is acceptable, the antecedent for *him* is in a different clause; but in (1b), which is unacceptable, the antecedent for *him* is in the same clause. Likewise, if we consider just the examples in (2), it is clear that the reflexive pronoun *himself* requires an antecedent *inside* of its clause. Note that in (2b), which is acceptable, the antecedent for *himself* is in the same clause; but in (2a), which is unacceptable, the antecedent for *himself* is in a different clause.

At this point, we might abstract away from the particular data in (1) and (2) and propose the following general theory governing the antecedents of personal and reflexive pronouns:

— The antecedent for a personal pronoun *cannot* be within the clause containing the pronoun.

— The antecedent for a reflexive pronoun *must* be within the clause containing the pronoun.

The next step would be to test our theory on additional examples containing personal and reflexive pronouns. If our theory predicts speakers' judgments about these other sentences, then it gains strength. If, on the other hand, it makes incorrect predictions, then we need to go back and revise the theory.

Let's consider a few other examples. The sentence *Mary lies to herself* is acceptable if *herself* refers to *Mary*; likewise, this sentence is unacceptable if *herself* refers to someone other than *Mary*. Both of these judgments are predicted by our theory: *herself* is a reflexive pronoun and thus must have an antecedent within the same clause, in this case *Mary*. Consider another example. The sentence *Mary lies to her* is acceptable only if *her* refers to someone other than *Mary*. Once again our theory predicts this judgment: *her* is a personal pronoun and thus cannot have an antecedent within the same clause; since *Mary* is in the same clause as *her*, it can't serve as the antecedent.

Both of these examples fit within the theory we have constructed, but what about a sentence like *John thinks that Mary hates himself*? This sentence is unacceptable regardless of whether *himself* refers to *John* or *Mary*. Our theory correctly predicts that *himself* cannot refer to *John*, since *himself* is reflexive and *John* appears in a different clause. However, our theory incorrectly predicts that *himself* should be able to refer to *Mary*, since *Mary* is in the same clause. The problem, of course, is that *himself* can refer only to words designating a male, and the word *Mary* normally designates a female. Thus, we would have to revise our rule to stipulate that pronouns and their antecedents must match in gender. This process of testing and revising the theory goes on until the theory predicts the data (in this case, speakers' judgments) exactly.

There are several points worth making about this process of theory construction. First, we have been able to account for some fairly puzzling phenomena (e.g., why can't *him* refer to *Bill* in *John thinks that Bill hates him*?) with two simple and apparently exceptionless statements concerning the distribution of antecedents for personal and reflexive pronouns. Second, in the process of devising these statements (or rules), we had to try several guesses (or hypotheses) before we hit upon one that seems to provide a reasonable explanation (or theory) of the data in (1) and (2). (In fact, the theory we ended up with is still not precise enough to predict every judgment a speaker can make about the distribution of antecedents for pronouns in English. For example, our revised theory, as it stands, cannot explain why *he* can refer to *John* in a sentence like *After he came home, John ate lunch*. Here the "antecedent" follows the pronoun, thus violating our theory.) Third, and most importantly, our theory is made up of categories (e.g., pronoun, antecedent, clause, gender) and rules (e.g., a reflexive pronoun must have an antecedent within the same clause) which are not part of the data themselves. Rather, these categories and rules are products of our own creation that enable us to account for the fact that speakers of English interpret sentences such as (1) and (2) in a specific, limited, and uniform manner. In short, this is what linguistic theory is all about: We try to form a theory of a psychological system that we cannot observe directly, by examining the superficial manifestations of this system (i.e., speakers' judgments about utterances).

This idea of trying to model what we cannot directly observe by drawing inferences from what we can observe is not restricted to linguistic theory. In 1938, the physicists Albert Einstein and Leopold Infeld wrote a book entitled *The Evolution of Physics*. In it they had this to say:

> In our endeavor to understand reality we are somewhat like a man trying to understand the mechanism of a closed watch. He sees the face and the moving hands, even hears its ticking, but he has no way of opening the case. If he is ingenious he may form some picture of a mechanism which could be responsible for all the things he observes, but he may never be quite sure his picture is the only one which could explain his observations. He will never be able to compare his picture with the real mechanism and he cannot even imagine the possibility of the meaning of such a comparison. (p. 31)

These physicists are essentially describing the same position that theoretical linguists are in: They are trying to formulate hypotheses about the structure of what they cannot observe, based upon what they can observe. In studying language, linguists cannot observe a speaker's mind. They can, however, observe the speaker's judgments about sentences. On the basis of these observable judgments, linguists can construct a theory of the unobservable psychological system that underlies these judgments. Moreover, they will never know for sure if their theory is correct; all they can do is continue to test it against an ever-expanding range of data and revise it as necessary.

To summarize, this book is intended to provide specialists in fields neighboring linguistics with a basic introduction to the principles and methods of linguistic theory. Under one common definition, linguistic theory is the study of the psychological system of language; that is, of the unconscious knowledge that lies behind our ability to produce and interpret utterances in a language. However, since this system cannot be observed directly, it must be studied indirectly. One common method is to infer properties of the system by analyzing speakers' judgments about utterances. The goal of this enterprise is to construct a theory of the psychological system of language. This theory is composed of categories, relationships, and rules, which are not part of the directly observable physical world. We will take up the topic of theories again in the final chapter.

REFERENCES

Einstein, A., and Infeld, L. (1938). *The evolution of physics*. New York: Simon and Schuster.

Chapter 2

Pragmatics

Pragmatics is the study of how language is used to communicate. Pragmatics is distinct from grammar, which is the study of the internal structure of language. (Grammar is generally divided into a number of particular areas of study: semantics, syntax, morphology, and phonology. These areas are covered in Chapters 3–6.) Keeping in mind this distinction between pragmatics (language use) and grammar (language structure), let's consider some observations that we can make about how language is used.

(1) The sentence *I apologize for stepping on your toe* can be used to constitute an act of apology. The sentence *John apologized to Mary* cannot.

(2) The sentence *I now pronounce you man and wife* can constitute an act of marriage if spoken by an appropriate authority, such as an ordained Catholic priest. The same sentence, if uttered by an eight year old child, cannot.

(3) An appropriate answer to the question *Can you tell me what time it is*? might be *7:15*; an inappropriate answer would be *Yes*.

(4) When a friend says something that you agree with, you might respond by saying *You can say that again*. But it would be inappropriate for your friend to then repeat what he or she originally said.

(5) If Jack says *Kathy's cooking dinner tonight*, and Jill replies with *Better stock up on Alka-Seltzer*, an observer might draw the conclusion that Kathy is not a good cook.

Observation (1) illustrates the fact that we can do things by uttering sentences, as well as say things. Observation (2) illustrates the fact that the nature of the participants in a verbal exchange can determine the effect of what is actually said. Observation (3) illustrates the fact that a correct answer to a question is not necessarily appropriate. Observation (4) illustrates the fact that sentences are sometimes used nonliterally.

Observation (5) illustrates the fact that sentences can imply things that are not actually stated.

All of these phenomena are essentially pragmatic in nature. That is, they have to do with the way we use language to communicate rather than the way language is structured internally. Moreover, we will assume that the phenomena in (1-5) are systematic; that is, they are governed by a system of principles. What we will now try to do is construct a set of categories and rules that will provide an explanation for these phenomena. Keep in mind that what follows is a theory (a set of hypotheses about unobservable categories and rules) designed to account for the data in (1-5) (a set of observable phenomena).

PERFORMATIVES

In 1955, the British philosopher John L. Austin delivered the William James Lectures at Harvard. (These lectures were published in 1962 as *How to Do Things with Words*.) Austin's fundamental insight was that an utterance can constitute an *act*. That is, he was the first to point out that in uttering a sentence, we can do things as well as say things. (Before Austin, philosophers held that sentences were used simply to say things.) For example, if I utter the sentence *I have five toes on my right foot*, I am simply saying something about my foot. However, uttering the sentences in (6) constitutes more than just saying something; they constitute doing something as well.

(6a)   I *promise* I'll be there on time.
(6b)   I *apologize* for the way I acted.
(6c)   I *name* this "The Good Ship Lollipop."
(6d)   I *give* and *bequeath* to John L. Jones all my earthly possessions.
(6e)   I *bet* you $100 that it'll rain before 6:00 p.m.
(6f)   I now *pronounce* you man and wife.

Note that, if said under the right circumstances, each of the sentences in (6a-f) constitutes the *performance* of an act: (6a) constitutes an act of promising; (6b) an act of apologizing; (6c) an act of naming; (6d) an act of giving; (6e) an act of betting; and (6f) an act of marrying. Consequently, the verbs in such sentences are known as **performatives**. Moreover, Austin noted that in order for a verb to be a performative, it must be *present tense* and it must have a *first person subject*. For example, consider sentences (7a-c).

(7a)   I *promise* that I won't be late.
(7b)   I *promised* that I wouldn't be late. (past tense)
(7c)   John *promises* that he won't be late. (third person subject)

Uttering (7a) constitutes performing an action (i.e., making a promise).

On the other hand, uttering (7b) or (7c) constitutes saying something: (7b) reports a past promise, and (7c) reports someone else's promise. Therefore, although (7a-c) all contain the same verb, only (7a) contains a performative.

FELICITY CONDITIONS

Austin further noted that a number of other conditions had to be met if uttering a performative is to constitute a *valid* act. These **felicity conditions** fall into three categories.

The Persons and Circumstances Must Be Appropriate. For example, an eight year old child cannot perform a valid act of marrying by saying *I now pronounce you man and wife* (even if the bride and groom are eligible to be married). Likewise, no clergyman or ship's captain can, under normal circumstances, perform a valid act of marriage between two males, two females, or two children. Similarly, an umpire at a baseball game can cause a player to be out by uttering *You're out!*; an excited fan in the bleachers, however, cannot. In all of these cases, either the persons or circumstances are inappropriate.

The Act Must Be Executed Completely and Correctly by All Participants. For example, if a policeman says to a suspect *I arrest you in the name of the law*, but fails to read the suspect his rights, then the act of arresting is not valid. Similarly, if I say *I bet you five dollars that the Tigers will win the World Series*, but you respond with *Sorry, I never gamble*, then the act of betting is not valid. Likewise, if, during a game of hide-and-go-seek, Suzy says to Billy *You're it*, and Billy responds with *I don't want to play*, then the act of naming is not valid. In all of these cases, the act is not executed either completely or correctly by all of the participants.

The Participants Must Have the Appropriate Intentions. For example, suppose that Smith and Jones are competing for the same job. Smith gets the job and Jones subsequently says *I congratulate you on your good fortune*. Jones, however, secretly hopes that Smith will develop beri-beri and be unable to perform the job. In this case, the act of congratulating is not valid. Likewise, if, after calling my neighbor every four-letter word in English, I say *I apologize for what I've said*, but I am actually delighted with my performance, then the act of apologizing is not valid. Finally, if I say to you *I promise that I'll meet you in your office at 10:00 a.m.*, but actually I plan to be on my way to Mexico at the time, then the act of promising is not valid. In all of these cases, the speaker lacks the appropriate intentions. (Note that this condition helps explain why it is so pointless for a parent to insist that a child "apologize" for something that the child is not sorry for.)

SPEECH ACTS

John Searle, one of Austin's students, wrote a doctoral dissertation in 1959 called *Sense and Reference*. (The substance of this work was published in 1969 as *Speech Acts*.) Searle developed and extended Austin's ideas by assuming that *all* utterances, not just those containing performative verbs, constitute acts. For example, consider the utterances in (8).

   (8a) I'm sorry for stepping on your toe.

   (8b) Big Bob said he was sorry for stepping on your toe.

Instead of treating (8a) as an instance of doing and (8b) as an instance of saying, Searle claims that both utterances under appropriate circumstances constitute acts: (8a) constitutes an act of apologizing and (8b) constitutes an act of stating. Thus, since under this theory every utterance of speech constitutes some sort of act, we have inherited the term **speech act**.

   Searle has expanded his theory by categorizing all speech events into different types of acts and then trying to determine the felicity (or validity) conditions on each type of speech act. Consider, for example, the act of *promising*. Searle would say that there are at least five different felicity conditions on this speech act.

   The Speaker Must Intend to Do What He Promises. For example, if I say *I promise I'll give you this book when I'm finished*, but I have no intention of doing so, then the speech act of promising is infelicitous (or invalid).

   The Speaker Must Believe (That the Hearer Believes) That the Action Is in the Hearer's Best Interest. For example, if an armed robber walks into a liquor store and says to the cashier *I promise I'll shoot you if you don't give me all of your money*, then the speech act of promising is infelicitous. In this case the robber cannot possibly believe (that the cashier believes) the shooting to be in the best interest of the cashier. Instead, this speech act might constitute a felicitous (or valid) act of threatening, a type of speech act governed by a different set of felicity conditions.

   The Speaker Must Believe That He Can Perform the Action. This implies that the action must be within the speaker's control. For example, if a sick child says to her mother, in anticipation of a weekend at the beach, *I promise I'll be well on Friday*, then the speech act of promising is infelicitous. The child has no way of controlling her physical condition on the appointed day. Instead, this speech act might constitute a felicitous act of predicting, again a type of speech act governed by a different set of felicity conditions.

   The Speaker Must Predicate a Future Action. For example, if a child comes home from school and tells his questioning mother *I promise I didn't spend my lunch money on candy*, then the speech act of promising is infelicitous. The child can't promise to do what is already done (or, in this case, not done).

The Speaker Must Predicate an Act of Himself. For example, if little Suzy, your four year old niece, says to her schoolmate *I promise my mommy will make a Halloween costume for you*, then the act of promising is infelicitous. Suzy is claiming that another person, her mother, will perform a particular action. Again, however, this might be a felicitous speech act of predicting.

In essence, then, Searle's theory states that everything we say constitutes some sort of speech act (promising, stating, apologizing, threatening, predicting, and so on). Furthermore, each type of speech act is governed by a set of felicity conditions which must be met if the speech act is to be valid. Finally, knowledge of these different speech acts and their felicity conditions constitutes part of our knowledge of the rules of language use.

LOCUTIONARY, ILLOCUTIONARY, AND PERLOCUTIONARY ACTS

In addition to developing the idea that every speech event constitutes a speech act, Searle also expanded the concept that every speech act consists of three separate acts: an act of saying something, an act of doing something, and an act of affecting someone (i.e., the listener). As a framework for investigating these different components, Searle adapted the following terminology from Austin.

Locutionary Act. This is the act of simply uttering a sentence from a language; it is a description of what the speaker *says*. It is the act of using a referring expression (e.g., a noun phrase) and a predicating expression (e.g., a verb phrase or adjective). For instance, if I say *My watch is broken*, the referring expression is *my watch* and the predicating expression is *is broken*. Locutionary acts, at least from our perspective here, are not very important for understanding speech acts.

Illocutionary Act. This is what the speaker intends to *do* by uttering a sentence. Illocutionary acts would include stating, promising, apologizing, threatening, predicting, ordering, and requesting. For example, if a mother says to her child *Take your feet off the table*, the illocutionary act is one of ordering. The intent associated with an illocutionary act is sometimes called the **illocutionary force** of the utterance. Thus, in the previous example, we might say that the illocutionary force of the mother's utterance is an order. Illocutionary acts, unlike locutionary acts, are at the very heart of our understanding of speech acts.

Perlocutionary Act. This is the *effect* on the hearer of what a speaker says. Perlocutionary acts would include such effects as persuading, embarrassing, intimidating, boring, irritating, or inspiring the hearer. For example, if a husband says to his wife ten times in five minutes *Hurry up, dear, we're going to be late for the party*, the illocutionary act might be one of urging but the perlocutionary act is likely to be one of irritating. As with illocutionary acts, the effect associated with a per-locutionary act is sometimes referred to as the **perlocutionary force** of the utterance. Although important to a complete understanding of speech acts, perlocutionary acts are, unfortunately, poorly understood at the present time.

As should be clear by now, speech acts (and their component acts) are extremely sensitive to the context of the utterance, in particular to the relationship between the speaker and the hearer. The following example may help to illustrate the importance of context.

Consider the utterance *You'd better do your homework*. Of course, the locutionary act (the act of uttering) remains the same regardless of context. Note, however, that the illocutionary act and the perlocutionary act change depending upon who is talking to whom. If a father utters this sentence to his school-age son, then the illocutionary act might be one of ordering and the perlocutionary act might be one of irritating (especially if this speech act is a daily occurrence). If a 20 year old college student utters this sentence to her roommate, then the illocutionary act might be one of urging and the perlocutionary act one of persuading (especially if it is right before final exams). If a high school teacher utters this sentence to a pupil, then the illocutionary act might be one of threatening and the perlocutionary act might be one of embarrassing (especially if the sentence is uttered in front of the entire class). Thus, it should be clear that the illocutionary and perlocutionary acts vary with context. This is, of course, what we should expect, given the fact that pragmatics deals with the use of language and, of necessity, we always use language in a particular context.

Note, too, incidentally, that in this example I have insisted on saying that the illocutionary or perlocutionary act "might" be such-and-such. This is because it is not always easy to tell precisely what the illocutionary or perlocutionary act is. For instance, in the context described above, where one roommate is speaking to another, it is difficult (if not impossible) to tell if the illocutionary act is one of urging or warning. The best we can do is try to delineate the class of possible illocutionary acts. Even though we may not be able to decide between these two (urging or warning), it is clearly not an act of ordering, since one roommate does not have the authority to order another to do anything.

DIRECT AND INDIRECT SPEECH ACTS

In "Indirect Speech Acts," published in 1975, Searle pointed out that one illocutionary act can be performed *indirectly* by performing another. For example, if I say to you *Bring me my coat*, I am performing a single illocutionary act of requesting. Thus, this would be a **direct speech act**. However, if I make the same request by saying *Could you bring me my coat?*, I am doing something quite different. Here, I am directly performing an illocutionary act of asking a question and indirectly performing an illocutionary act of making a request. Thus, this would be an **indirect speech act**. It turns out, fortunately enough, that there is a simple way of differentiating direct and indirect speech acts.

Direct Speech Acts. In general, the syntactic form of an utterance reflects the direct illocutionary act. Consider the following examples.

UTTERANCE	SYNTACTIC FORM	DIRECT ILLOCUTIONARY ACT
(9a) The earth is round.	declarative	stating
(9b) What time is it?	interrogative	asking
(9c) Get off my foot.	imperative	ordering or requesting

In each of these examples, the syntactic form of the utterance matches the direct illocutionary act. In (9a) a declarative form is used to make a statement; in (9b) an interrogative form is used to ask a question; and in (9c) an imperative form is used to give an order or make a request. Thus, the direct speech act (or direct illocutionary act) is the one that matches the syntactic form of the utterance.

Indirect Speech Acts. In general, the syntactic form of an utterance does not reflect any indirect illocutionary act associated with it. The best way to tell if you are dealing with an indirect illocutionary act is to respond to the *direct* illocutionary act. If the response seems inappropriate, then the utterance is probably being used to perform an *indirect* illocutionary act. For example, suppose you are in a diner, sitting at the counter; the salt shaker is out of your reach, so you turn to a stranger sitting next to you and say *Can you pass the salt?* He says *Yes* but, rather than passing the salt, turns back to his lunch. His response is inappropriate because he responded to the direct illocutionary act (asking a question) rather than to the indirect illocutionary act (making a request).

Let's take a look at a few more examples of indirect speech acts (i.e., utterances used to perform indirect illocutionary acts).

(a) Suppose Mrs. Olsen is in her kitchen baking brownies, and a tramp comes to the back door and says *I haven't had anything to eat in three days.* Is this an indirect speech act? Yes. The syntactic form of the utterance is declarative; thus, the direct illocutionary act is one of stating. If Mrs. Olsen were to respond to the direct act, she might say *Gee, I just had six brownies; they were delicious!* and then close the door. Such a response, however, would be inappropriate in this context; so she assumes that the tramp is using the utterance to perform an indirect act, namely one of requesting. She then might respond to the indirect act by saying *Let me get you something to eat.* In this example, the tramp is using a declarative structure to make a request.

(b) It's 8:00 p.m. and bedtime for Junior, who is watching television. His mother says *Don't you think it's time to go to bed?* Again, this is an indirect speech act. The syntactic form of the utterance is interrogative; thus, the direct illocutionary act is one of asking a question. However, were Junior to respond to the direct act, he might simply say *No* (or he might even say *Yes* and continue watching television). In either case, his response would be inappropriate. The reason, of course, is that his mother is using her utterance to perform an indirect illocutionary act, namely one of ordering (or at least requesting). In this example, the mother is using an interrogative structure to give an order.

(c) Suppose Bob goes over to his friend Bill's apartment, and Bill is in his bedroom combing his hair. Bill yells to Bob *Get yourself a beer out of the refrigerator.* This, too, is an indirect speech act. The syntactic form of the utterance is imperative; thus, the direct illocutionary act is one of making a request. However, if Bob were to respond to the direct act, he might say *Do I have to?* or *What'll you do if I don't?* Either of these responses would be inappropriate; so Bob assumes that Bill is using the utterance to perform an indirect act, namely one of making an offer. Bob might respond by saying *Thanks* and getting himself the beer. In this example, Bill is using an imperative structure to make an offer.

Thus, we have a fairly straightforward way of differentiating direct and indirect speech acts. The syntactic form of an utterance generally reflects the direct illocutionary act. If a response to the direct illocutionary act is inappropriate, then the utterance is probably being used to perform an indirect illocutionary act.

An apparent problem with this rule arises with interrogative structures. For example, if I walk up to a stranger on the street and say *Do you have the time?*, he might respond by saying *It's 7:20* (an appropriate response) or he might simply say *Yes* and walk away (an inappropriate response). Note, however, that I am using an interrogative structure to ask a question, and both of the stranger's responses are answers to that question. Why, then, is one response appropriate and the other inappropriate? The answer is that English differentiates between two types of interrogative structures: *yes-no* interrogatives and *wh*-interrogatives. A *yes-no* interrogative is one to which you can respond *Yes* or *No*—for example, *Have you eaten lunch yet?* A *wh*-interrogative, on the other hand, is one to which you cannot respond *Yes* or *No*—for example, *What did you have for lunch?* (*wh*-interrogatives contain what is called a *wh*-word: *who, what, when, where, how; yes-no* interrogatives do not).

With this information we have a ready explanation for the seemingly anomalous interchange between the stranger and myself. When I ask the stranger *Do you have the time?*, I am performing an indirect speech act. The syntactic form of the utterance is a *yes-no* interrogative; thus, the direct illocutionary act is one of asking a *yes-no* question. If the stranger were to respond to the direct act, he might say *Yes*. Such a response, however, would be inappropriate, so the stranger assumes that I am using the utterance to perform an indirect act, namely one of asking a *wh*-question. He then responds to the indirect act by saying *It's 7:20*. In this example, I am using a *yes-no* interrogative structure to ask a *wh*-question.

LITERAL AND NONLITERAL SPEECH ACTS

Another phenomenon that our theory of language use has to account for is the fact that speakers sometimes mean what they say *literally* and sometimes not. For example, if I eat eight jelly donuts and then announce *I feel just awful*, I mean exactly what I say. Thus, this utterance constitutes a **literal speech act**. On the other hand, imagine a student in a physics class who does not know a photon from a fireplug. As he begins the midterm exam, he turns to his friend and says *I just love taking physics tests*. He does not mean what he says. This utterance, then, would constitute a **nonliteral speech act**.

INTERACTION OF DIRECT-INDIRECT AND LITERAL-NONLITERAL SPEECH ACTS

We have seen that speech acts can vary along two dimensions: directness and literalness. The fact that each of these dimensions has two values means that we should be able to identify four different types of speech acts: literal and direct, nonliteral and direct, literal and indirect, and nonliteral and indirect. The following examples illustrate each type.

Literal and Direct. Suppose you are having a physical examination and the doctor says *Stick out your tongue*. This is a literal and direct speech act. It is literal because the doctor means exactly what these words say (i.e., the doctor wants you to stick out your tongue). It is direct because an imperative structure is being used to perform a direct illocutionary act, namely making a request.

Nonliteral and Direct. Suppose Joe and Jack are leaving a four-hour anatomy and physiology exam. Joe says to Jack *That was the most miserable test I've ever taken.* Jack responds by saying *You can say that again.* This is a nonliteral direct speech act. It is nonliteral because Jack does not mean exactly what his words say (i.e., he does not want Joe to repeat his original statement). It is direct because Jack is using a declarative structure to perform a direct illocutionary act, namely making a statement (i.e., something like *I agree with you*).

Literal and Indirect. Imagine that you and a friend are seated at a table in a restaurant. The butter is on your friend's side of the table, out of your reach. You say *I'd like some butter.* This is a literal and indirect speech act. It is literal because you mean what your words say (i.e., you *would* like some butter). It is indirect because you are using a declarative structure to perform a direct illocutionary act of stating and an indirect illocutionary act of requesting. Note that if your friend were to respond to the direct illocutionary force of your utterance by simply making a statement (e.g., *And I'd like a million dollars*) it would be inappropriate.

Nonliteral and Indirect. Suppose Mr. White is sitting in the waiting room of a doctor's office. A woman and her six year old daughter walk in and sit down. After a few minutes the little girl begins to run around the waiting room, yelling at the top of her lungs. She then stops right in front of Mr. White and lets out her best war whoop. Mr. White says *Why don't you yell a little louder?* This is a nonliteral and indirect speech act. It is nonliteral because Mr. White does not mean what his words say (i.e., he does not want her to yell louder). It is indirect because Mr. White is using an interrogative structure to perform the indirect illocutionary act of making a request (i.e., that the little girl be quiet). Note that if the child were to respond to the direct illocutionary act by saying *Because I'm already yelling as loud as I can!*, it would be inappropriate.

The relationship between directness and literalness in speech acts is summarized in Figure 2–1.

DIRECT	LITERAL	EXAMPLE	SYNTACTIC FORM	DIRECT SPEECH ACT	INDIRECT SPEECH ACT
yes	yes	A. Doctor to patient: *Stick out your tongue.*	Imperative	Requesting	None
yes	no	B. One student to another: *You can say that again.*	Declarative	Stating	None
no	yes	C. One diner to another: *I'd like some butter.*	Declarative	Stating	Requesting
no	no	D. Adult to boisterous child: *Why don't you yell a little louder?*	Interrogative	Questioning	Requesting

Figure 2–1. Relation between directness and literalness in speech acts.

IMPLICATURE

In a 1975 article entitled "Logic and Conversation," the philosopher Paul Grice pointed out that an utterance can *imply* a proposition (i.e., a statement) that is not part of the utterance and that does not follow as a necessary consequence of the utterance. Grice called such implied statements **implicatures**. Consider the following example. John says to his wife Mary *Uncle Chester is coming over for dinner tonight*, and Mary responds with *I guess I'd better lock up the liquor*. An observer of this interchange might draw the inference that Uncle Chester has a drinking problem. Thus, in Grice's terms, we might say that Mary's utterance *raises the implicature* that Uncle Chester has a drinking problem.

It is important to make three points about this example of implicature. First, the implicature (Uncle Chester has a drinking problem) is not part of Mary's utterance (*I guess I'd better lock up the liquor*). Second, the implicature does not follow as a necessary consequence from Mary's utterance. A necessary consequence of an utterance is called an **entailment** and will be covered in the chapter on semantics. Consider an example of entailment: The sentence *John fried some fish* entails *John cooked some fish*, since it is impossible to fry fish without cooking them. In entailment, if the first sentence is true then the second one must be true, but not vice versa. (Note that it is possible to cook fish without frying them—they could be broiled, for instance.) However, an implicature, as opposed to an entailment, does not follow as a necessary consequence from the utterance which implies it. Third, it is possible for an utterance to raise more than one implicature, or to raise different implicatures if uttered in different contexts. For instance, in the previous example, Mary's response (*I guess I'd better lock up the liquor*) might raise the implicature that Uncle Chester is a teetotaler and a prohibitionist. That is, the mere sight of alcohol and its consumption offends Uncle Chester, so Mary is locking it up to keep it out of sight. Thus, in this respect, implicatures are just like illocutionary acts; they both are heavily dependent upon the context and the participants.

Let's look at a few more examples of implicature.

(a) John and Joe are friends of Bill, but only passing acquaintances of each other. Bill moves away rather suddenly. John later sees Joe on the street and says *Do you know where Bill moved?* Joe responds with *Somewhere on the east coast*. Joe's response raises an implicature, namely that he doesn't know the city or state that Bill moved to.

(b) Muffy says to Sissy *How was your blind date last night?* Sissy responds with *Well, he had on a nice pair of shoes*. Sissy's response raises an implicature, namely that the person she went out with was dull.

(c) The Dean says to the Chancellor *Professor Smith is sure he'll get tenure*. The Chancellor responds with *Yeah, and my pet turtle is sure it'll win the Kentucky Derby*. The Chancellor's response raises an implicature, namely that Professor Smith is unlikely to get tenure.

Each of these examples illustrates the fact that utterances can imply statements that are neither part of the utterance itself nor entailed by the utterance; that is, utterances can raise implicatures. However, we have not yet constructed any hypotheses about how these implicatures arise. We will now consider what such a theory might look like.

CONVERSATIONAL MAXIMS

Grice proposes that conversations are governed by what he calls the Cooperative Principle, namely that participants in a conversation cooperate with each other. This Cooperative Principle, in turn, consists of four **conversational maxims: Quantity**—a participant's contribution should be as informative as is required; **Quality**—a participant should not say that which is false or that which the participant lacks evidence for; **Relation**— a participant's contribution should be relevant; and **Manner**—a participant's contribution should be direct; it should not be obscure, ambiguous, or wordy. Grice's claim, however, is not that we strictly adhere to these maxims when we converse; rather, he claims that we interpret what we hear *as if* it conforms to these maxims. That is, when a maxim appears to be violated, we draw an inference (i.e., an implicature) which makes the utterance conform to these maxims. This, then, would constitute a theory of how implicatures arise. Let's now consider how this theory of conversational implicature applies in some hypothetical cases (adapted from Grice, 1975 and Levinson, 1983).

Maxim of Quantity. This maxim states that each participant's contribution to a conversation should be just as informative as is required; it should not be less informative or more informative. Suppose Bob has worked for Mr. Green in the accounting department of a major retail outlet for six months. Bob is moving to another city and applying for a similar job, where his boss will be Ms. Brown. Mr. Green writes a letter of recommendation for Bob to Ms. Brown. The letter says (in its entirety), *Bob speaks perfect English; he doesn't smoke in the office; and I have never known him to use foul language*. When Ms. Brown reads the letter, an implicature is raised. Ms. Brown reasons (unconsciously) as follows: Green's letter doesn't mention Bob's accounting ability or his performance on the job; in short, Green is giving me less information than he should under these circumstances. He appears to be violating the Maxim of Quantity; there must be a reason for this lack of information. The inference (i.e., the implicature) I draw is that Bob is a poor accountant.

Maxim of Quality. This maxim states that each participant's contribution should be truthful and based on sufficient evidence. Suppose an undergraduate in a geography class says, in response to a question from the instructor, *Reno's the capital of Nevada, isn't it?* The instructor, Mr. Barbados, then says *Yeah, and London's the capital of New Jersey.* The student reasons (unconsciously) as follows: Mr. Barbados said that London is the capital of New Jersey; he knows that is not true. He appears to be violating the Maxim of Quality; there must be a reason for him saying something patently false. The inference (i.e., the implicature) I draw is that my answer was false (i.e., Reno is not the capital of Nevada).

Maxim of Relation. This maxim states that each participant's contribution should be relevant to the subject of the conversation. Suppose I get out of bed in the morning and ask my wife *What time is it?* She responds with *Well, the paper's already come.* My wife's statement raises an implicature. I reason (unconsciously) as follows: I asked about the time and she told me about something seemingly unrelated—the arrival of the newspaper. She appears to be violating the Maxim of Relation; there must be some reason for her seemingly irrelevant comment. The inference (i.e., the implicature) I draw is that she doesn't know the exact time but the arrival of the newspaper has something to do with the time, namely that it is now past the time of day that the newspaper usually comes (i.e., 7:00 a.m.).

Maxim of Manner. This maxim states that each participant's contribution should be reasonably direct; that is, it should not be vague, ambiguous, or excessively wordy. Suppose Mr. and Mrs. Jones are out for a Sunday drive with their two preschool children. Mr. Jones says to Mrs. Jones *Let's stop and get something to eat.* Mrs. Jones responds with *Okay, but not M-c-D-o-n-a-l-d-s.* Mrs. Jones' statement raises an implicature. Mr. Jones reasons (unconsciously) as follows: She spelled out the word *McDonald's,* which is certainly not the most direct way of making a statement. She appears to be violating the Maxim of Manner; there must be a reason for her indirectness. Since the kids cannot spell, the inference (i.e., the implicature) I draw is that she wants to keep that part of her statement from the children.

SUMMARY

Let's review what we have done. We started with five observations about the way language is used to communicate. However, we had no ready explanation for these phenomena. Thus, we constructed a (partial) theory of pragmatics to account for our original observations. This theory makes use of such concepts as performative verb, felicity conditions, speech act (including locutionary, illocutionary, and perlocutionary acts), direct and indirect speech acts, literal and nonliteral speech acts, implicature, and conversational maxims (including quantity, quality, relation, and manner). These theoretical constructs were developed by such people as Austin, Searle, and Grice in order to help explain the observations noted in (1–5). This theory may turn out to require revision, but it is the best we have at the present time.

Moreover, it is important to realize that there is much more to the study of pragmatics than what has been presented in this one short chapter. However, you have now been exposed to some of the basic ideas in the field; if you want to learn more about the subject, see the readings at the end of the chapter. Following this summary is a set of exercises which you can use to check your understanding of the material in this chapter.

EXERCISES

(1)   Explain why each of the italicized verbs in the following sentences is *not* functioning as a performative.
   (a)   I *warned* you not to go to that movie.
   (b)   *Promise* me anything, but give me Arpege.
   (c)   He is *begging* you not to leave.

(2)   For each of the following utterances, state (i) the syntactic form, (ii) the direct speech act, and (iii) the indirect speech act.
   (a)   A mother says to her child *I wish you would finish your dinner*.
   (b)   A mother says to her child *Why don't you stop hitting your brother?*
   (c)   One friend says to another *Have some candy*.
   (d)   A husband says to his wife *Shouldn't we leave soon?*
   (e)   One friend says to another *I wonder if Jerry knows that*.

(3)   Assume that each of the following utterances constitutes a non-felicitous (i.e., invalid) act of apologizing. From these examples construct three felicity conditions on apologizing.
   (a)   *I apologize for what I'm about to do.*
   (b)   *I apologize for not running you over with my car.*
   (c)   *I apologize for Little Freddie's having dumped potato soup in your lap.*
   (d)   *I apologize for having given you an A on the last test.*

(4) In this chapter, we discussed the felicity conditions on acts of promising. What follows are felicity conditions on acts of *requesting*. Try to construct an example that violates each of them.

    (a) The speaker sincerely wants the hearer to carry out some action.

    (b) The speaker believes the hearer is capable of carrying out some action.

(5) You are sitting at a table in a restaurant with your mother-in-law, who, as you know, has crippled hands due to rheumatoid arthritis, and you ask her to hand you the crackers.

    (a) Is this a felicitous (i.e., valid) act of requesting?

    (b) Why or why not?

(6) You are trying to study and your roommate has the stereo as loud as it will go. You have reached the end of your rope, so you scream *Could you turn it up a little?*

    (a) What is the direct speech act?

    (b) What is the indirect speech act (if any)?

    (c) Is the direct speech act literal or nonliteral?

(7) Give an example of an interrogative sentence that has the indirect illocutionary force of a request.

(8) You are driving down the street and see a sign that says *Construction Ahead*. What is the illocutionary force of the indirect speech act?

(9) You walk into your office and ask your secretary, Big Bob, to go up to the third floor and get you some typing paper. However, you know that Big Bob has a severe case of claustrophobia and that the only way to get to and from the third floor is by a tiny elevator run by four mice and a rubber band.

    (a) Is this a felicitous act of requesting?

    (b) Why or why not?

(10) You go to a movie and the Warthog family comes in and sits down behind you. They crumple candy wrappers and talk for the first 20 minutes of the movie. Finally you have had enough, and you turn to them and say *I don't want to have to call the manager*. What kind of speech act is your utterance?

    (a) direct and literal

    (b) indirect and literal

    (c) direct and nonliteral

    (d) indirect and nonliteral

(11) Assume the context is the same as in question (10), except you say *I can still hear the movie; would you mind speaking up?* What kind of speech act is your utterance?
 (a) direct and literal
 (b) indirect and literal
 (c) direct and nonliteral
 (d) indirect and nonliteral

(12) A neighbor's five year old child is visiting you. You have just finished baking a German chocolate cake. You say to the child *Try some cake.* The child responds with *Do I have to?* instead of with, for example, *No, thanks.* Explain the child's misinterpretation of your utterance.

(13) Some return envelopes have the following statement in the upper right-hand corner: *Place stamp here.* What kind of speech act is this?
 (a) direct and literal
 (b) indirect and literal
 (c) direct and nonliteral
 (d) indirect and nonliteral

(14) Assume that you are teaching a course. A fellow instructor approaches you after you have graded a test and asks *How did Mr. Jones do?* You respond with *Well, he wrote something down for every question.*
 (a) Which of Grice's maxims does your response appear to violate?
 (b) What is the implicature raised by your response?

(15) You ask a friend *Do you know where Billy Bob is?* The friend responds with *Well, he didn't meet me for lunch like he was supposed to.*
 (a) Which of Grice's maxims does your friend's statement appear to violate?
 (b) What is the implicature raised by your friend's statement?

ANSWERS TO EXERCISES

The following answers are by no means the only possible ones; they are meant solely to be suggestive. Discussion of other possible answers is part of the exercises.

(1) (a) *warned* is not present tense.
  (b) *promise* does not have a first person subject.
  (c) *is begging* does not have a first person subject.

(2) (a) (i) declarative (ii) stating (iii) ordering/requesting
  (b) (i) interrogative (ii) asking (iii) ordering/requesting
  (c) (i) imperative (ii) requesting (iii) offering
  (d) (i) interrogative (ii) asking (iii) suggesting
  (e) (i) declarative (ii) stating (iii) asking

(3) (a) Speaker can apologize only for a past action.
  (b, d) Speaker can apologize only for an action that he believes the hearer believes is not in the hearer's best interest.
  (c) Speaker can apologize only for an action that he himself committed.

(4) (a) A girlfriend is quarreling with her boyfriend. The girlfriend says *Go ahead and date other girls; see if I care.*
  (b) An instructor knows that a particular student in his class has not done the homework, and he says to that student *Please put the answer to problem six on the board.*

(5) (a) No.
  (b) You (the speaker) do not believe that your mother-in-law (the hearer) is capable of carrying out the request.

(6) (a) asking a question
  (b) requesting
  (c) nonliteral

(7) *Could you get me a cup of coffee?*

(8) warning

(9) (a) No.
  (b) You (the speaker) do not believe Big Bob (the hearer) is capable of carrying out the request.

(10) (b) indirect and literal

(11) (d) indirect and nonliteral

(12) Your utterance takes the syntactic form of an imperative; thus, the direct illocutionary act is one of ordering or requesting. The child responds to the direct illocutionary act, rather than to the indirect act of offering.

(13) (a) direct and literal

(14) (a) Maxim of Manner (or Quantity)
  (b) Mr. Jones did not do well on the test.

(15) (a) Maxim of Relation
  (b) Your friend does not know where Billy Bob is.

SUPPLEMENTARY READINGS

Primary

1. Austin, J. L. (1962). *How to do things with words*. Oxford: Clarendon Press.
2. Grice, H. P. (1975). Logic and conversation. In P. Cole and J. L. Morgan (Eds.), *Syntax and semantics 3: Speech acts* (pp. 41-58). New York: Academic Press.
3. Searle, J. R. (1969). *Speech acts*. Cambridge, England: Cambridge University Press.
4. Searle, J. R. (1975). Indirect speech acts. In P. Cole and J. L. Morgan (Eds.), *Syntax and semantics 3: Speech acts* (pp. 59-82). New York: Academic Press.
5. Searle, J. R. (1976). The classification of illocutionary acts. *Language in Society, 5,* 1-24.

Secondary

6. Bach, K., and Harnish, R. M. (1979). *Linguistic communication and speech acts*. Cambridge, MA: MIT Press.
7. Gazdar, G. (1979). *Pragmatics: Implicature, presupposition, and logical form*. New York: Academic Press.
8. Levinson, S. (1983). *Pragmatics*. Cambridge, England: Cambridge University Press.

You are now prepared to read all of the primary works. The secondary works are more advanced and require a minimum background of an introductory course in linguistics. Levinson (8) is the most recent and detailed textbook on pragmatics; since it has a detailed index and bibliography, you can also use it as a reference tool.

Chapter 3

Semantics

Semantics is the study of linguistic meaning; that is, the meaning of words, phrases, and sentences. Unlike pragmatics, semantics is part of grammar proper, the study of the internal structure of language. (Other areas of grammar are syntax, morphology, and phonology; these are covered in Chapters 4–6.) Unfortunately, because semantics is the most poorly understood component of grammar, it can be one of the most difficult areas of linguistics to study. The fact is that no one has yet developed a comprehensive, authoritative theory of linguistic meaning. Nonetheless, we can discuss some of the phenomena that have been thought to fall within the domain of semantics and some of the theories that have been developed to explain them. It is important to keep in mind, however, that much of what follows is tentative and subject to a great deal of debate.

Let's first consider some observations we can make about the meaning of words and sentences.

(1)   The word *fly* has more than one meaning in English. The word *moth* does not.

(2)   The word *hide* can mean the same thing as *conceal*.

(3)   The meaning of the word *fear* includes the meaning of the word *emotion*, but not vice versa.

(4)   The words *sister* and *niece* seem to be closer in meaning than are the words *sister* and *girl*.

(5)   In the sentence *Jimmy Carter was the 39th president of the United States*, the phrases *Jimmy Carter* and *the 39th president of the United States* refer to the same person. The phrases, however, don't "mean" the same thing.

(6)   In the sentence *Monica believes that she is a genius*, *she* can refer either to *Monica* or to someone else. However, in the sentence *Monica believes herself to be a genius*, *herself* can refer only to *Monica*.

(7)   If someone were to ask you to name a bird, you would probably think of a robin before you would think of an ostrich.

(8)   The sentences *A colorless gas is blue* and *Oxygen is blue* are both false, but they are false for different reasons.

(9)   The sentence *John's wife is six feet tall* is neither true nor false, if John does not have a wife.

The observations in (1–9) are all essentially semantic in nature. That is, they have to do with the meaning of words and sentences. As is standard procedure in linguistics, we will assume that these phenomena are systematic; that is, they are rule-governed. What we will try to do now is construct a set of categories and principles that will at least partially explain these phenomena. Keep in mind that what follows is a (partial) theory designed to account for the observations in (1–9). It may eventually be replaced by other theories, but it is the best we have, given the present state of the art.

BACKGROUND

Contributions to semantics have come essentially from two sources— linguistics and philosophy. Linguists have contributed primarily to the study of the core meaning or **sense** of individual words. One method that they have used to characterize the sense of words is called **lexical decomposition**. This method represents the sense of a word in terms of the **semantic features** that comprise it. For example, consider the words *man*, *woman*, *boy*, and *girl*. The sense of each of these words can be partly characterized by specifying a value (+ or −) for the features [±adult] and [±male], as follows.

	man	*woman*	*boy*	*girl*
[adult]	+	+	−	−
[male]	+	−	+	−

Lexical decomposition, as a method for characterizing the sense of words, has several advantages. First, it explains our intuitions as speakers of English that the meanings of *man* and *boy* are more closely related than are the meanings of *man* and *girl*. *Man* and *boy* have the same value for one of these features [±male], whereas *man* and *girl* do not have the same value for either of these features. Second, it is easy to characterize the senses of additional words by adding features. For example, we can account for part of the meanings of *stallion, mare, colt,* and *filly* simply by adding the feature [±human], as follows.

	man	woman	boy	girl	stallion	mare	colt	filly
[adult]	+	+	−	−	+	+	−	−
[male]	+	−	+	−	+	−	+	−
[human]	+	+	+	+	−	−	−	−

Finally, this method allows us, at least in principle, to characterize the senses of a potentially infinite set of words with a finite number of semantic features. (Note that in the previous example, we were able to differentiate the senses of eight words with only three features.) In general, the fewer the number of statements required by a theory to account for a given set of observations, the more highly valued the theory.

On the other hand, lexical decomposition has several practical limitations. First, linguists have been unable to agree on exactly how many and which features constitute the universal set of semantic properties. Once we go beyond the handful of features already mentioned, there is a great deal of disagreement. Moreover, nouns, especially concrete nouns, seem to lend themselves to lexical decomposition more readily than do other categories of words (i.e., parts of speech). For example, what features could be used to characterize the sense of *carefully*, *belligerent*, and *assassinate*, not to mention *the*, *of*, and *however*? In sum, then, lexical decomposition in terms of semantic features provides a useful, if somewhat limited, account of the meaning of words.

Philosophers, on the other hand, have contributed primarily to the study of the meaning of sentences. However, rather than trying to characterize the core meaning or sense of sentences directly—which, as we have just seen, is a difficult undertaking—they have approached the semantics of sentences from two other directions: the study of **reference** and the study of **truth conditions**. Reference is essentially the study of what objects linguistic expressions (i.e., words, phrases, sentences, and so on) refer to. For example, in the sentence *Mulroney is the Prime Minister of Canada*, the expression *Mulroney* and the expression *the Prime Minister of Canada* refer to the same entity, namely Brian Mulroney. Truth conditional semantics, on the other hand, is essentially the study of the conditions under which a statement can be judged true or false. In actuality, much of what goes under the name of truth conditions involves truth relations that hold between sentences. For example, if the sentence *Fred is 80 years old* is true, then the sentence *Fred is over 50 years old* is necessarily true.

Like lexical decomposition, both the study of reference and the study of truth conditions have advantages as well as limitations. The major advantage of both avenues of inquiry is that they have very restricted domains, which can be probed in a reasonable amount of detail. Rather than dealing with the sense of linguistic expressions in general, they focus, respectively, on the reference of linguistic expressions and the conditions under which linguistic expressions can be judged true or false. The drawback, of course, is that both of them overlook a great deal of what might fall within the domain of "meaning." For example, in the sentence *Brian Mulroney is the Prime Minister of Canada*, determining the referents of *Mulroney* and *the Prime Minister of Canada* skirts the question of what these expressions "mean."

So far, we have considered semantics from the point of view of the contributors to the theory: linguists, who have studied meaning through lexical decomposition, and philosophers, who have tried to characterize meaning through the study of reference and truth conditions. (I should add that the research of these groups is not, in practice, as discrete and compartmentalized as I have suggested. There has been a great deal of cross-fertilization between linguistics and philosophy, especially in the last decade or so.) Nonetheless, as I pointed out earlier, semantics is the most poorly understood area of grammar. Therefore, it should not be surprising that a certain amount of disagreement exists among researchers in the field and that, consequently, a great deal of confusion can exist in the mind of anyone trying to learn the field. All we can do is try to impose some order on the diverse array of approaches to the subject. If we abstract away from the material we've been discussing, we can divide the study of semantics into three areas: **sense**, **reference**, and **truth**. Let's now consider each one in turn.

SENSE

The study of sense (or meaning) can be divided into two areas: speaker-sense and linguistic-sense. **Speaker-sense** is the speaker's intention in producing some linguistic expression. For example, if I utter the sentence *Fred is a real genius* sarcastically, then the speaker-sense of the sentence might be 'Fred is below average in intelligence.' Speaker-sense, because it has to do with nonliteral meaning, is outside the domain of semantics; rather, it is part of pragmatics (discussed in Chapter 2). Consequently, no further mention of speaker-sense will be made in this chapter. **Linguistic-sense**, on the other hand, is the meaning of a linguistic expression as part of a language. For example, if the sentence *Fred is a real genius* means literally something like 'Fred has a truly superior intellect,' then the linguistic-sense, in contrast to speaker-sense, is within the domain of semantics, since it deals solely with literal meaning and is independent of speaker, hearer, and situational context. Note, however, that in this example we presently have no better way of indicating the linguistic-sense of a sentence than by simply paraphrasing it. All we have done so far is differentiate situationally dependent meaning (speaker-sense, part of pragmatics) from situationally independent meaning (linguistic-sense, part of semantics).

Now let's consider some sense properties and relations that any descriptively adequate theory of semantics should account for.

Lexical Ambiguity. A word is lexically ambiguous if it has more than one sense or meaning. For example, the English noun *fly* is ambiguous because it has more than one sense: an insect, a zipper on a pair of pants, or a baseball hit into the air with a bat. Thus, the sentence *Waldo saw a fly* is three-ways ambiguous. One way a semantic theory might account for this fact is to list the word *fly* in the **lexicon** of English (i.e., a dictionary listing of all English words) three times, once with each sense of the word. It is not clear, however, exactly what form each of these **lexical entries** should take. For the time being, we will assume that each one takes the form of a paraphrase, e.g., *fly*: (i) an insect having the following characteristics . . .; (ii) a zipper . . .; (iii) a ball . . . .

Note, however, that not all cases of ambiguity are lexical. Consider the phrase *American history teacher*, which can mean either 'a teacher of American history' or 'a history teacher who is American.' The ambiguity here does not derive from the ambiguity of a particular word, as it did in the case of *fly*. Neither *American*, nor *history*, nor *teacher* has more than one sense. Instead, the ambiguity of *American history teacher* is syntactic, in that we can assign two different structures or bracketings to the phrase: for example [[American history] teacher] = 'a teacher of American history,' and [American [history teacher]] = 'a history teacher who is American.' Syntactic ambiguity will be discussed in Chapter 4.

Synonymy. Two words are synonymous if they have the same sense; that is, if they have the same values for all of their semantic features. For example, the pairs *conceal* and *hide*, *stubborn* and *obstinate*, and *big* and *large* seem to be synonymous in English. Presumably, the meaning of each pair consists of the same set of features marked for the same value. Note, however, that it is not at all clear what the relevant features are for each of these pairs. As mentioned earlier, one of the major difficulties in the study of sense (or core meaning) is determining exactly what constitutes the universal set of semantic properties or features; that is, the dimensions human beings use to characterize the sense of words. Moreover, in all likelihood there are no two words in any language that constitute absolute synonyms, that is, words that mean exactly the same thing in all contexts. For example, even though *big* and *large* are (near) synonyms, the phrases *my big sister* and *my large sister* certainly do not have the same meaning.

Hyponymy. A **hyponym** is a word whose meaning contains the entire meaning of another word, known as the **superordinate**. For example, *oak*

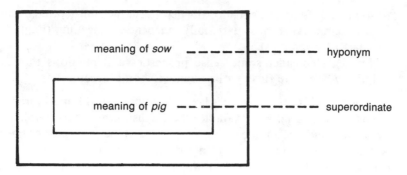

Figure 3-1. Representation of hyponymy.

is a hyponym of the superordinate *tree*; *fear* is a hyponym of the superordinate *emotion*; and *sow* is a hyponym of the superordinate *pig*. Note, for instance, that part of the meaning of the word *sow* is the entire meaning of the word *pig*. This relationship is schematized in Figure 3-1. In general, there are a number of hyponyms for each superordinate. For example, *boar* and *piglet* are also hyponyms of the superordinate *pig*. That is, the meaning of each of the three words *sow*, *boar*, and *piglet* "contains" the meaning of the word *pig*. (Note that in defining a word like *sow*, *boar*, or *piglet*, the superordinate word *pig* is often used as part of the definition: "*A sow* is an adult female *pig*.") Thus, it is not surprising that hyponymy is sometimes referred to as **inclusion**. This same relationship is schematized somewhat differently in Figure 3-2.

A potential source of confusion derives from the terms *superordinate* and *hyponym* themselves. The prefix *super-* in *superordinate* indicates 'above' (cf. *supervisor*) and *hypo-* in *hyponym* indicates 'below' (cf. *hypotension* 'low blood pressure'). However, as we have seen, the actual spatial representation of these terms depends on how we choose to diagram them. The point to remember is that, somewhat paradoxically, the superordinate is the included word and the hyponym is the including one.

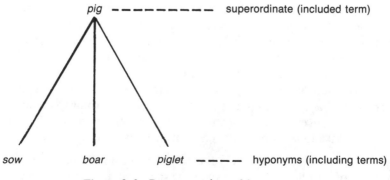

Figure 3-2. Representation of hyponymy.

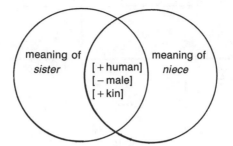

Figure 3–3. Illustration of overlap.

Overlap. Two words overlap in meaning if they have the same value for some (but not all) of the semantic features that constitute their meaning. For example, the words *sister, niece, aunt,* and *mother* overlap in meaning. This phenomenon can be accounted for by stating that part of the meaning of each of these words is characterized as [+human/−male/+kin]. If we were to add the words *nun* and *mistress* to the list above, then the meanings of this set of words would overlap by virtue of the fact that they are all marked [+human/-male]. If we were to further add *mare* and *sow* to this list, then the meanings of this set would overlap by being marked [−male]. And so on. This relationship is displayed in the following diagram.

	sister	niece	aunt	mother	nun	mistress	mare	sow
[human]	+	+	+	+	+	+	−	−
[male]	−	−	−	−	−	−	−	−
[kin]	+	+	+	+	−	−	−	−

It is important, however, to distinguish overlap from hyponymy. With hyponymy, the meaning of one word is entirely included in the meaning of another. (The meaning of *pig* is entirely included in the meaning of *sow*; i.e., all sows are pigs, but not all pigs are sows.) With overlap, on the other hand, the meanings of two words intersect, but neither one includes the other. The meanings of *sister* and *niece* intersect, but neither includes the other: Not all sisters are nieces, and not all nieces are sisters. Overlap is schematized in Figure 3–3.

Antonymy. Two words are antonyms if their meanings differ only in the value for a single semantic feature. The following pairs are all antonyms: *dead* and *alive, above* and *below, hot* and *cold,* and *fat* and *skinny.* The meanings of the members of each pair are presumably identical, except for opposite values of some semantic feature. The meanings of *dead* and *alive,* for instance, are identical except that *dead* is marked [−living] and *alive* is marked [+living]. Once again, however,

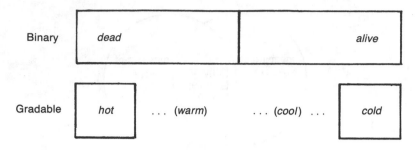

Figure 3–4. Illustration of binary and gradable antonyms.

note the difficulty in determining the relevant semantic feature that distinguishes the members of each pair.

Antonyms, moreover, fall into two groups. **Binary antonyms** are pairs that exhaust all possibilities along some scale. *Dead* and *alive* are examples of binary antonyms. Everything that can be dead or alive is, in fact, either dead or alive: There is no middle ground between the two. All men, for example, are either dead or alive. **Gradable antonyms**, on the other hand, are pairs that describe opposite ends of a continuous scale. *Hot* and *cold* are examples of gradable antonyms. Not everything that can be hot or cold is, in fact, either hot or cold. A liquid, for example, may be neither hot nor cold; it can be in between, say, warm or cool. The difference between binary and gradable antonyms is schematized in Figure 3–4.

REFERENCE

The study of reference, like the study of sense, can be divided into two areas: speaker-reference and linguistic-reference. **Speaker-reference** is what the speaker is referring to by using some linguistic expression. For example, if I utter the sentence *Here comes President Reagan* facetiously, to refer to a bag lady coming down the sidewalk, then the speaker-reference of the expression *President Reagan* is the bag lady. Speaker-reference, because it varies according to the speaker and context, is outside the domain of semantics; instead it is part of pragmatics. **Linguistic-reference**, on the other hand, is the systematic denotation of some linguistic expression as part of a language. For example, the linguistic expression *President Reagan* in the sentence *Here comes President Reagan* refers in fact to the public figure Ronald Reagan. Linguistic-reference, in contrast to speaker-reference, is within the domain of semantics, since it deals with reference that is a systematic function of the language itself, rather than of the speaker and context.

Let's now consider some concepts that seem to be useful in thinking and talking about reference (**referent**, **extension**, **prototype**, and

stereotype); then we will take a look at some different types of linguistic reference (**coreference, anaphora,** and **deixis**).

Referent. The entity identified by the use of a referring expression such as a noun or noun phrase is the referent of that expression. If, for example, I am standing in my back yard and point to a particular yellow-bellied sapsucker and say *That bird looks sick*, then the referent for the referring expression *That bird* is the particular yellow-bellied sapsucker I am pointing at.

Extension. Extension refers to the set of all potential referents for a referring expression. For example, the extension of *bird* is the set of all entities (past, present, and future) that could systematically be referred to by the expression *bird*. In other words, the extension of *bird* is the set of all birds.

Prototype. A "typical" member of the extension of a referring expression is a prototype of that expression. For example, a robin or a bluebird might be a prototype of *bird*; a pelican or an ostrich, since each is somewhat atypical, would not be.

Stereotype. A list of characteristics describing a prototype is said to be a stereotype. For example, the stereotype of *bird* might be something like: has two legs and two wings, has feathers, is about six to eight inches from head to tail, makes a chirping noise, lays eggs, builds nests, and so on.

Coreference. Two linguistic expressions that have the same extralinguistic referent are said to be coreferential. Consider, for example, the sentence *The Earth is the third planet from the Sun*. The expressions *the Earth* and *the third planet from the Sun* are coreferential because they both refer to the same extralinguistic object, namely the heavenly body that we are spinning around on right now. Note, however, that the expressions *the Earth* and *the third planet from the Sun* do not "mean" the same thing. Suppose, for example, a new planet were discovered between Mercury (now the first planet from the Sun) and Venus (now the second planet from the Sun). If so, then the Earth would become the fourth planet from the Sun, and Venus would become the third. Thus, the linguistic expressions *the Earth* and *the fourth planet from the Sun* would become coreferential. Note, moreover, that if we were to claim that these two expressions "mean" the same thing, then we should be able to substitute *the third planet from the Sun* for *the Earth* in a sentence like *The Earth is the fourth planet from the Sun*, assuming, of course, our discovery of a new planet between Mercury and Venus. This substitution procedure would give us **The third planet from the Sun is the fourth planet from the Sun*. (Recall that an asterisk indicates an unacceptable form.)

As this example illustrates quite clearly, the fact is that *the Earth* and *the third planet from the Sun* each have separate meanings in English, even though they now happen to be coreferential.

This notion that coreference is distinct from meaning is slippery, so let's look at another example. Consider the following questions: (a) *Does a likeness of Andrew Jackson appear on a $20 bill?*; (b) *Does a likeness of the seventh president of the United States appear on a $20 bill?* The fact is that Andrew Jackson was the seventh president of the United States. Thus, the expressions *Andrew Jackson* and *the seventh president of the United States* are coreferential. However, if the two expressions had the same "meaning," then it would be impossible to explain the fact that there are fluent speakers of English who can answer question (a) correctly, but not question (b). (I, for one, couldn't have answered (b) without looking it up!)

Anaphora. A linguistic expression that refers to another linguistic expression is said to be anaphoric or an anaphor. Consider the sentence *Mary wants to play whoever thinks himself capable of beating her.* In this sentence the linguistic expression *himself* necessarily refers to *whoever*; thus *himself* is being used anaphorically in this case. Note, moreover, that it would be inaccurate to claim that *whoever* and *himself* are coreferential (i.e., that they have the same extralinguistic referent). This is because there may in fact not be anyone who thinks himself capable of beating Mary; that is, there may not be any extralinguistic referent for *whoever* and *himself*.

It is common, however, for coreference and anaphora to coincide. Consider, for example, the sentence *Roger Mudd thinks that President Reagan believes himself to be invincible.* The expressions *President Reagan* and *himself* are coreferential since they refer to the same extralinguistic object, namely Ronald Reagan. At the same time, *himself* is an anaphor since it necessarily refers to the expression *President Reagan*. Note that there is no reading of this sentence such that *himself* can be construed as referring to the expression *Roger Mudd*. In sum, coreference deals with the relation of a linguistic expression to some entity in the real world, past, present, or future; anaphora deals with the relation between two linguistic expressions.

Deixis. An expression that has one meaning but refers to different entities as the extralinguistic context changes is said to be deictic. Obvious examples are expressions such as *yesterday*, *today*, and *tomorrow*, whose referents change every 24 hours. If, on November 28, 1946, X says to Y *I'll see you tomorrow*, then the referent for *tomorrow* is November 29, 1946. If, on the other hand, X says the same thing to Y on June 6, 1965, then the referent for *tomorrow* is June 7, 1965; and so on. Among the most interesting deictic expressions in English are the personal pronouns: *I*, *me*, *you*, *he*, *him*, and so on. If, for example, I say to my cat Midnight Muffaletta *I see you*, then *I* refers to Frank Parker and *you* refers to Midnight Muffaletta. If, however, President Reagan says the same thing to his wife, then *I* refers to Ronald Reagan and *you* refers to Nancy Reagan; and so on. In other words, deictic expressions have a "pointing" function; they point to entities within the context of the utterance.

Note, however, that anaphora and deixis can intersect. Consider, for example, the sentence *President Reagan believes that he is invincible*. The expression *he* can refer either to the expression *President Reagan* or to some other male in the context of the utterance. When, as in the first case, a pronoun refers to another linguistic expression, it is used anaphorically; when, as in the second case, it refers to some entity in the extralinguistic context, it is used deictically.

TRUTH

The study of truth or truth conditions in semantics falls into two basic categories: the study of different types of truth embodied in individual sentences (**analytic**, **contradictory**, and **synthetic**) and the study of different types of truth relations that hold between sentences (**entailment** and **presupposition**).

Analytic Sentences. An analytic sentence is one that is necessarily true as a result of the words in it. For example, the sentence *A bachelor is an unmarried man* is true not because the world is the way it is, but because the English language is the way it is. Part of our knowledge of ordinary English is that *bachelor* "means" *an unmarried man*; thus to say that one *is* the other must necessarily be true. We do not need to check on the outside world to verify the truth of this sentence. We might say that analytic sentences are "true by definition." Analytic sentences are sometimes referred to as **linguistic truths**, because they are true by virtue of the language itself.

Contradictory Sentences. Contradictory sentences are just the opposite of analytic sentences. While analytic sentences are necessarily true as a result of the words in them, contradictory sentences are necessarily false for the same reason. The following sentences are all contradictory: *A bachelor is a married man*, *A blue gas is colorless*, *A square has five equal sides*. In each case, we know the sentence is false because we know the meaning of the words in it: Part of the meaning of *bachelor* is 'unmarried'; part of the meaning of *blue* is 'has color'; part of the meaning of *square* is 'has four sides.' It is not necessary to refer to the outside world in order to judge each of these sentences false. Consequently, contradictory sentences are sometimes referred to as **linguistic falsities,** because they are false by virtue of the language itself.

Synthetic Sentences. Sentences that may be true or false depending upon how the world is are called synthetic. In contrast to analytic and contradictory sentences, synthetic sentences are not true or false because of the words that comprise them, but rather because they do or do not accurately describe some state of affairs in the world. For example, the sentence *My next door neighbor, Bud Brown, is married* is a synthetic sentence. Note that you cannot judge its truth or falsity by inspecting the words in the sentence. Rather, you must verify the truth or falsity of this sentence empirically, for example by checking the marriage records at the courthouse. Other examples of synthetic sentences include *Nitrous oxide is blue*, *Nitrous oxide is not blue*, *Bud Brown's house has five sides*, and *Bud Brown's house does not have five sides*. In each case, the truth or falsity of the sentence can be verified only by consulting the state of affairs that holds in the world. Thus, synthetic sentences are sometimes referred to as **empirical truths** or **falsities,** because they are true or false by virtue of the state of the extralinguistic world.

The examples that we have considered so far seem fairly straightforward. Analytic and contradictory sentences are true and false, respectively, by definition. Synthetic sentences, however, are not—they must be verified or falsified empirically. Nevertheless, some sentences do not fall neatly into one of these two groups. Consider, for example, the sentence *Oxygen is not blue*. It is true. But is it analytic—true by virtue of the words that make it up (i.e., part of the meaning of *oxygen* is 'having no color')? Or is it synthetic—true because it coincides with the state of the world (i.e., because it just so happens that oxygen has no color)? This can get to be a thorny issue and the experts don't always have a uniform answer to such questions. However, it would probably be reasonable to treat such cases as synthetic truths rather than analytic truths, at least for the time being. This is because it is easy to imagine conditions under which the sentence *Oxygen is not blue* would be false. For example, suppose scientists froze oxygen and found that solid oxygen is in fact blue. Such a finding would not cause a change in the meaning of the word *oxygen*, but rather a change in our understanding of the substance oxygen. In contrast, consider the sentence *A colorless gas is not blue*. It is impossible, at least for me, to imagine a situation in which this sentence would be false. If a gas is colorless, it cannot be blue; if it is blue, it cannot be colorless. Thus it seems reasonable, at least until more light can be shed on the subject, to consider sentences like *Oxygen is not blue* as synthetically true.

Entailment. One sentence entails another if the meaning of the first sentence includes the meaning of the second. (Note the similarity between entailment and hyponymy. Just as hyponymy describes an inclusive relation between two words, so entailment describes an inclusive relation between two sentences.) The test for entailment is as follows: Sentence (a) entails sentence (b) if the truth of sentence (a) insures the truth of sentence (b) and if the falsity of sentence (b) insures the falsity of sentence (a). Consider the following sentences: (a) *Bill suffered a fatal heart attack* and (b) *Bill is dead.* In this case, sentence (a) entails sentence (b) because the truth of (a) insures the truth of (b) (if Bill suffered a fatal heart attack, he necessarily is dead), and the falsity of (b) insures the falsity of (a) (if Bill is not dead, he necessarily didn't suffer a fatal heart attack). The relationship of entailment is represented schematically in Figure 3-5. That is, sentence (a) entails sentence (b) if the truth of (a) insures the truth of (b) and the falsity of (b) insures the falsity of (a).

Note, however, that the relation of entailment is unidirectional. For instance, consider our example sentences again, but in the opposite order: (b) *Bill is dead* and (a) *Bill suffered a fatal heart attack.* In this case, sentence (b) does *not* entail (a) (if Bill is dead, he did not necessarily die of a heart attack—he may have died of kidney failure or he may have been hit by a bolt of lightning); and the falsity of (a) does not insure the falsity of (b) (if Bill did not suffer a fatal heart attack, it is not necessarily the case that he is not dead—he may, once again, have died of kidney failure or he may have been hit by a bolt of lightning). In short, then, it should be clear that the relation of entailment is unidirectional.

This is not to say, however, that there cannot be a pair of sentences such that each entails the other. Rather, when such a relation holds, it is called **paraphrase**. For example, the sentences *Biff and Tammy are good scouts* and *Tammy and Biff are good scouts* are paraphrases of each other. Likewise, *Tammy was driven home by Biff* is a paraphrase of *Biff drove Tammy home.*

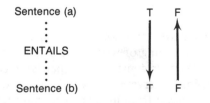

Sentence (a)

ENTAILS

Sentence (b)

Figure 3-5. Representation of entailment.

Presupposition. One sentence presupposes another if the falsity of the second renders the first without a truth value. A sentence without a truth value is one that cannot be judged true or false. Questions, for example, are typical of sentences without truth values. What sense would it make to say that a sentence like *Do you have blue eyes?* is true or false? Likewise, imperatives have no truth value. It wouldn't make any sense to say that a sentence like *Shut up!* is either true or false.

Now, let's consider an example of presupposition and examine how this concept relies on the notion of "sentence without a truth value." As stated before, one sentence presupposes another if the falsity of the second renders the first without a truth value. Consider the following sentences: (a) *Unicorns have horns* and (b) *There are unicorns.* Sentence (a) presupposes (b) because if (b) is false, then (a) has no truth value. Note that if (b) is false—that is, if there are no unicorns—then it doesn't make sense to say that (a) *Unicorns have horns* is true or false. For (a) to be true, there would have to be such things as unicorns and they would have to have horns. On the other hand, for (a) to be false, there would have to be such things as unicorns and they would have to *not* have horns. Consider another example: The sentence *The King of Canada is tall* presupposes the sentence *There is a King of Canada* (or some other sentence expressing the same proposition: *The King of Canada exists*). Note that if *There is a King of Canada* is false, then *The King of Canada is tall* cannot be judged true or false.

Another property of presupposition is that a sentence and its denial (i.e., the negative version of the sentence) have the same set of presuppositions. Thus if sentence (a) *Unicorns have horns* presupposes sentence (b) *There are unicorns*, then the denial of sentence (a) *Unicorns do not have horns* also presupposes sentence (b). If there are no unicorns, then *Unicorns do not have horns* cannot be judged true or false.

It might be of some comfort to know that presupposition is a much more slippery concept than entailment. Consequently, more investigators agree on the semantic concept of entailment than on that of presupposition.

SUMMARY

Let's go back over what we have done. We started with a number of observations about the meaning of words and sentences that we had no ready explanation for. We then constructed a (partial) theory of semantics to account for our original observations. Contributions to this theory have come from two main sources: from linguists who have traditionally been interested in the core meaning or sense of linguistic expressions (especially words) and from philosophers who have traditionally been concerned with the reference of linguistic expressions and the truth of sentences. The study of sense makes use of such concepts as lexical decomposition, semantic features, lexical ambiguity, synonymy, hyponymy, overlap, and antonymy. The study of reference utilizes concepts such as referent, extension, prototype, stereotype, coreference, anaphora, and deixis. Finally, the study of truth conditions relies on the notions of analytic, contradictory, and synthetic sentences, as well as entailment and presupposition. These theoretical constructs were developed by linguists and philosophers, too numerous to name here, to help explain the observations in (1–9). This theory, fragmented and incomplete as it is, will undoubtedly turn out to need revision in some of its details; however, it is the best we have for the time being. Think of the discussion in this chapter as a (partial) working hypothesis concerning the nature of semantic structure.

In addition, it is important to keep in mind that there is much more to the study of semantics than has been presented so briefly here. Nonetheless, you have now had some exposure to most of the basic concepts in the field; if you want to investigate the subject further, consult the reading list at the end of the chapter. Also, you might want to check your understanding of the ideas in this chapter by working through the following exercises.

EXERCISES

(1) What semantic feature or property differentiates the following sets of nouns?
   (a) *niece, daughter, sister* vs. *nun, woman, girl*
   (b) *mailman, nephew, priest* vs. *gander, stag, bull*
   (c) *hen, ewe, cow* vs. *rooster, ram, bull*
   (d) *table, chair, pencil* vs. *love, thought, idea*
   (e) *table, chair, pencil* vs. *water, dirt, cream*

(2) *Riddle*: A father and a son are riding in a car. The car hits a truck. The father dies and the son is rushed to the emergency room of a nearby hospital. The doctor comes in and says, "I can't operate on this boy. He's my son." What is the relationship between the doctor and the boy?
   Answer: The doctor is the boy's mother.
   A listener's inability to answer this riddle rests on his or her semantic representation of the word *doctor*. Explain.

(3) What sense relation is illustrated by the following words: *rectangle, parallelogram,* and *square*?

(4)   What reference relation holds between the italicized expressions in each of the following sentences?
    (a)   George will give a fat lip to *anyone who* wants one.
    (b)   *Maxine* has been named *secretary of the Student Government Association.*

(5)   What truth relation holds between the following sentences? How can it be demonstrated?
    (a)   *Fred is mortal.*
    (b)   *Fred is a man.*

(6)   What truth relation holds between the following sentences? How can it be demonstrated?
    (a)   *Fred's wife is ten feet tall.*
    (b)   *Fred is married.*

(7)   What kind of truth is illustrated by each of the following sentences?
    (a)   *Waldo's living room has four right angles.*
    (b)   *A square has four right angles.*

(8)   True/False.
    (a)   Philosophers' most important contributions to the study of semantics have been in the area of sense.
    (b)   *Fat* and *skinny* are binary antonyms.
    (c)   The meaning relation illustrated by *hen*, *cow*, *mare*, and *vixen* is overlap.
    (d)   The phrase *French literature teacher* constitutes a case of lexical ambiguity.
    (e)   The relationship that holds between the italicized expressions in "*George Bush* has been elected *Vice-President of the United States*" is reference.
    (f)   The sentence *John killed Bill* presupposes the sentence *Bill died.*
    (g)   The following sentence is analytic: *If George killed the deer, then the deer died.*
    (h)   Two words overlap in meaning if they share the same specifications for at least one semantic feature.
    (i)   The pronoun in the following sentence is deictic: *Sam is extremely pleased with himself.*
    (j)   The sentence *Buckaroo Bonzai loves his wife* entails the sentence *Buckaroo Bonzai is married.*
    (k)   The pronouns in the following sentence are anaphoric: *I like her a lot.*
    (l)   *Smart* and *stupid* are gradable antonyms.
    (m)   The sense relation illustrated by *rooster, bull, stallion,* and *buck* is hyponymy.

ANSWERS TO EXERCISES

The following answers are by no means the only possible ones; they are meant solely to be suggestive. Discussion of other possible answers is part of the exercises.

(1) (a) [±kin]
     (b) [±human]
     (c) [±male]
     (d) [±abstract] (or [±concrete])
     (e) [±count] Note: *table*, *chair*, and *pencil* each have a plural form and thus are called count nouns. *Water*, *dirt*, and *cream* don't have a plural form and consequently are called non-count nouns. However, what's going on when someone goes into a restaurant, orders coffee, and asks for *two creams*?

(2) The listener's semantic representation of *doctor* apparently includes the feature specification [+male]. This would then preclude the listener from associating *doctor* with a female referent, in this case the boy's mother.

(3) Hyponymy or inclusion. Note: *parallelogram* means 'four-sided figure with opposite sides parallel'; *rectangle* means 'four-sided figure with opposite sides parallel, containing four right angles'; *square* means 'four-sided figure with opposite sides parallel, containing four right angles and four equal sides.' Thus, the meaning of *square* includes the meaning of *rectangle*, which in turn includes the meaning of *parallelogram*, but not vice versa.

(4) (a) anaphora
     (b) coreference

(5) (b) entails (a). Note: If *Fred is a man* is true, then *Fred is mortal* must be true; likewise, if *Fred is mortal* is false, then *Fred is a man* must be false.

(6) (a) presupposes (b). Note: If *Fred is married* is false, then *Fred's wife is ten feet tall* has no truth value.

(7) (a) empirical (synthetic sentence)
     (b) linguistic (analytic sentence)

(8) (a) F (reference and truth)
     (b) F (gradable)
     (c) T
     (d) F (syntactic)
     (e) F (coreference)

(f)   F (entailment)
(g)   T
(h)   T
(i)   F (anaphoric)
(j)   F (presupposition)
(k)   F (deictic)
(l)   T
(m) F (overlap)

SUPPLEMENTARY READINGS

1.   Allwood, J., Andersson, L. -G., and Dahl, Ö. (1977). *Logic in linguistics*. Cambridge, England: Cambridge University Press.
2.   Fodor, J. D. (1977). *Semantics: Theories of meaning in generative grammar*. New York: Thomas Y. Crowell.
3.   Hurford, J. R., and Heasley, B. (1983). *Semantics: A coursebook*. New York: Cambridge University Press.
4.   Katz, J. J. (1972). *Semantic theory*. New York: Harper and Row.
5.   Kempson, R. (1977). *Semantic theory*. Cambridge, England: Cambridge University Press.
6.   Lyons, J. (1977). *Semantics* (2 vols.). New York: Cambridge University Press.
7.   Palmer, F. R. (1976). *Semantics: A new outline*. New York: Cambridge University Press.

All of these readings are, or can be used as, textbooks. However, they differ in the amount of preparation you will need in order to benefit from them. You are ready to read Hurford and Heasley (3), Kempson (5), and Palmer (7) right now. Allwood et al. (1) and Lyons (6) require a minimum background of an introductory course in linguistics, and Fodor (2) and Katz (4) require an additional course in syntax. I would urge you to begin with Hurford and Heasley (3). Not only is it recent, but it is also the most lucid and informative introduction to semantics that I have ever come across.

Chapter 4

Syntax

Syntax is the study of the architecture of phrases, clauses, and sentences; that is, of the way they are constructed. In contrast to semantics, syntax is one of the better understood areas within linguistics. In fact, during the last 30 years, more has probably been written about syntax than about any other area within linguistics. This interest in syntax has stemmed largely from the pioneering work of Noam Chomsky, who in 1957 first set out his ideas in a little book (117 pages) entitled *Syntactic Structures*. Since then, Chomsky's name has become almost synonymous with the study of generative grammar in general. However, the fact that syntactic theory has undergone such rapid and detailed development over the past several decades raises a problem for us here. What points can we discuss in just a few pages that will provide a basic grasp of the core elements of the theory of syntax? As usual, we can begin by considering some observations that we can make about the structure of phrases, clauses, and sentences.

(1) The phrase *the biggest house* is acceptable English; *theest big house* is not.

(2) The sentence *Sergeant Preston was shot in the arm by an Indian* is acceptable English; *Sergeant Preston in the arm was shot by an Indian* is not.

(3) The interrogative *What will Tiny Abner put on his head?* is acceptable in English; *What will Tiny Abner put a hat on his head?* is not.

Observation (1) can be used to illustrate the fact that the words in a language are organized into different **categories** or, in traditional terms, parts of speech. Observation (2) can be used to illustrate the fact that words in sentences are not just strings of elements arranged in left-to-right order, but are also arranged in hierarchical **constituent structures**. Observation

47

(3) can be used to illustrate the fact that sentence structures are related by **transformations**: operations that move a category from one location to another within a structure.

All of these phenomena are essentially syntactic in nature. That is, they all have to do with the internal architecture of phrases, clauses, and sentences. Moreover, we will make the now familiar assumption that the phenomena in (1–3) are systematic; that is, they are governed by a system of principles stated in terms of theoretical constructs. What we will do now is investigate three of these constructs (categories, constituent structure, and transformations), without which we cannot even begin to account for the observations in (1–3). It is important to bear in mind that what follows is part of an (unobservable) theory designed to account for the (observable) data in (1–3).

CATEGORIES

The classification of words into categories or parts of speech goes back at least as far as Plato, who first mentioned the categories **noun, verb,** and **sentence.** (He, of course, used the Greek terms *noma, rhema,* and *logos,* respectively.) Even today, school children learn that there are eight parts of speech in English. However, because categories have been with us so long, it is easy to be misled into thinking that they are part of the *observable* aspect of language. Nothing could be farther from the truth: Categories are theoretical constructs, part of the *unobservable* theory of syntax. Linguists have historically classified words into categories solely because postulating such categories helps them explain phenomena that they otherwise could not explain. For example, one such phenomenon is that some words can be made plural (*table-tables, boy-boys, idea-ideas*), whereas others cannot (*quick-*quicks, of-*ofs, the-*thes*) (note that an asterisk in front of a form means that it is not acceptable in the language in question; it is ungrammatical or ill-formed). One way of accounting for this phenomenon is to categorize English words into two groups: nouns (which can be made plural) and others (which cannot be made plural). Now we can make a general statement about English: Nouns can be made plural; other words can't. Note that if we did not postulate a category such as noun, we would have to state as an idiosyncratic fact about each word in English whether or not it can be made plural.

Two further points are worth making before we leave this example. First, there is nothing sacred about the term *noun* itself. If we wanted to, we could call this group of words that can be made plural *category one,* or make up some other term, such as *dook.* The point is that words in human languages can be categorized in terms of their behavior; what we choose to call these categories is immaterial. Second, the ability to be made plural is just one "test" for determining whether or not a word is a noun. Another test for nouns is whether they can be preceded by an article: Nouns generally can be; other words generally cannot. For example, *honesty* cannot be made plural (**honesties*); however, it can be preceded by an article (*The honesty of Fred's employees reinforces his faith in them*). Thus, classifying words into categories often calls for several tests of properties peculiar to a particular class, rather than just one test.

Consider another example. Children are taught in school that articles are a type of adjective. Is this, however, a legitimate claim? The answer, unfortunately, is "no." The reason is that adjectives and articles behave differently; that is, they have different properties. First, adjectives can be made comparative and superlative (*tall-taller-tallest*), whereas articles can't (*the-*theer-*theest, a-*aer-*aest, an-*aner-*anest*). Second, if both an adjective and an article modify a noun, then the article must precede the adjective (*the tall man, a tall man, *tall the man, *tall a man*). Finally, a noun can be modified by more than one adjective, but not by more than one article (*a short, fat man; a short, fat, bald man; *the a fat man; *a the fat man*).

Let's go back and take a look at what we've done here. First, we have justified postulating a category **adjective** by virtue of the fact that some words can be made comparative and superlative (*short-shorter-shortest*, and so on) whereas others can't (*boy-*boyer-*boyest, of-*ofer-*ofest, and-*ander-*andest*). Second, we have provided three different pieces of evidence that articles are not a type of adjective simply because they do not behave like adjectives. There is in fact reason to believe that articles are members of another category **determiner**, which includes demonstratives (*this, that, these,* and *those*) as well as perhaps possessive personal pronouns (*my, your, his, her, its, our, their*). Try the tests we've discussed on these words, and see what you think.

The point of this section on categories is straightforward. First, we cannot make even the most commonplace statement about the observations in (1) without reference to the concept **category**. Second, we can group words in a language into categories based on their behavior (e.g., the types of endings they allow and their position in phrases and sentences).

Before leaving this section, we should further note that linguists have grouped words into two corresponding types of categories: **lexical** (or word) **categories**, which include items such as nouns, verbs, adjectives, and adverbs; and **phrasal categories**, which include items such as noun phrases, adjective phrases, and adverb phrases. For example, the sentence *The fat man ate* contains a noun phrase (NP) *the fat man*, which in turn contains the noun (N) *man*. The theory is that every phrasal category contains at least one lexical category of the same basic type. For example, every NP contains at least an N, every VP contains at least a V, and so on. Conversely, every lexical category belongs to a phrasal category of the same basic type: Every N belongs to an NP, and so on. As usual, however, even such straightforward claims such as these can be problematic. For example, in the sentence *To win is everything*, the words *to win* seem to be functioning as the subject NP of the sentence yet that NP does not contain an N (*to win* is a verb form). One way around this problem might be to claim that *to win* is not a member of the category NP at all, but rather a reduced S(entence). Note, incidentally, that *to win* can take a subject and an object just like an S can: *For the Cubs to win the pennant is everything*. Regardless of how this particular problem is resolved, however, the point is that it is representative of the types of problems linguists run into in theorizing about categories.

CONSTITUENT STRUCTURE

Phrases, clauses, and sentences are more than just a set of words or, as we have just discussed, categories arranged in left-to-right order. Rather, they are sets of categories organized into a *hierarchical* structure. As was the case with categories, linguists have postulated hierarchical structures for sentences solely in order to account for phenomena that they otherwise could not explain. For example, consider the phrase *American history teacher*, which was mentioned briefly in the chapter on semantics. As any native speaker of English can verify, this phrase is ambiguous: It can mean either 'a teacher of American history' or 'a history teacher who is American.' However, we saw earlier that this ambiguity is not lexical; none of the words (*American*, *history*, or *teacher*) has more than one sense. If this is the case, how then are we to account for the ambiguity of *American history teacher*?

One way to explain this phenomenon is to assume that phrases are organized into hierarchical structures and that there are cases where more than one such structure can be assigned to a particular phrase. Such cases are said to exhibit **structural ambiguity**. Under this hypothesis, *American history teacher* can be assigned two different structures and, therefore, is structurally ambiguous. The two structures are given in Figure 4-1. An informal explanation of how these structures account for the ambiguity of *American history teacher* is as follows. In (i), *American* modifies *history*. In alternative terms, we might say that *American history* is a **constituent**. Two or more words form a constituent if there is a point in their associated tree structure that dominates all and only these words. In structure (i),

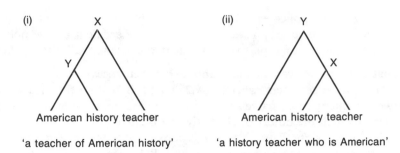

Figure 4-1. Structural ambiguity.

there is a point Y which dominates all and only the words *American history*. Note also that there is no such point in (i) which dominates all and only the words *history teacher*. Thus, in (i) *history* does not modify *teacher* or, in alternative terms, *history teacher* is not a constituent. Moreover, note that structure (i), in which *American history* is a constituent, corresponds exactly to the interpretation of (i), namely that *American* describes *history*.

Now consider structure (ii). Here *history teacher* is a constituent, whereas *American history* is not. There is a point X in (ii) which dominates all and only *history teacher*; there is not a point which dominates all and only *American history*. Structure (ii), in turn, corresponds exactly to the interpretation of (ii), namely that *history* describes *teacher*.

Before moving on, it is worth mentioning several points about these two structures. First, they are theoretical constructs (i.e., part of a theory) postulated by linguists in order to account for the fact that the phrase *American history teacher* has two different senses or interpretations. Second, without postulating these hierarchical structures, there is no transparent explanation for the ambiguity of *American history teacher*. (As we saw earlier, this is not a case of lexical ambiguity.) Third, the justification for these two hierarchical structures is independent of the justification for categories. Note that, in these two structures, the words *American*, *history*, and *teacher* are not labeled for categories. In fact, it is immaterial what category each of these words falls into. The point is that the structures are motivated independently of the need for categories. Note, incidentally, that the argument for categories discussed in the first section of this chapter was completely independent of the argument for hierarchical structure.

However, the concepts of categories and constituent structure do interact in many syntactic phenomena. Consider the following sentences.

(A.1)   An Indian shot Sergeant Preston in the arm.
(A.2)   Sergeant Preston was shot in the arm by an Indian.
(A.3)   *Sergeant Preston in the arm was shot by an Indian.

(B.1) The police examined a photograph of the accident.

(B.2) *A photograph was examined of the accident by the police.

(B.3) A photograph of the accident was examined by the police.

What observations can we make about these sentences? First, (A.1) and (B.1) are **active** sentences, whereas (A.2–3) and (B.2–3) are their respective **passive** counterparts. (Active and passive sentences are paraphrases of each other in which the object of the active verb corresponds to the subject of the passive verb. Thus, *X saw Y* is active and *Y was seen by X* is the corresponding passive.) Second, (A.1) and (B.1) seem to contain the same categories arranged in the same order, as illustrated here.

NP	V	NP	PP
			(Prepositional Phrase)
A.1 An Indian	shot	Sergeant Preston	in the arm
B.1 The police	examined	a photograph	of the accident

Third, in (A.2) the NP *Sergeant Preston* is the subject; in (A.3) the NP-PP sequence *Sergeant Preston in the arm* is the subject. In (B.2) the NP *a photograph* is the subject; in (B.3) the NP-PP sequence *a photograph of the accident* is the subject. Fourth, (A.2) is an acceptable passive version of (A.1), but (A.3) isn't. On the other hand, (B.3) is an acceptable passive version of (B.1), but (B.2) isn't. It is this last observation that seems to have no ready explanation. That is, why should the acceptable passive version of (A.1) have only an NP (*Sergeant Preston*) as its subject but the acceptable passive version of (B.1) have an NP-PP sequence (*a photograph of the accident*) as its subject?

This state of affairs can be explained if we make three assumptions. First, a passive sentence will have the direct object of its active version as subject. That is, the direct object of the active becomes the subject in the passive. Second, the direct object of an active sentence is the NP directly under VP (or, in more technical terms, the NP **directly dominated** by VP). Third, (A.1) and (B.1) have different constituent structures, as shown in Figure 4–2. These structures provide a simple account of the problem we noted earlier, namely that in the acceptable passive of (A.1), the NP *Sergeant Preston* is the subject, but in the acceptable passive of (B.1), the NP-PP sequence *a photograph of the accident* is the subject. Note that in diagram (A.1), *Sergeant Preston* is the direct object (the NP directly under VP) and thus becomes the subject in the passive version (A.2). On the other hand, in diagram (B.1), *a photograph of the accident* is the direct object (i.e., *a photograph of the accident* is all part of the NP directly under VP) and thus becomes the subject in the passive version (B.3). (As an informal exercise, try to explain how the diagram in (A.1) rules out the

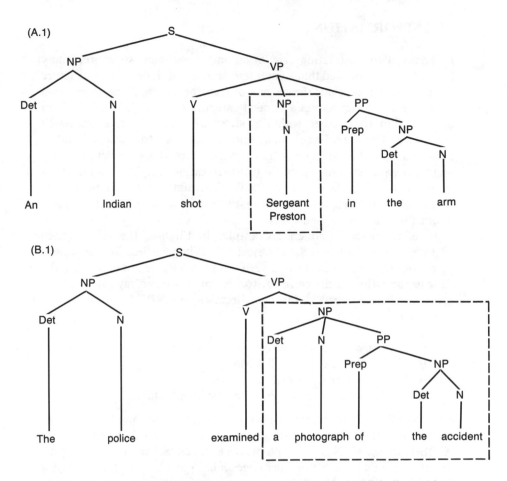

Figure 4-2. Constituent structures of (A.1) and (B.1), indicating their direct objects.

unacceptable passive in (A.3) and how the diagram in (B.1) rules out the unacceptable passive in (B.2).)

The main point of this example is that our explanation of the data in (A.1–3) and (B.1–3) is crucially dependent on the concepts of categories and constituent structure. Note our reference to categories (e.g., a direct object is the NP directly under VP) and to constituent structure (e.g., the PP in (B.1) is part of the direct object NP, whereas the PP in (A.1) is not). As this example shows, it is difficult, if not impossible, to make even the most commonplace observations about syntactic phenomena without using notions such as categories and constituent structure.

TRANSFORMATIONS

In addition to postulating categories and constituent structure, many linguists have proposed that a complete account of the syntactic structure of sentences must include the concept of **transformation**. A transformation is an operation that moves a phrasal category (e.g., NP, VP, PP) from one location to another within a structure. As with categories and constituent structure, linguists have postulated transformations in order to account for phenomena that they otherwise could not explain. In other words, no one has ever "seen" a transformation (or, for that matter, a syntactic structure or a category). Transformations are simply handy theoretical constructs that linguists assume exist in order to explain facts about the behavior of sentences.

Let's consider a concrete example. In English, the verb *conceal* requires one and only one direct object NP. When we describe the phrasal categories that can occur after a verb within a VP, we are describing the **subcategorization** of the verb; so, for example, we can say that the verb *conceal* is subcategorized for one direct object NP. This property is illustrated in (C.1–4).

(C.1)   Tiny Abner concealed the document.
(C.2)   Tiny Abner concealed Mary.
(C.3)   *Tiny Abner concealed.
(C.4)   *Tiny Abner concealed the document Mary.

Sentences (C.1–2) are acceptable because *conceal* is followed in each case by one and only one direct object (*the document* in (C.1) and *Mary* in (C.2)). Sentence (C.3) is unacceptable because *conceal* has no direct object, and (C.4) is unacceptable because *conceal* has more than one direct object (*the document* and *Mary*). We can account for these facts very simply with the following generalization: Any sentence containing the verb *conceal* will be acceptable if it contains one and only one direct object NP; conversely, any sentence containing the verb *conceal* will be unacceptable if it contains no direct object or more than one direct object.

In passing, it is worth mentioning that sentences such as *Tiny Abner concealed the document and the microfilm* appear to violate this generalization, since there seem to be two direct objects, *the document* and *the microfilm*. One method linguists have used to solve this apparent problem is to assume that sentences containing compound NP's (e.g., *the document and the microfilm*) are actually reduced versions of compound sentences (e.g., *Tiny Abner concealed the document and Tiny Abner concealed the microfilm*). Note that in this example each half of the compound sentence has one occurrence of *conceal* and exactly one direct object, which conforms to our generalization.

Now let's look at some *wh*-interrogatives containing the verb *conceal*. (A *wh*-interrogative is one introduced by a *wh*-word: *who, what, when, where, why,* or *how.*) Examples are given in (D.1–4.)

(D.1)   What did Tiny Abner conceal?
(D.2)   Who did Tiny Abner conceal?
(D.3)   *What did Tiny Abner conceal Mary?
(D.4)   *Who did Tiny Abner conceal the document?

These sentences seem to present a problem. Note that our generalization about the declarative sentences in (C.1–4) makes exactly the *wrong* predictions about (D.1–4). The generalization predicts that (D.1–2) should be unacceptable, since neither of these sentences apparently has a direct object, and that (D.3–4) should be acceptable, since each of these sentences apparently has one and only one direct object. (Recall our definition of direct object as an NP directly under VP.) Actually, the facts are just the reverse: (D.1–2) are perfectly acceptable, and (D.3–4) are absolutely unacceptable.

One way out of this predicament would be to say that sentences containing the verb *conceal* are subject to two different generalizations, depending upon whether they are declaratives or interrogatives. We can state these generalizations as follows:

Generalization 1: A declarative sentence containing the verb *conceal* is acceptable if it contains one and only one direct object.
Generalization 2: An interrogative sentence containing the verb *conceal* is acceptable if it contains no direct object.

This solution, however, although it seems to work, raises three additional problems. First, it requires us to double our number of generalizations concerning sentences containing *conceal*. This problem is not insurmountable, but it does make our analysis suspect, since it opens the door to proliferating the number of generalizations we need to cover various types of sentences. Second, there are interrogative sentences such as *Where did Tiny Abner conceal the document?* that contain the verb *conceal* and do have a direct object. Third, there are other interrogative sentences (non-*wh*-interrogatives) that conform to Generalization 1 (the one for declaratives) rather than to Generalization 2 (the one for interrogatives). Consider the non-*wh*-interrogatives in (E.1–4).

(E.1)   Did Tiny Abner conceal the document?
(E.2)   Did Tiny Abner conceal Mary?
(E.3)   *Did Tiny Abner conceal?
(E.4)   *Did Tiny Abner conceal the document Mary?

Note that these interrogative sentences do not behave like the interrogatives in (D.1–4), but instead like the declaratives in (C.1–4). That is,

Generalization 2, the one concerning interrogatives, *incorrectly* predicts that (E.1–2) are unacceptable, since they contain a direct object; and that (E.3) is acceptable, because it contains no direct object. On the other hand, Generalization 1, the one concerning declaratives, *correctly* predicts that (E.1–2) are acceptable, since they contain one and only one direct object; that (E.3) is unacceptable, because it contains no direct object; and that (E.4) is unacceptable, because it contains more than one direct object. How can we avoid these problems?

We could, of course, state that (for some unknown reason) declaratives and non-*wh*-interrogatives behave one way with respect to *conceal* and that *wh*-interrogatives behave another way. This solution would describe some of the facts, but it doesn't really explain them. That is, it doesn't give us any insight into why the facts are the way they are.

Let's consider another, completely different way of analyzing the *wh*-interrogatives in (D.1–4). Let's assume that our original generalization about *conceal* was correct, namely that *conceal* requires one and only one direct object. Let's further assume that *wh*-words do not originate in sentence-initial position, but instead originate elsewhere in the structure and are moved into sentence-initial position by a transformation that is stated something like this: Move the *wh*-word into sentence-initial position. Let's call the structure that exists before the *wh*-word is moved the **underlying structure** and that which exists after the *wh*-word is moved the **surface structure**. Finally, let's stipulate that our original generalization— that the verb *conceal* requires one and only one direct object—applies only to underlying structures.

Now we are in a position to provide a straightforward account of *wh*-interrogatives containing the verb *conceal*. The underlying structure of (D.1) *What did Tiny Abner conceal?* is given in Figure 4–3. Note that this underlying structure is consistent with our original generalization, namely that *conceal* requires one and only one direct object NP (the direct object here is the NP *what*). The *wh*-Movement transformation applies to the underlying structure in Figure 4–3, transforming it into the surface structure in Figure 4–4.

The *wh*-Movement transformation accounts for the fact that even though *what* originated as the direct object in the underlying structure, it ends up in sentence-initial position in the surface structure. The main point is that this analysis provides a unified treatment of sentences (C.1), (D.1), and (E.1), repeated here.

(C.1)   Tiny Abner concealed the document.
(D.1)   What did Tiny Abner conceal?
(E.1)   Did Tiny Abner conceal the document?

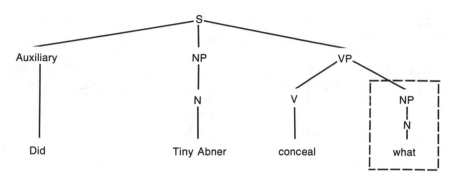

Figure 4-3. Underlying structure of sentence (D.1).

The underlying structure of all three sentences contains one and only one direct object, and thus meets the criterion for acceptability set out in our original generalization, namely that *conceal* requires one and only one direct object. The direct object in (D.1) (i.e., *what*) is moved to sentence-initial position by the *wh*-Movement transformation. The direct object in both (C.1) and (E.1) (i.e., *the document*) remains in its original position since it is not a *wh*-word and thus is not subject to the *wh*-Movement transformation.

Note, too, that our transformational analysis provides a straightforward account of the unacceptability of (D.3) **What did Tiny Abner conceal Mary?* The underlying structure of this sentence is given in Figure 4-5. This structure violates our generalization that *conceal* requires one and only one direct object NP in the underlying structure. Even though the *wh*-Movement transformation would move *what* to sentence-initial position, leaving only one direct object (i.e., *Mary*) in the surface structure, the "damage" is already done. Our generalization applies to underlying structures, not to surface structures.

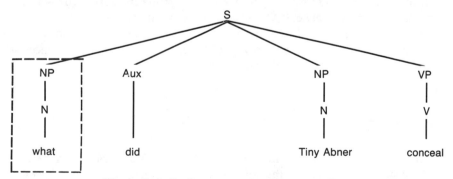

Figure 4-4. Surface structure of sentence (D.1).

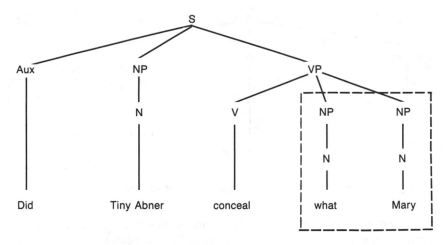

Figure 4–5. Underlying structure of sentence (D.3).

To conclude this section, we have looked at the motivation for positing transformations as part of a theory of syntax. Like the concepts of categories and constituent structure, the concept of transformations is postulated in order to account for phenomena that otherwise could not be explained, at least in any systematic, principled way. Before leaving the subject of transformations, let me again emphasize that transformations are part of an (unobservable) theory of syntax—that is, part of a method for describing and analyzing the structure of sentences. It would be a mistake to assume that transformations are involved in the **performance** of sentences, that is, in their actual production and perception by speakers and listeners. In other words, the fact that sentences can be described in terms of their underlying and surface structures should not be interpreted as meaning that a speaker "starts out" with an underlying structure and "transforms" it into a surface structure during the act of producing a sentence. A theory that includes the notions of transformations, underlying structures, and surface structures does not make any direct claims about how speakers go about producing sentences, but instead about how sentences themselves can be analyzed.

SUMMARY

Let's review the main points of this chapter. We began with three observations concerning the syntax or "architecture" of sentences. However, we had no transparent explanation for these phenomena. We therefore constructed a (partial) theory of syntax to account for our original observations. This theory makes use of three crucial concepts: category, constituent structure, and transformation. These theoretical constructs are postulated solely to help us account for phenomena that otherwise would go unexplained. Of course, some of the details surrounding these concepts may turn out to need revision; however, they enable us to account for syntactic phenomena better than any competing theory that has been proposed so far.

Since the study of syntax has received more attention than any other area of linguistics during the past 30 years, it is especially important to understand that there is much more to the study of syntax than we have been able to cover here. However, you have now been exposed to some of the seminal concepts that form the basis of syntactic investigation. If you want to learn more, take a look at some of the supplementary readings at the end of this chapter. As usual, it would be wise to check your understanding of the material in this chapter by attempting to do the following exercises.

EXERCISES

(1)   Our unconscious knowledge of categories and constituents enables us to recognize the grammaticality (i.e., the syntactic well-formedness) even of sentences containing nonsense words. Which of the following sentences appears to be syntactically well formed?
   (a)   *Brillig slithey* 'twas the and *toves gyre* in *wabe* the *gimble.*
   (b)   'Twas *brillig* and the *slithey toves* did *gyre* and *gimble* in the *wabe.*
   Now try to label the category (i.e., part of speech) of each of the italicized words in the well-formed sentence.

(2)   English contains a group of words called **reflexive pronouns**. These pronouns are formed by adding the suffix *-self* or *-selves* to a form of the personal pronoun (e.g., *I* = nominative, *me* = objective, *my* = possessive).
   (a)   Based on the following data, which form of the personal pronoun is *-self* or *-selves* added to in order to form a reflexive pronoun?
   > *myself   ourselves*
   > *yourself   yourselves*
   (b)   Based on your answer to question (a), try to explain why some nonstandard dialects of English use the following reflexive pronouns:
   > *hisself* (instead of *himself*)
   > *theirselves* (instead of *themselves*)

(3)   Each of the following phrases is structurally ambiguous—that is, it can be assigned two different constituent structures. For each phrase, use tree diagrams to show the two different structures. Also, provide a paraphrase which indicates the meaning associated with each tree structure.
(a)   abnormal psychology professor
(b)   red oak table
(c)   foreign student organization
(d)   second language teacher
(e)   big truck driver

(4)   Consider the following sentence: *Where has John put the car?* How can the following data be used to argue that *where* originated after *the car* in the underlying structure (i.e., *John has put the car where*) and was moved to sentence-initial position in the surface structure?
(a)   John has put the car in the garage.
(b)   *John has put.
(c)   *John has put the car.
Hint: Both *where* and *in the garage* indicate location.

(5)   Negative sentences in English follow a predictable pattern in terms of where *not* can occur within the sentence. Based on the following data, state a generalization about where *not* can occur.
(a)   (1)   John has put the car in the garage.
       (2)   *John *not* has put the car in the garage.
       (3)   John has *not* put the car in the garage.
       (4)   *John has put *not* the car in the garage.

(b)   (1)   John must have put the car in the garage.
       (2)   *John *not* must have put the car in the garage.
       (3)   John must *not* have put the car in the garage.
       (4)   *John must have *not* put the car in the garage.
       (5)   *John must have put *not* the car in the garage.

(c)   (1)   John must have been putting the car in the garage.
       (2)   *John *not* must have been putting the car in the garage.
       (3)   John must *not* have been putting the car in the garage.
       (4)   *John must have *not* been putting the car in the garage.
       (5)   *John must have been *not* putting the car in the garage.
       (6)   *John must have been putting *not* the car in the garage.

(6)   The following two sentences appear to have the same structure:
(a)   John threw away the magazine.
(b)   John walked down the street.
However, certain tests can be used as evidence that one of these sentences contains a one-word verb followed by a prepositional

phrase, while the other sentence contains a two-word verb followed by an object noun phrase. Try each of the following tests on these two sentences. What conclusions can you draw about which sentence has which structure?

    (A) A prepositional phrase can be moved to sentence-initial position (e.g., *Up the chimney* he went _____).

    (B) A two-word verb can be separated by its object noun phrase (e.g., John picked _____ the garbage *up*).

ANSWERS TO EXERCISES

The following answers are meant only to be suggestive; discussion of other possible answers is part of the exercises.

(1) Sentence (b) (from Lewis Carroll's poem "Jabberwocky") is syntactically well formed.
brillig = adjective; *slithey* = adjective; *toves* = noun; *gyre* = verb; *gimble* = verb; *wabe* = noun.
What clues in the sentence structure enable you to assign these nonsense words to categories? Note: Assigning the italicized words in sentence (a) to categories is much more difficult, if not impossible.

(2) (a) *myself* = possessive + *self*   *ourselves* = possessive + *selves*
          yourself = possessive + *self*   *yourselves* = possessive + *selves*
    (b) The general rule (first and second persons) is to add -*self* or -*selves* to the possessive form of the pronoun. The exception (third person) is to add -*self* or -*selves* to the objective form. The nonstandard dialects simply extend the general rule (possessive + *self/selves*) to the third person (*his* + *self*; *their* + *selves*).

(3) (a)

abnormal psychology professor = 'professor of abnormal psychology'

abnormal psychology professor = 'psychology professor who is abnormal'

    (b)

red oak table = 'table made of red oak'

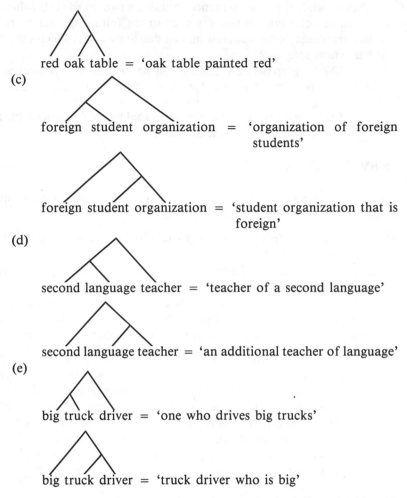

red oak table = 'oak table painted red'

(c)

foreign student organization = 'organization of foreign students'

foreign student organization = 'student organization that is foreign'

(d)

second language teacher = 'teacher of a second language'

second language teacher = 'an additional teacher of language'

(e)

big truck driver = 'one who drives big trucks'

big truck driver = 'truck driver who is big'

(4) Sentences (a-c) indicate that the verb *put* must be followed (although not immediately) by a phrase indicating location (e.g., *in the garage*). In the sentence *Where has John put the car?*, there is no phrase indicating location following *put*, yet the sentence is perfectly acceptable. One way to account for the acceptability of this sentence is to assume that *where* (a phrase indicating location) originated to the right of *put* in the underlying structure (i.e., *Has John put the car where*) and was later moved into sentence-initial position by the rule of *wh*-Movement.

(5) *Not* can occur after the first verb form in a sentence. (Actually, we might say after the first auxiliary verb, since forms of *must*, *have*, and *be* are auxiliary verbs and *put* is a main verb.)

Note that some of the starred sentences may be acceptable to you (e.g., (b-4),(c-4), (c-5)). If you assume that these sentences are acceptable, along with the unstarred ones, how would you have to state the generalization concerning the occurrence of *not*?

(6) (a)   = two-word verb + direct object noun phrase
     (b)   = one-word verb + prepositional phrase

     (a)   John threw away the magazine.
     (A)   *Away the magazine John threw.
     (B)   John threw the magazine away.

     (b)   John walked down the street.
     (A)   Down the street John walked.
     (B)   *John walked the street down.

SUPPLEMENTARY READINGS

Primary

1. Leiber, J. (1975). *Noam Chomsky: A philosophic overview*. New York: St. Martin's Press.
2. Lightfoot, D. (1982). *The language lottery: Toward a biology of grammars*. Cambridge, MA: MIT Press.
3. Lyons, J. (1977). *Noam Chomsky*. New York: Penguin.
4. Newmeyer, F. J. (1980). *Linguistic theory in America: The first quarter-century of transformational generative grammar*. New York: Academic Press.
5. Newmeyer, F. J. (1983). *Grammatical theory: Its limits and its possibilities*. Chicago: University of Chicago Press.

Secondary

6. Akmajian, A., and Heny, F. W. (1975). *An introduction to the principles of transformational syntax*. Cambridge, MA: MIT Press.
7. Radford, A. (1981). *Transformational syntax: A student's guide to extended standard theory*. Cambridge, England: Cambridge University Press.

So much has been written about syntax that it is a difficult area to break into on your own. My best advice is to take an elementary course in syntax, where you will read Akmajian and Heny (6) or Radford (7), or something like them. Then read (1–5). If you are in a position where you cannot take a course, read these books in the following order. Lyons (3) and Leiber (1) provide an introduction to Chomsky's thought; Akmajian and Heny (6) and Radford (7) are texts dealing with Chomsky's "standard" and "extended standard" theories of syntax, respectively; Newmeyer (4) discusses the social and intellectual context surrounding the development of syntactic theory from the mid 1950's up to 1980; and Lightfoot (2) and Newmeyer (5) provide overviews of current thought in syntax.

Chapter 5

Morphology

Morphology is the study of word formation. (The word *morphology* itself comes from the Greek word *morphē* which means 'form.') Morphology is to words what syntax is to sentences. That is, morphology is the study of the architecture of words, just as syntax is the study of the architecture of sentences. The study of morphology, at least in the Western tradition, can be traced as far back as Franz Bopp, a German, who in 1816 published a comparative study of verbal endings of a number of related language families, including Germanic (which in turn includes English). Even though the study of morphology has been eclipsed in the twentieth century by the study of syntax (Chapter 4) and phonology (Chapter 6), there are, nevertheless, a number of interesting observations we can make about the internal structure of words.

Let's begin by considering some of the observations we can make about the structure of words in English.

(1) *Boldest* can be divided into two parts (i.e., *bold* + *est*), each of which has a meaning; *bold* cannot.

(2) The word *boy* has a meaning in and of itself; the word *at* does not. Rather, *at* indicates a relationship between two meaningful expressions (e.g., *The man at the door*).

(3) The form *serve* can stand alone as a word; the form *pre-* (as in *preserve*) cannot.

(4) *Friendliest* is a word; *friendestly* is not.

Observation (1) illustrates the fact that words are made up of meaningful units (**morphemes**). Observation (2) illustrates the fact that some morphemes have meaning in and of themselves (**lexical morphemes**), while others specify the relationship between one lexical morpheme and another (**grammatical morphemes**). Observation (3) illustrates the fact that some morphemes, called **free morphemes**, can stand alone as words, while others, called **bound morphemes,** cannot. Observation (4) can be used to argue that bound morphemes can be divided into two types, **inflectional** and **derivational.**

All of these phenomena are essentially morphological in nature. That is, they have to do with the internal architecture of words. Moreover, we will make our standard assumption that the phenomena in (1–4) are governed by a system of rules. What we will do now is attempt to construct a set of concepts and principles that will help us account for the phenomena in (1–4). As usual, keep in mind that what follows is a theory designed to account for the data in (1–4).

MORPHEMES

A **morpheme** can be loosely defined as a minimal unit having more or less *constant meaning* associated with more or less *constant form*. Consider, for example, a transparent case: the word *buyers* is made up of three morphemes, {buy} + {er} + {s}. (Braces are sometimes used to indicate morphemes.) Each of these morphemes has a unique meaning: {buy} = verb 'buy' (however it might be represented semantically); {er} = 'one who performs an action'; {s} = 'more than one.' Together they mean something like 'more than one person who buys things.' The strongest evidence that each of these word parts is a morpheme is the fact that each one can occur with other morphemes without changing its core meaning. For example, {buy} occurs in *buy, buying,* and *buys,* as well as in *buyers.* {er} occurs in *farmer, driver,* and *mover,* as well as in *buyers.* {s} occurs in *boys, girls,* and *dogs,* as well as in *buyers.*

There are three points to note with respect to morphemes. First, they are distinct from semantic features, in that morphemes have a more or less constant form, which is usually reflected by their spelling. (After covering the chapter on phonology [Chapter 6], we will be able to define morphemes a little more precisely in terms of pronunciation rather than spelling.) For example, the senses of the words *man, boy, stallion,* and *colt* all might be specified with the semantic feature [+ male], yet all four words constitute different morphemes. One way of looking at the difference between semantic features and morphemes would be to say that features combine vertically to form morphemes, and morphemes combine horizontally to form words. The semantic and morphological structure of the word *girls* is illustrated in the following diagram. (The dotted line represents other semantic features, whatever they may be, that are necessary for specifying the meaning of {girl}.)

[– adult]
[– male]
[+ human]
.
.
.
.
.
.
.

{girl}   + {s} = *girls*

Moreover, note that words such as *conceal* and *hide* constitute different morphemes (because they have different forms or spellings), even though their senses might be represented by identical sets of semantic features.

Second, the definition of a morpheme as a minimal unit with *more or less* constant meaning associated with *more or less* constant form should be taken as a general rule of thumb rather than a hard and fast criterion. For example, the words *boys* and *girls* conform to this definition rather closely. That is, *boys* can be divided into {boy} + {s} and *girls* can be divided into {girl} + {s}, where the -*s* in each word represents the same plural morpheme. (The plural morpheme is often symbolized {PLU} rather than {s} to distinguish it from other morphemes spelled with -*s*, such as the possessive morpheme in *boy's*.) The word *men*, however, does not seem to be as easily divisible into morphemes, where plurality is marked not by the addition of an -*s* but rather by a change in vowel (from *man*). What are we to do in cases like this? Do we want to say that *men* has nothing in common with *boys* and *girls*, simply because there is no consistency in form (i.e., spelling)? Probably not. This solution would overlook the obvious generalization that the meaning relationship between *man* and *men* is identical to that between *boy* and *boys*, *girl* and *girls*, and so on, even though the form (or spelling) relationship between such pairs is not identical. In order to capture such obvious meaning relationships, some linguists have opted for representing the morphological structure of *men* as {man} + {PLU}. Note, moreover, that we will have ample opportunity to make further use of this type of abstraction. For example, *went* is to *go* as *walked* is to *walk*. Thus, *went* might be represented morphologically as {go} + {PAST}, just as *walked* would be characterized as {walk} + {PAST}. In short, all exceptional cases (e.g., *men* and *went*) can be treated on analogy with regular cases (e.g., *boys* and *walked*).

Third, it is important to note that identical spellings do not necessarily indicate identical morphemes. For example, consider *buyer* and *shorter*, each of which ends in -*er*. Note, however, that the -*er* in *buyer* means something like 'one who,' while the -*er* in *shorter* means something like 'to a greater degree than.' Note, moreover, that the -*er* which means 'one who' always attaches to a verb (e.g., *buy*) and the -*er* which means 'to a greater degree than' always attaches to an adjective (e.g., *short*). Thus, even though the two -*er*'s have the same form or spelling, they have different meanings, and we therefore have to treat them as different morphemes. The former is sometimes called the agentive morpheme (abbreviated {AG}), since it indicates one who performs an action, and the latter is termed the comparative morpheme ({COMP}), since it indicates the comparative degree of an adjective.

Let's summarize the main point of this section. A morpheme is a linguistic unit that is defined by a (more or less) constant core meaning associated with a (more or less) constant form.

LEXICAL AND GRAMMATICAL MORPHEMES

The distinction between lexical and grammatical morphemes is not well defined, although many linguists seem to agree that it is a useful division to make. **Lexical morphemes** have a sense (i.e., meaning) in and of themselves. Nouns, verbs, and adjectives (e.g., {boy}, {buy}, and {big}) are typical of lexical morphemes. **Grammatical morphemes**, on the other hand, don't really have a sense in and of themselves; instead, they express some sort of relationship *between* lexical morphemes. Prepositions, articles, and conjunctions (e.g., {of}, {the}, and {but}) are typical of grammatical morphemes.

FREE AND BOUND MORPHEMES

In contrast to the division between lexical and grammatical morphemes, the distinction between free and bound morphemes is straightforward. **Free morphemes** are those that can stand alone as words. They may be lexical (e.g., {serve}, {press}) or they may be grammatical (e.g., {at}, {and}). **Bound morphemes**, on the other hand, cannot stand alone as words. Likewise, they may be lexical (e.g., {clude} as in *exclude, include,* and *preclude*) or they may be grammatical (e.g., {PLU} = plural as in *boys, girls,* and *cats*).

INFLECTIONAL AND
DERIVATIONAL MORPHEMES

This distinction applies only to the class of bound, grammatical morphemes. (See the right-hand branch of Figure 5–1.) The more familiar term for the class of bound grammatical morphemes is **affix**. Affixes, in turn, can be subdivided into **prefixes** and **suffixes**, depending upon whether they are attached to the beginning of a lexical morpheme, as in *depress* (where {de} is a prefix), or to the end of a lexical morpheme, as in *helpful* (where {ful} is a suffix). Note that this division of affixes into prefixes and suffixes appears to present a bit of a problem in cases such as *men* = {man} + {PLU}, which technically has neither a prefix nor a suffix. What we are forced to say here is that the plural morpheme in English *generally* appears as a suffix, never as a prefix. A summary of these divisions is presented schematically in Figure 5–1.

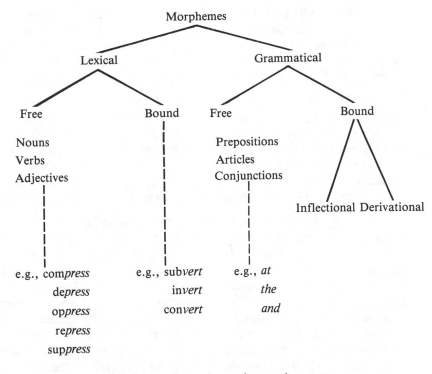

Figure 5–1.   Division of morphemes into various types.

Inflectional Affixes

Let's now return to the distinction between inflectional and derivational affixes (i.e., bound, grammatical morphemes). English has eight inflectional affixes; all other affixes are derivational. The eight inflectional affixes are listed in the following table, along with the type of root (i.e., lexical morpheme) that each one attaches to, and a representative example.

INFLECTIONAL AFFIX	ROOT	EXAMPLE
{PLU} = plural	Noun	boy*s*
{POSS} = possessive	Noun	boy'*s*
{COMP} = comparative	Adjective	old*er*
{SUP} = superlative	Adjective	old*est*
{PRES} = present	Verb	walk*s*
{PAST} = past	Verb	walk*ed*
{PAST PART} = past participle	Verb	driv*en*
{PRES PART} = present participle	Verb	driv*ing*

Each one of these requires some comment.

{*PLU*}. All plural nouns in English can be represented morphologically as consisting of a root + {PLU}, regardless of how the plural morpheme is actually spelled or pronounced. For example, *boys* = {boy} + {PLU}, *men* = {man} + {PLU}, and even the plural of *sheep* (as in *Those sheep have big noses*) = {sheep} + {PLU}.

{*POSS*}. All possessive nouns in English can be represented morphologically as consisting of a root + {POSS}. For example, *boy's* = {boy} + {POSS}, and *man's* = {man} + {POSS}. (The reason that {PLU} and {POSS} are both generally spelled with -*s* in Modern English is the result of historical accident. The plural -*s* comes from the Old English masculine nominative-objective plural suffix -*as*, while the possessive -*s* comes from the Old English masculine possessive singular suffix -*es*.)

{*COMP*} *and* {*SUP*}. All comparative and superlative adjectives in English can be represented morphologically as consisting of a root + {COMP} or {SUP}. For example, *happier* = {happy} + {COMP}, and *happiest* = {happy} + {SUP}. Note, even *good, better,* and *best* can be represented in this fashion: *good* = {good}, *better* = {good} + {COMP}, and *best* = {good} + {SUP}. On the other hand, it isn't clear how best to handle forms like *most beautiful*. Under some circumstances it might be reasonable to treat them as a root plus an affix (e.g., *most beautiful* = {beautiful} + {SUP}), on analogy with regular cases such as *prettiest* = {pretty} + {SUP}. However, *most* in *most beautiful* is clearly not an affix, as is -*est* in *prettiest*; rather, it's a free grammatical morpheme. Since linguists do not always agree on how to handle forms such as *most beautiful*, we will simply leave this as an open question.

{*PRES*}. All present tense verbs in English can be represented morphologically as consisting of a root + {PRES}. For example, *loves* (as in *John loves Mary*) = {love} + {PRES}. Note, however, that the only time this -*s* surfaces (i.e., is spelled out) is when there is a third person singular subject (i.e., *he, she, it,* or an NP for which one of these can substitute—for example, *John, Mary, the dog*). With all other subjects (e.g., *I, you, we, they, John and Mary,* and so on), the present tense verb has no surface affix. Nonetheless, the verb *love* (as in *John and Mary love each other*) can be represented as {love} + {PRES}.

{*PAST*}. All past tense verbs in English can be represented morphologically as consisting of a root + {PAST}. For example, *walked* (as in *John walked on hot coals*) = {walk} + {PAST}. Thus, any past tense verb, regardless of its spelling, can be represented in this fashion. For example, *drove* = {drive} + {PAST}. Note, moreover, that in English (as in all Germanic languages), the first and only the first verb form in a simple sentence is inflected for tense (i.e., {PRES} or {PAST}); no verb following the first is ever inflected for tense. Thus, for example, in the sentence *I think*, *think* is inflected for tense ({think} + {PRES}); in *I have thought*, *have* is inflected for tense ({have} + {PRES}); in *I am thinking*, *am* is inflected for tense ({be} + {PRES}); and so on.

{*PAST PART*}. All past participles in English can be represented morphologically as consisting of a root + {PAST PART}. For example, *driven* (as in *John has driven his mother crazy*) = {drive} + {PAST PART}. One potential problem in identifying past participles results from the fact that there is so much variation in their spelling. For example, *gone* = {go} + {PAST PART}, *come* (as in *They've come home*) = {come} + {PAST PART}, *hit* (as in *He's hit three home runs*) = {hit} + {PAST PART}, and *walked* (as in *He's walked three miles for that Camel*) = {walk} + {PAST PART}. Nonetheless, there is a very simple method for identifying a past participle in a simple active sentence: A past participle always follows the auxiliary verb *have*. Thus, in the sentence *They have walked home*, *walked* is a past participle since it immediately follows a form of *have*. However, in the sentence *They walked home*, *walked* is not a past participle since it does not follow a form of *have*. In fact, it is a tensed form (here past), since it is the first verb form in the sentence.

{*PRES PART*}. All present participles in English can be represented morphologically as consisting of a root + {PRES PART}. For example, *drinking* = {drink} + {PRES PART}. Unlike other verb forms in English, present participles always appear in a constant form (i.e., with an -*ing* suffix). In addition, the present participle in a simple active sentence can be identified as the verb form following a form of the auxiliary verb *to be*, as in *They were laughing*.

Let me add a footnote at this point concerning verb forms in English. In simple, active sentences there are five different types of verbs that can occur: main verbs and four different auxiliary verbs (modal verbs, forms of *have*, forms of *be*, and forms of *do*). We will take these up one at a time.

The **main verb** is always the verb farthest to the right in a simple sentence. Thus, in the sentence *John should have gone*, *gone* is the main verb; in *John might have a cold*, *have* is the main verb; and so on. Note that forms of *have, be,* and *do* in English can function as both main verbs and auxiliaries. If they are farthest to the right, they are main verbs; if not, they are auxiliaries.

The primary **modal verbs** are *can/could, shall/should, will/would, may/might,* and *must.* Modals are characterized by the absence of the third person singular *-s* that occurs on all other types of verbs in the present tense. For example, in the sentence *John has seen Mary*, note the *-s* on *has*. However, in the sentence *John may see Mary*, note that there is no *-s* on *may* (cf. **John mays see Mary*). Furthermore, when a modal occurs in a sentence, it is always the first verb form and it is always followed by an uninflected verb form; for example, in *John will be going*, the modal *will* is first in the series, and the following verb *be* is uninflected (cf. **John is will go* and **John will been going*).

If the auxiliary *have* occurs in a simple active sentence, it is always followed by a past participle. For example, in the sentence *John has eaten*, *eaten* follows *have* and thus is a past participle; in the sentence *John has been eating*, *been* follows *have* and thus is a past participle; and so on. Moreover, if both a modal and the auxiliary *have* occur in the same sentence, *have* follows the modal; for example, in *We may have gone*, *have* follows the modal *may* (cf. **We have may gone*).

If the auxiliary *be* occurs in a simple active sentence, it is always followed by a present participle. For example, in the sentence *John is eating, eating* follows a form of *be* (*is*) and thus is a present participle; in the sentence *John will be eating, eating* follows *be* and thus is a present participle; and so on. Furthermore, if both the auxiliary *have* and the auxiliary *be* occur in the same sentence, the form of *be* always follows the form of *have*; for example, in *We have been eating*, the form of *be* (i.e., *been*) follows the form of *have* (cf. **We are have eating*).

The auxiliary *do* never occurs with any of the other auxiliary verbs in a simple, active sentence. When two items (e.g., *do* and the other auxiliaries) never occur in the same environment (e.g., in a simple active sentence), the two items are said to be in **complementary distribution**. In other words, auxiliary *do* occurs only with a main verb, never with another auxiliary verb. For example, in the sentence *I do eat corn, do* is an auxiliary and *eat* is a main verb (cf. **I do may eat corn, *I do have eaten corn, *I* *do am eating corn*). Moreover, the main verb that appears with *do* is always uninflected. For example, in the sentence *We did see that movie, see* is the main verb and thus is uninflected (cf. **We did saw that movie, *We did seen that movie, *We did seeing that movie*).

In short, then, verbs in English are perfectly systematic. For example, using the sentence *Someone may have been knocking at the door*, we can make several observations based on this system. First, *knocking* is the main verb, because it is the right-most verb. Moreover, it is a present participle, because it immediately follows a form of *be*. Second, *been* is an auxiliary verb, because it is not the right-most verb. Furthermore, it is a past participle, because it immediately follows a form of *have*. Third, *have* is an auxiliary verb, because it is not the right-most verb. Also, it is uninflected, because it immediately follows a modal (*may*). Fourth, *may* is a modal, because it lacks the third person singular *-s*. Moreover, it is inflected for present tense (*might* would be past), since the first and only the first verb in a simple sentence in English is inflected for tense.

Before ending this footnote to the section on inflectional affixes, let me say something about **tense**. As I have been using the term, it refers to a particular form of a verb. All Germanic languages (including English) have two inflected tenses: present and past. Furthermore, a past tense verb in English is generally characterized by a *-t* or *-d* suffix. Thus, *may* is present and *might* is past; *can* is present and *could* is past; and so on. The main point to note, however, is that inflected tense does not correlate perfectly with time reference. That is, a past tense verb form does not always indicate past time. For example, the sentence *I might go with you tonight* contains a past tense verb form (*might*) but the sentence refers to future time. Likewise, a present tense verb form does not always indicate present time. For instance, the sentence *Yesterday this guy comes up to me on the street* contains a present tense verb form (*comes*) but the sentence refers to past time. Since inflected tense and time reference do not always coincide, the term **aspect** is sometimes used to describe the time reference of a verb.

Derivational Affixes

After this rather long detour into inflectional affixes, let's return to their counterparts, the derivational affixes. Unlike the inflectional affixes, which number only eight in English, the set of derivational affixes is open-ended; that is, there are a potentially infinite number of them (although the number is finite at any one time for a particular speaker). Since it would be impossible to enumerate them exhaustively, let us look at a few representative examples. The suffix {ize} attaches to a noun and turns it into the corresponding verb, as in *criticize, simonize, rubberize, vulcanize, pasteurize, mesmerize,* and so on. (This suffix can also be added to adjectives, as in *normalize, realize, finalize, vitalize, equalize, solemnize, mysticize,* and so on.) The suffix {ful} attaches to a noun and changes it into the corresponding adjective, as in *helpful, playful, thoughtful, careful, wishful,* and so on. The suffix {ly} attaches to an adjective and turns it into the corresponding adverb, as in *quickly, carefully, swiftly, mightily,* and so on. Note that there is another separate derivational affix, also spelled *-ly,* which attaches to a noun and changes it into the corresponding adjective, as in *friendly, manly, neighborly,* and so on. Obviously, we would need to come up with two different morphological symbols for these two derivational affixes spelled *-ly,* just as we came up with {AG} and {COMP} for the two affixes generally spelled *-er.*

In addition to these derivational suffixes, English also has derivational prefixes. The following all exhibit some variation on the meaning 'not.' The prefix {un} appears in forms like *unhappy, unwary, unassuming,* and *unforgettable.* The prefix {dis} occurs in words such as *displeasure, disproportionate, dislike,* and *distrust.* The prefix {a} appears in forms such as *asymmetrical, asexual, atheist,* and *atypical.* And the prefix {anti} occurs in words like *anti-American, anti-Castro,* and *anti-aircraft.*

DIFFERENCES BETWEEN TYPES OF AFFIXES

So far, we have simply assumed that there are two classes of bound grammatical morphemes: inflectional and derivational. Let's now consider some evidence for this division. Remember that one of our fundamental assumptions is that if two items exhibit different behavior under the same conditions, they must belong to different categories.

Historical Development. All inflectional affixes are native to English (i.e., they have been part of English since Old English was spoken—around 500-1000 AD). On the other hand, many (but not all) derivational affixes are borrowings from other languages, in particular Latin and Greek. For example, {ize} is borrowed from Greek: {dis}, {de}, and {re} are borrowed from Latin; and {a} and {anti} are borrowed from Greek through Latin. Moreover, while derivational prefixes tend to show a high percentage of borrowings, there are still a number of derivational affixes (especially suffixes) that are native to English. For example, {ful}, {ly} (both varieties), {like}, and {AG} all derive ultimately from Old English. Thus we can make the generalization that if an affix is borrowed, it is derivational (i.e., all borrowed affixes are derivational).

Distribution. All inflectional affixes are suffixes; derivational affixes may be suffixes or prefixes. That is, {PLU}, {POSS}, {COMP}, {SUP}, and the four verbal inflectional affixes all appear as suffixes, at least in the unexceptional cases. (Recall that the exceptional cases are analyzed on analogy with the regular cases; for example, *sang* = {sing} + {PAST}, since *walked* = {walk} + {PAST}.) On the other hand, it should be clear by now that derivational affixes may be either prefixes or suffixes. For example, *unfriendly* consists of the free lexical morpheme {friend} plus the derivational prefix {un} and the derivational suffix {ly}. In sum, we can say that if an affix is a prefix, then it is derivational (i.e., all prefixes are derivational).

Range of Application. Inflectional affixes have a relatively wide range of application, while derivational affixes have a wide to narrow range of application. Wide application means that if an affix joins with a particular category of morpheme, then it joins with (almost) all members of that category. Inflectional affixes have this property. For example, the inflectional affix {PLU} adjoins to (almost) all members of the category noun. Note that it is difficult to find a noun in English that cannot be made plural. Even proper names can be made plural (for example, *There are two Marthas in my syntax class*). Derivational affixes, on the other hand, have a varying range of applications. Many of them (especially prefixes) have a fairly narrow range of application. For example, the derivational prefix {a} can be prefixed to a very limited number of lexical morphemes: *asexual, atypical, asymmetrical, atheist, agnostic, amoral, apolitical, aseptic, aphasia.* We quickly begin to exhaust the roots that can take the prefix {a}. The derivational prefix {un} seems to have a somewhat wider range of application. It is prefixed to adjectives (among other things) to form the negative: *unhappy, unmanageable, unreliable, unpatriotic, unpopular, unbearable, unimportant, untouchable, unremarkable,* and so on. Note, however, that not all adjectives will take this prefix: **unshort, *unsad, *untall, *ungullible,* and so forth. Other derivational affixes, especially the suffixes, tend to have a wider range of application. For example, the {AG} affix can be suffixed to a wide range of verbs: *doer, achiever, thinker, builder, baker, pusher,* and so on. On the other hand, some derivational suffixes have a very limited range of application. For example, {hood} appears in the kinship terms *motherhood, fatherhood, sisterhood,* and *brotherhood,* but not **aunthood, *unclehood, *niecehood,* or **nephewhood.* In short, we can make the following generalization: If an affix has a narrow range of application, it is derivational.

Order of Appearance. Inflectional suffixes follow derivational suffixes. That is, if a word contains both a derivational and an inflectional suffix, then the inflectional suffix comes last. For example, the word *friendliest* can be broken down as follows (R = root, D = derivational, and I = inflectional).

$$\{friend\} + \{ly\} + \{SUP\}$$
$$\quad R \qquad D \qquad I$$

Note that reversing the suffixes results in the unacceptable form *friendestly*. Consider another example. The word *lovers* consists of the following morphemes.

$$\{love\} + \{AG\} + \{PLU\}$$
$$\quad R \qquad D \qquad I$$

As in the previous case, reversing the suffixes results in the unacceptable form *loveser*.

This principle of inflectional suffixes following derivational suffixes, in turn, accounts for some apparently problematic cases. Consider, for example, the forms *spoonsful* and *spoonfuls*. Proponents of prescriptive or "school" grammar would claim that *spoonsful* is "correct" and *spoonfuls* is "incorrect." On the other hand, many (if not most) speakers of English would unselfconsciously say *spoonfuls* rather than *spoonsful*. Our principle governing the order of derivational and inflectional affixes helps explain what is going on here. Historically, *spoon* and *ful* (from *full*) were two separate lexical morphemes, as in *a spoon full of castor oil*. Thus, since *spoon* was a noun and nouns take the {PLU} affix, an -*s* was added to *spoon* to make the phrase plural, as in *two spoons full of castor oil*. However, over time *spoon full* (two lexical morphemes) was reanalyzed as *spoonful* (a lexical morpheme plus a derivational suffix). Note that if you were to hear *spoon full* or *spoonful* spoken, you wouldn't be able to tell if it were one word or two. Once *full* was reanalyzed as a derivational suffix attached to the noun *spoon*, then our principle would predict that the plural morpheme would be attached to the right of the derivational affix *ful*, yielding *spoonfuls* as follows.

$$\{spoon\} + \{ful\} + \{PLU\}$$
$$\quad R \qquad D \qquad I$$

Note that *spoonsful* is a violation of the principle governing the order of suffixes.

$$*\{spoon\} + \{PLU\} + \{ful\}$$
$$\quad R \qquad I \qquad D$$

In short, the morphological rules of English dictate that *spoonfuls* will eventually supplant *spoonsful*. An identical argument could be used to explain the preference for *cupfuls* over *cupsful* and *mother-in-laws* over *mothers-in-law*.

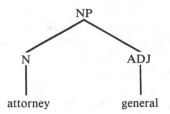

Figure 5-2. Structure of *attorney general* in French.

Consider a related example. What is the plural of *attorney general*: *attorneys general* or *attorney generals*? Again the purists would probably claim that *attorneys general* is "correct," since *attorney* is a noun and thus takes the plural suffix, while *general* is an adjective and thus should not be inflected for {PLU}. On the other hand, most speakers of English would unselfconsciously say *attorney generals* for the plural form. As in our earlier example, this can be explained as a by-product of reanalysis. English borrowed the term *attorney general* from French, a language in which an adjective generally follows the noun it modifies. Thus, this phrase in French would have the structure shown in Figure 5-2. As a result, since the plural inflection is affixed to nouns, the plural form in French would be *attorneys general*. English, on the other hand, is a language in which an adjective generally *precedes* the noun it modifies. Thus, *attorney general*, once borrowed, has been reanalyzed to conform to English structure as shown in Figure 5-3. Given this structure, it is perfectly predictable that English speakers will pluralize *attorney general* as *attorney generals*. In short, then, inflectional and derivational affixes are governed by a system of principles that predict both their order and the categories to which they can be attached.

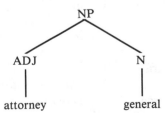

Figure 5-3. Structure of *attorney general* in English.

Effect on Syntactic Category. Inflectional suffixes do not change the syntactic category (i.e., part of speech) of the root they are attached to; derivational suffixes generally do. First, let's consider some inflectional suffixes. *Boy* is a noun and *boys* ({boy} + {PLU}) is also a noun. *Short* is an adjective and *shorter* ({short} + {COMP}) is likewise an adjective. *Drive* is a verb and *driven* ({drive} + {PAST PART}) is also a verb. Now consider some derivational suffixes. *Critic* is a noun, but *criticize* ({critic} + {ize}) is a verb. *Quick* is an adjective, but *quickly* ({quick} + {ly}) is an adverb. *Read* is a verb, but *readable* ({read} + {able}) is an adjective. It is important to realize, however, that some derivational suffixes do not change the category of the root. For example, *brother* is a noun and so is *brotherhood* ({brother} + {hood}). Also, derivational prefixes do not change the category of the root. For example, *do* is a verb and so are *undo* ({un} + {do}) and *redo* ({re} + {do}). Therefore, we can make the following generalization: If a suffix changes the syntactic category of the lexical morpheme to which it is attached, the suffix is derivational.

Number of Allowable Affixes. No more than one inflectional morpheme can be affixed to a particular syntactic category; however, there is no limit to the number of derivational morphemes that can be affixed to one category. Let's first consider the inflectional affixes. In nontechnical terms, this principle essentially says that no noun, adjective, or verb can have more than one inflectional affix at any one time. Thus, for example, **happierest* ({happy} + {COMP} + {SUP}) is correctly predicted by this principle to be unacceptable, since the adjective {happy} has been inflected for two inflectional affixes: {COMP} and {SUP}. Likewise, the verb form **droven* ({drive} + {PAST} + {PAST PART}) is ungrammatical for the same reason.

However, what about a form like *men's*, which appears to violate this principle? That is, it looks like the form *men's* is constructed from a noun plus *two* inflectional affixes: {man} + {PLU} + {POSS}. Actually, neither this example nor plural possessive nouns in general violate our principle. It turns out that {PLU} and {POSS} do not affix to the same category at all. In fact, {PLU} affixes to N's (nouns), while {POSS} affixes to NP's (noun phrases). To see this, consider the NP *the man on the moon*, which contains the head N *man*. If we want to make this phrase plural, we inflect the N *man* for plurality: *the men on the moon*; we do not add a plural suffix to the end of the NP: **the man on the moons*. The significant point is that {PLU} attaches to the N *man*, not to the whole NP *the man on the moon*. On the other hand, if we want to make the phrase possessive, we inflect the entire NP: *the man on the moon's wife*; we do not inflect the N *man* for {POSS}: **the man's on the moon wife*. In short, then, *men's* does not violate our principle that there can be no more than one inflectional affix per syntactic category. Rather, the morphological structure of *men's* is represented as follows.

$$[\; [\{man\}] + \{PLU\}] + \{POSS\}$$
NP N

Thus, the N *man* is inflected for {PLU} and the NP *man* is inflected for {POSS}.

Derivational affixes, on the other hand, are subject to no such constraint; a given syntactic category can take an infinite number of derivational affixes, at least in theory. For example, {cover} is a verb and from it we can build, by way of derivational affixes, the following forms: *coverable, recover, recoverable, uncover, unrecoverable, recoverability, unrecoverability,* and so on. Thus, we can make the following generalization: A syntactic category can be inflected for a (theoretically) infinite number of derivational affixes, but no more than one inflectional affix.

SUMMARY

Let's review what we've done in this chapter. We started with four observations about the internal structure of words. At first, however, we had no obvious explanation for these phenomena. We then constructed a (partial) theory of morphology to account for our original observations. Central to this theory is the concept of morpheme, as well as the distinctions between lexical and grammatical morphemes, bound and free morphemes, and inflectional and derivational morphemes. These theoretical constructs have been developed by linguists in order to help explain the observations in (1–4).

This, of course, is only part of the theory of morphology; there is much more to this subject than what has been discussed in this one short chapter. However, you have now been exposed to some of the basic ideas in the field. If you want to investigate the subject further, take a look at the reading list at the end of the chapter. You may also want to check your understanding of this chapter by working through the following exercises.

EXERCISES

(1) List the morphemes that make up the following Spanish words, and assign a meaning to each morpheme. (For example, the meaning of {re} in *rewrite* and *reenter* might be 'perform an action again.')

tío	'uncle'	*hermano*	'brother'
muchacha	'girl'	*abuelo*	'grandfather'
abuela	'grandmother'	*nieta*	'granddaughter'
nieto	'grandson'	*tía*	'aunt'
hermana	'sister'	*muchacho*	'boy'

(2) Divide the following words into morphemes. For each morpheme, identify the type (lexical or grammatical, free or bound, prefix or suffix, inflectional or derivational), where applicable.
   (a) *restate*
   (b) *strongest*
   (c) *actively*
   (d) *precede*

(3) Give an example (other than the one in this chapter) which illustrates the principle that in English the plural inflection attaches to nouns and the possessive inflection attaches to noun phrases. (Hint: You will need an NP containing a head N such that the boundaries of the NP and the N are not the same.)

(4) State the morphological principle that each of the following forms violates.
   (a) *cupsful* for *cupfuls*
   (b) **loveding* for *loved* or *loving*
   (c) **photographser* for *photographers*
   (d) **two coffee blacks* for *two coffees black*

(5) What kind of evidence could be used to argue that *action* and *package* each contain two morphemes: {act} + {ion} and {pack} + {age}? (Hint: A morpheme can appear independently in other words.)

(6) What kind of evidence could be used to argue that {age} in *package* is a derivational morpheme?

ANSWERS TO EXERCISES

The following answers are by no means the only possible ones; they are meant solely to be suggestive. Discussion of other possible answers is part of the exercises.

(1) {a} 'female'
   {o} 'male'
   {muchach} 'child'
   {abuel} 'grandparent'
   {niet} 'grandchild'

{herman} 'sibling'
{tí} 'parent's sibling'

(2) (a) *restate* = {re} + {state}
    {re} = grammatical, bound, prefix, derivational
    {state} = lexical, free
  (b) *strongest* = {strong} + {SUP}
    {strong} = lexical, free
    {SUP} = grammatical, bound, suffix, inflectional
  (c) *actively* = {act} + {ive} + {ly}
    {act} = lexical, free
    {ive} = grammatical, bound, suffix, derivational
    {ly} = grammatical, bound, suffix, derivational
  (d) *precede* = {pre} + {cede}
    {pre} = grammatical, bound, prefix, derivational
    {cede} = lexical, bound (Note: {cede} is a separate morpheme
        because it appears in other words: *secede, intercede,* and
        so forth.)

(3) The kid*s* next door'*s* pool = [the [kid] + {PLU} next door] +
                         NP N

{POSS}

(4) (a) Inflectional suffixes must follow any derivational suffixes.
  (b) No more than one inflectional affix per syntactic category.
  (c) Same as (a).
  (d) {PLU} attaches to nouns, not to noun phrases.

(5) {act} occurs in *act, actor, active, react.*
  {ion} occurs in *construction, projection, inflection, rejection.*
  {pack} occurs in *pack, packs, packed, packing, packer.*
  {age} occurs in *wreckage, baggage, breakage.*

(6) *packages, packaged, packaging.* An inflectional morpheme can be added
after {age}. Since a lexical morpheme can take only one inflectional
affix, {age} must be derivational.

SUPPLEMENTARY READINGS

Primary

1. Aronoff, M. (1976). *Word formation in generative grammar.* Cambridge, MA: MIT Press.
2. Marchand, H. (1969). *The categories and types of present-day English word-formation* (2nd ed.), Munich: Beck.
3. Selkirk, E. O. (1982). *The syntax of words.* Cambridge, MA: MIT Press.

Secondary

4. Adams, V. (1973). *An introduction to modern English word formation*. London: Longmans.
5. Matthews, P. H. (1974). *Morphology: An introduction to the theory of word-structure*. Cambridge, England: Cambridge University Press.

You are now prepared to tackle either of the secondary readings: Adams (4) and Matthews (5) are general introductions to the field of morphology; however, (4) is restricted to English. The primary readings are more advanced and require at least an introductory course in linguistics. (A course each in phonology and syntax would enable you to get more out of these works.) Aronoff (1) is a revised and expanded version of his MIT doctoral dissertation and deals primarily with derivational morphology. Selkirk (3) is a monograph based on developments in morphology and syntax since 1977. Marchand (2) is probably the most comprehensive work written on the subject of English morphology.

Chapter 6

Phonology

Phonology is the study of the sound system of language: the rules that govern pronunciation. (The word *phonology* itself comes from the Greek word *phōnē*, which means 'voice'.) The study of phonology in the Western tradition goes back almost 200 years, to the early 1800's, when European linguists began studying sound change by comparing the speech sounds in a variety of related languages. However, the emphasis in modern phonology, as it has developed over the last 30 years, has been primarily on the *psychological system* that underlies pronunciation, and secondarily on the actual physical articulation of speech.

In order to see how phonology works, let's begin by considering some observations we can make about the sound system of English.

(1) The first sound in the word *fight* is produced by bringing together the top teeth and the bottom lip, and then blowing air between them.

(2) The word *can't* is produced with one continuous motion of the vocal tract (lungs, tongue, lips, and so on), yet we interpret this motion as a series of four separate speech sounds, *k-a-n-t*.

(3) The words *pea, see, me,* and *key* all have the same vowel, even though the vowel in each word is spelled differently.

(4) *p* and *b* are alike in that they are both pronounced with the lips; *p* and *k* are different in that *k* is not pronounced with the lips.

(5) The vowels in the words *cab* and *cad* are longer than the same vowels in *cap* and *cat*.

Observation (1) illustrates the fact that we use our **vocal tract** to produce speech. Observation (2) illustrates the fact that words are physically one continuous motion but are psychologically a series of discrete units called **segments**. Observation (3) illustrates that a single segment can be represented by a variety of spellings. Observations (2) and (3) can, in turn, be used to justify a **phonemic alphabet**, a system of

83

transcription in which one symbol uniquely represents one segment. Observation (4) illustrates the fact that segments are composed of smaller units called **distinctive features**. Thus "labial" (referring to the lips) is a distinctive feature shared by *p* and *b*, but not by *p* and *k*. Observation (5) illustrates that two segments can be the same on one **level of representation** but different on another. Thus, the vowels in *cab, cad, cap,* and *cat* are the same on one level (the vowel *a*), but different on another level (long *a* in *cab* and *cad*; short *a* in *cap* and *cat*). (Note that the terms *long* and *short* are not used here in the same way as they are in phonics. In phonology, they indicate differences in duration.) These systematic variations between levels of representation can, in turn, be stated in terms of **phonological rules** (e.g., vowels are lengthened in a particular context).

All of the phenomena in (1–5) are essentially phonological in nature, in that they have to do with the system underlying the pronunciation of words. In addition, we will make the by now familiar assumption that these phenomena are governed by a system of rules. What we will do now is attempt to develop a set of concepts and principles to help us explain the observations in (1–5). Bear in mind that what follows is an (unobservable) theory designed to account for the (observable) data in (1–5).

VOCAL TRACT

The vocal tract consists of the passageway between the lips and nostrils on one end and the larynx, which contains the vocal cords, on the other. The vocal tract is important to the study of phonology for two reasons. First, human beings use the vocal tract to produce speech. Second, and more importantly, terms which refer to physical properties of the vocal tract are used to describe the psychological units of phonology. A cross-section of the vocal tract is given in Figure 6–1.

Let's go over the landmarks in this figure one by one: (1) **lips**; (2) **teeth**; (3) **tongue**; (4) **alveolar ridge**, the bony ridge right behind the upper teeth; (5) **palate**, the bony dome constituting the roof of the mouth; (6) **velum**, the soft tissue immediately behind the palate; (7) **uvula**, the soft appendage hanging off the velum (you can see it if you open your mouth wide and look in a mirror); (8) **pharynx**, the back wall of the throat behind the tongue; (9) **epiglottis**, the soft tissue which covers the vocal cords during eating, thus protecting the passageway to the lungs; (10) **esophagus**, the tube going to the stomach; (11) **larynx**, containing the vocal cords; and (12) **trachea**, the tube going to the lungs.

Speech is produced by pushing air from the lungs up through the vocal tract and manipulating several variables at the same time. These variables

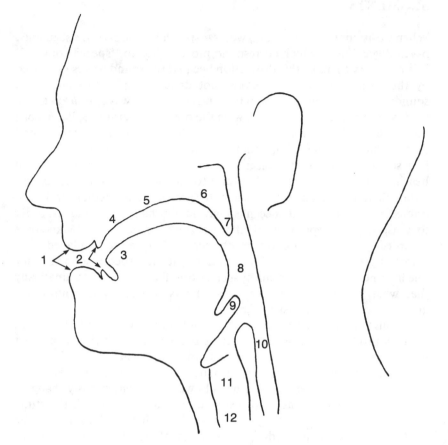

Figure 6-1. Cross-section of the vocal tract.

include whether or not the vocal cords are vibrating; whether the velum is raised (forcing all of the air through the mouth) or lowered (allowing some of the air to escape through the nose); and whether or not the air flow is stopped or impeded at some point between the lips and the larynx. In short, the vocal tract is a tube which produces sound when air from the lungs is pumped through it. Different speech sounds are produced by manipulating the lips, tongue, teeth, velum, pharynx, and vocal cords, thus changing the shape of this tube. For our purposes, however, the primary importance of the vocal tract is the fact that phonological units and rules are described in terms of these physical properties of the vocal mechanism.

SEGMENTS

When we listen to someone talk, we *hear* speech but we *perceive* segments, psychological units which correspond more or less to "speech sounds." It is necessary to make this distinction because the sound waves produced by the vocal tract are *continuous* (not divided neatly into individual sounds); however, our interpretation of these sound waves is *discrete* (we perceive distinct sounds, one following the other). For example, if someone utters the word *can't* within our hearing, what we actually hear is a sound that gradually changes shape though time. What we perceive, however, is a series of four discrete segments: *k-a-n-t*. This distinction between hearing and perceiving is fundamental to an appreciation of phonology, although it is not an easy concept to grasp. In particular, it is not immediately evident that speech is a gradually changing sound. In order to grasp this concept, you might try a simple experiment: Take some recorded speech (e.g., a phonograph record) designed to be played at 45 rpm and play it at 16 rpm. You'll notice that the "speech sounds" blur one into the other. An experiment such as this illustrates quite dramatically that what we perceive as discrete segments is actually a continuous, gradually changing, physical signal.

Thus, the main point to keep in mind is that when we talk, we are actually producing a continuous set of movements with the vocal tract which result in a continuous set of sound waves; what we think we are doing (unconsciously, of course) is producing a series of discrete segments. Likewise, when we listen to someone talk, we hear a continuously changing set of sound waves; what we perceive are segments. **Speech** is the study of what we are actually doing when we talk and listen; **phonology** is the study of the segments and rules in terms of which we organize our interpretation of speech. In short, speech is the study of physical or physiological phenomena, and phonology is the study of mental or psychological phenomena.

PHONEMIC ALPHABET

One type of segment that we perceive when we hear speech is termed the **phoneme**. As we have already seen, however, conventional orthography (i.e., spelling) does not provide an adequate means of representing the phonological structure of words. For example, *pea* and *key* both contain the same vowel, but in *pea* the vowel is spelled *ea* and in *key* it is spelled *ey*. In order to get around this problem, linguists have developed a phonemic alphabet, in which one symbol always corresponds to a single phoneme. So, for example, in our phonemic alphabet we might choose to represent the vowel in *pea, see, me,* and *key* as /i/. (Phonemic transcription is always enclosed in slashes to distinguish it from conventional orthography.) Thus, we can capture the fact that we perceive all of these words as having the same vowel by transcribing them as follows: *pea* /pi/, *see* /si/, *me* /mi/, and *key* /ki/.

Now that we've established this principle, let's consider the entire phonemic alphabet of English.

Vowels

PHONEMIC SYMBOL	EXAMPLE
/i/	s*ea*t
/ɪ/	s*i*t
/e/	s*ay*
/ɛ/	s*ai*d
/æ/	s*a*d
/ʌ/ (unstressed = /ə/)	s*u*ds (sof*a*)
/a/	s*o*d
/u/	s*ui*t
/ʊ/	s*oo*t
/o/	s*ew*ed
/ɔ/	s*ough*t
/aɪ/	s*igh*t
/aʊ/	s*ou*th
/ɔɪ/	s*oy*

These vowel phonemes (which, remember, are percepts—psychological units) are described in terms of the following physical dimensions.

Tongue Height. For any articulation corresponding to one of these vowel phonemes, the tongue is either relatively *high* in the mouth (/i,ɪ,u,ʊ/), *mid* (/e,ɛ,ʌ(ə),o/), or *low* (/æ,a,ɔ/). Compare *he* (high) and *hay* (mid).

Frontness. For any articulation corresponding to one of these vowel phonemes, the tongue is either relatively *front* (/i,ɪ,e,ɛ,æ/) or *back* (/ʌ(ə),a,u,ʊ,o,ɔ/). Compare *he* (front) and *who* (back).

Lip Rounding. For any articulation corresponding to one of these vowel phonemes, the lips are either relatively *round* (/u,ʊ,o,ɔ/) or *spread* (/i,ɪ,e,ɛ,æ,ʌ(ə),a/). Compare *hoe* (round) and *hay* (spread).

Tenseness. For any articulation corresponding to one of these vowel phonemes, the vocal musculature is either relatively *tense* (/i,e,u,o,ɔ/) or *lax* (/ɪ,ɛ,æ,ʌ(ə),a,ʊ/). Compare *aid* (tense) and *Ed* (lax).

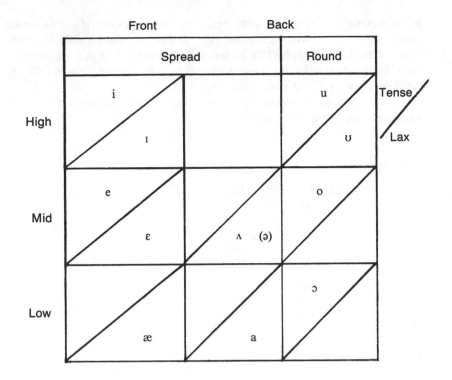

Figure 6–2.   Vowel phonemes of English.

Figure 6–2 charts the vowel phonemes of English in terms of these four physical dimensions.

Thus, for example, /i/ in the upper right-hand corner is high, front, tense, and spread. On the other hand, /ɔ/ in the lower right-hand corner is low, back, tense, and round. And so on.

Moreover, viewed from this perspective, it becomes apparent that each of these vowel phonemes is not really an indivisible unit, but rather a composite of values (+ or −) along one of several dimensions. Each such dimension constitutes a **distinctive feature**. The vowel chart in Figure 6–2 can be broken down into the following distinctive features: [±HIGH], [±LOW], [±BACK], [±TENSE], and [±ROUND]. Thus, for example, /i/ and /ɔ/ are not really units in themselves, but rather a bundle of features, as follows.

$$
/i/ \;=\; \begin{bmatrix} +\text{HIGH} \\ -\text{LOW} \\ -\text{BACK} \\ +\text{TENSE} \\ -\text{ROUND} \end{bmatrix}
\qquad
/ɔ/ \;=\; \begin{bmatrix} -\text{HIGH} \\ +\text{LOW} \\ +\text{BACK} \\ +\text{TENSE} \\ +\text{ROUND} \end{bmatrix}
$$

If you have tried to articulate words containing these vowels while you were reading the chart, you may have noticed that it is hard to determine the exact configuration of your vocal tract during any particular articulation. For example, is /i/ really tense and is /ɪ/ really lax? Actually, this is of no great importance. Keep in mind that phonemes and distinctive features are theoretical constructs within a theory of phonology. Phonemes are abstract entities postulated to account for the fact that speakers of English perceive the vowels in *seat* and *sit*, for example, to be different. Likewise, distinctive features are postulated to account for the fact that these segments are different along a particular dimension, here what we have somewhat arbitrarily decided to call [±TENSE]. The fact that phonemes and distinctive features are described in physical terms is of no real consequence. It results from the fact that modern phonology developed from the study of sound change, which in turn was thought to be a direct function of the vocal tract. In short, even though phonemes and distinctive features are described in physical terms, they are actually psychological entities: *No one has ever uttered a phoneme or a distinctive feature*. Rather, when we talk, we utter a physical speech signal which we *interpret* as containing phonemes, which in turn consist of distinctive features.

Consonants

For each consonant phoneme in the following table, there are three examples: one each for the occurrence of the phoneme in word-initial, word-medial, and word-final position. A blank indicates that the phoneme does not occur in that position in English.

PHONEMIC SYMBOL	EXAMPLE
/p/	*p*at, zi*pp*er, ca*p*
/b/	*b*at, fi*bb*er, ca*b*
/t/	*t*ab, ca*tt*y, ca*t*
/d/	*d*ab, ca*dd*y, ca*d*
/k/	*c*ap, di*ck*er, ta*ck*
/g/	*g*ap, di*gg*er, ta*g*
/f/	*f*at, sa*f*er, belie*f*
/v/	*v*at, sa*v*er, belie*v*e
/θ/	*th*in, e*th*er, brea*th*
/ð/	*th*en, ei*th*er, brea*the*
/s/	*s*ue, la*c*y, pea*c*e
/z/	*z*oo, la*z*y, pea*s*
/š/	*sh*oe, thre*sh*er, ru*sh*
/ž/	----, trea*s*ure, rou*g*e
/h/	*h*am, a*h*ead, ----

/č/	*ch*ain, ske*tch*y, besee*ch*
/ǰ/	*J*ane, e*dg*y, besie*ge*
/m/	*m*itt, si*mm*er, see*m*
/n/	*kn*it, si*nn*er, see*n*
/ŋ/	----, si*ng*er, si*ng*
/l/	*l*ight, te*ll*er, coa*l*
/r/	*r*ight, te*rr*or, co*r*e
/w/	*w*et, lo*w*er, ----
/y/	*y*et, la*y*er, ----

(Note: English words which appear to end in /w/ and /y/ are analyzed as ending in vowels in this system. For example, *cow* = /kaʊ/ and *sky* = /skaɪ/.)

As was the case with vowels, these consonant phonemes (which, once again, are percepts—psychological units) are described in terms of physical dimensions, as follows.

Place of Articulation.   For any articulation corresponding to one of these consonant phonemes, the vocal tract is constricted at one of the following points.

(a)   **Bilabial** (from *bi* 'two' + *labial* 'lips'). The primary constriction is at the lips (/p,b,m,w/). Compare *pea* (bilabial) and *tea* (non-bilabial).

(b)   **Labiodental** (from *labio* 'lip' + *dental* 'teeth'). The primary constriction is between the lower lip and upper teeth (/f,v/). Compare *fee* (labiodental) and *see* (non-labiodental).

(c)   **Interdental** (from *inter* 'between' + *dental* 'teeth'). The primary constriction is between the tongue and the upper teeth (/θ,ð/). Compare *thigh* (interdental) and *shy* (non-interdental).

(d)   **Alveolar** (from *alveolar ridge*). The primary constriction is between the tongue and the alveolar ridge (/t,d,s,z,n,l/). Compare *tea* (alveolar) and *key* (non-alveolar).

(e)   **Palatal** (from *palate*). The primary constriction is between the tongue and the palate (/š,ž,č,ǰ,r,y/). Compare *shoe* (palatal) and *sue* (non-palatal).

(f)   **Velar** (from *velum*). The primary constriction is between the tongue and the velum (/k,g,ŋ/). Compare *coo* (velar) and *two* (non-velar).

(g)   **Glottal** (from *glottis*, which refers to the space between the vocal cords). The primary constriction is at the glottis (/h/). Compare *hoe* (glottal) and *so* (non-glottal).

Manner of Articulation.   For any articulation corresponding to one of these consonant phonemes, the vocal tract is constricted in one of the following ways.

(a) **Stops.** Two articulators (lips, tongue, teeth, etc.) are brought together such that the flow of air through the vocal tract is completely blocked (/p,b,t,d,g,k/). Compare *tea* (stop) and *see* (non-stop).

(b) **Fricatives.** Two articulators are brought near each other such that the flow of air is impeded but not completely blocked. The air flow through the narrow opening creates friction, hence the term *fricative* (/f,v,θ,ð,s,z,š,ž,h/). Compare *zoo* (fricative) and *do* (non-fricative).

(c) **Affricates.** Articulations corresponding to affricates are those that begin like stops (with a complete closure in the vocal tract) and end like fricatives (with a narrow opening in the vocal tract) (/č,ǰ/). Compare *chew* (affricate) and *shoe* (non-affricate). Because affricates can be described as a stop plus a fricative, some phonemic alphabets transcribe /č/ as /tš/ and /ǰ/ as /dž/.

(d) **Nasals.** A nasal articulation is one in which the airflow through the mouth is completely blocked but the velum is lowered, forcing the air through the nose (/m,n,ŋ/). Compare *no* (nasal) and *doe* (non-nasal).

(e) **Liquids** and **Glides.** Both of these terms describe articulations that are mid-way between true consonants (i.e., stops, fricatives, affricates, and nasals) and vowels, although they are both generally classified as consonants. Liquid is a cover term for all *l*-like and *r*-like articulations (/l,r/). Compare *low* (liquid) and *doe* (non-liquid). The term glide refers to an articulation in which the vocal tract is constricted, but not enough to block or impede the airflow (/w,y/). Compare *way* (glide) and *bay* (non-glide).

Voicing. For any articulation corresponding to one of these consonant phonemes, the vocal cords are either vibrating (/b,d,g,v,ð,z,ž,ǰ,m,n,ŋ, l,r,w,y/) or not (/p,t,k,f,θ,s,š,h,č/). Compare *zoo* (voiced) and *sue* (voiceless). Stops, fricatives, and affricates come in voiced and voiceless pairs (except for /h/); nasals, liquids, and glides are all voiced, as are vowels.

Figure 6–3 plots the consonant phonemes of English in terms of these three physical dimensions: place of articulation, manner of articulation, and voicing. Thus, for example, /p/ is a voiceless bilabial stop; /v/ is a voiced labiodental fricative; /č/ is a voiceless palatal affricate; /ŋ/ is a voiced velar nasal; and so on.

Moreover, as was the case with vowels, each of these consonant phonemes is not really an indivisible unit, but rather a composite of values along each of these three dimensions. Once again, each such dimension constitutes a **distinctive feature**. Thus, for example, from one perspective

		Bilabial	Labiodental	Interdental	Alveolar	Palatal	Velar	Glottal
Stops	voiceless	p			t		k	
	voiced	b			d		g	
Fricatives	voiceless		f	θ	s	š		h
	voiced		v	ð	z	ž		
Affricates	voiceless					č		
	voiced					ǰ		
Nasals	voiceless							
	voiced	m			n		ŋ	
Liquids	voiceless							
	voiced				l	r		
Glides	voiceless							
	voiced	w				y		

Figure 6–3.   Consonant phonemes of English.

/p/ and /ŋ/ are not really units in themselves, but rather a bundle of feature values, as follows.

$$/p/ \; = \; \begin{bmatrix} +\text{BILABIAL} \\ +\text{STOP} \\ -\text{VOICE} \end{bmatrix} \qquad /ŋ/ \; = \; \begin{bmatrix} +\text{VELAR} \\ +\text{NASAL} \\ +\text{VOICE} \end{bmatrix}$$

Once again, it is important to keep in mind that phonemes and distinctive features are theoretical constructs within a theory of phonology. Phonemes are postulated to account for the fact that the consonants in *pea* and *bee*, for example, are different. Likewise, distinctive features are postulated to account for the fact that they are different along a particular dimension, namely [±VOICE].

Before leaving this section, it may be useful to clear up several points of potential confusion. First, the specific symbols used in a phonemic alphabet are of no particular theoretical importance. For example, the symbols /p/ and /b/ in English could, in theory, be replaced by /1/ and

/2/. All that is necessary is that one symbol be used to represent each segment that is perceived as unique by speakers of the language in question.

Second, a number of phonemic alphabets for English are currently in use. Thus, for example, you will see the initial phoneme in *yes* sometimes transcribed as /y/ and other times transcribed as /j/. Likewise, you will see the vowel phoneme in *pea* sometimes transcribed as /i/ and other times transcribed as /iy/. This is simply a fact of life that anyone who deals with phonology has to get used to. (Actually, with a little practice, it is quite easy to go from one transcription system to another.) Similarly, there are several different distinctive feature systems in current use. The one we have discussed for vowels ([±HIGH], [±LOW], [±BACK], [±ROUND], and [±TENSE]) is fairly standard. The one for consonants ([PLACE], [MANNER], and [±VOICE]) is somewhat oversimplified, but is adequate for our purposes here. The "best" set of distinctive features for describing segments found in human languages is a matter of current debate and need not concern us here.

Third, you will see some of the phonemes of English charted slightly differently (recall the vowel and consonant charts discussed earlier) depending upon who you read. Thus, the phoneme /h/, which we have characterized as a fricative, is sometimes classified as a glide. Likewise, the phoneme /ɔ/, which we have characterized as a low vowel, is sometimes classified as a mid vowel. And so on. Again, for our purposes these differences are of no great theoretical consequence. What is important is that each phoneme be given a *unique* representation in terms of distinctive features. After all, by calling something a phoneme, we are saying that it is different from any other segment in the language in question.

Fourth, the phonemic representation of the words in a language is not identical for every speaker of that language. For example, the vowels in *cot* and *caught* are different for some speakers of English (*cot* has /a/ and *caught* has /ɔ/) but the same for others (both *cot* and *caught* have /a/). Likewise, some speakers of English perceive the final consonant in *garage* as /ž/, while others perceive it as /ǰ/. Such differences between speakers, however, are more noticeable among the vowels. For example, in the word *think*, some speakers have /ɪ/, others have /i/, and still others (I, for one) have /e/! When such differences are found, they typically involve phonemes that are near each other in articulatory terms. Note, for instance, that /i/, /ɪ/, and /e/ are adjacent on the vowel chart.

Fifth, different languages have different sets of phonemes. English contains phonemes not found in some other languages; and, conversely, English lacks phonemes which are found in other languages. For example, English contains the interdental fricatives /θ/ and /ð/, which are relatively rare among the world's languages. Modern Greek has them, but French,

German, Italian, Persian, and Russian (among others) do not. On the other hand, English entirely lacks front rounded vowels. French, however, has three: /ü/ (high) as in *sucre* 'sugar', /ö/ (mid) as in *jeu* 'game', and /œ/ (low) as in *oeuf* 'egg'. (To pronounce the vowel in *sucre*, for example, try to say the vowel in *see* while rounding your lips.)

LEVELS OF REPRESENTATION

At the beginning of this chapter, we discussed the idea that two segments might, at the same time, be both the same and different. In order to reconcile this apparent paradox, linguists have developed the notion of **level of representation**. By recognizing more than one such level, we are able to say that two segments are identical on one level of representation, yet different on another. As an illustration of this concept, let's take the fact that specific properties of a phoneme vary according to its position in a word. This variation is sometimes referred to as **allophonic variation**. Consider, for example, the following English words and phrases, each of which contains an instance of the phoneme /t/: *Tim, stem, hit, hit me*, and *Betty*. Each of these instances of /t/ differs systematically from the others. These systematic variations of /t/ are called **allophones** of /t/ and are transcribed in square brackets ([]).

The /t/ in *Tim* is aspirated; that is, there is a puff of air following the release of the /t/. (You can test this by holding the palm of your hand about three inches from your lips and saying *Tim*. Feel the rush of air as you release the /t/?) Aspirated /t/ is transcribed [tʰ].

The /t/ in *stem* is released; that is, there is no puff of air following the release of the /t/. (You can test this by using the "palm" test just described; say *Tim* and *stem* alternately. Note that there is no rush of air with the /t/ in *stem*.) Released /t/ is transcribed [t].

The /t/ in *hit* can be released or unreleased. If it is unreleased, the tip of the tongue stops at the alveolar ridge. (You can test this by saying *hit* and leaving your tongue at the alveolar ridge after the word is pronounced.) Unreleased /t/ is transcribed [t˥].

The /t/ in *hit me* may be unreleased or it may be a glottal stop. If it is a glottal stop, there is no contact between the tip of the tongue and the alveolar ridge; instead, the vocal cords are brought together and the airflow is stopped momentarily. (You can test this by saying *hit me* without ever raising your tongue to the alveolar ridge. The /t/ you perceive is actually a stop formed with the vocal cords.) A glottal stop is transcribed [ʔ].

The /t/ in *Betty* is an alveolar flap; that is, it is formed by raising the tip of the tongue to the alveolar ridge very rapidly and releasing it. An alveolar flap is more rapid than either [t] or [d]. (You can test this by saying *Betty* with an alveolar flap, which sounds like the normal American pronunciation; then with a [t], which sounds British, like Cary Grant; and then with a [d], which sounds like *beddy*.) An alveolar flap is transcribed [ɾ].

Each of these allophones of /t/ is predictable, in that it typically occurs in a particular position within a word or phrase. For example, [tʰ] as in *Tim* occurs when /t/ begins a syllable and is followed by a stressed vowel. [t] as in *stem* occurs when /t/ is followed by a vowel, but does not begin a syllable. [t˥] as in *hit* occurs when /t/ occurs at the end of an utterance. [ʔ] as in *hit me* occurs when /t/ follows a vowel and precedes a consonant. [ɾ] as in *Betty* occurs when /t/ follows a stressed vowel and precedes an unstressed vowel.

Notice, however, the consequences of what we have done. We have essentially justified two levels of phonological representation: the **phonemic**, where phonemes are described, and the **phonetic**, where allophones (i.e., systematic variants) of phonemes are described. This situation is summarized in Figure 6-4, which illustrates the fact that speakers of English perceive the words *Tim, stem, hit, hit me,* and *Betty* as containing instances of the same phoneme, /t/. Yet each instance of /t/ differs on the phonetic level, depending on the context in which /t/ occurs. Thus, by using the concept **level of representation**, we are able to capture the fact that two segments can be both the same (i.e., phonemically) and different (i.e., phonetically).

This discussion, of course, raises the side issue of how to tell whether two segments are allophones of different phonemes or allophones of the same phoneme. The basic test is to substitute one phone for another. If the substitution changes one word into another, then the two phones **contrast** and are allophones of different phonemes. If they do not, then they are in **free variation** and are allophones of the same phoneme. Consider, for example, *hit* [hɪt˥]. If we substitute [d˥] for [t˥], we get a different word, *hid*. Thus, [t˥] and [d˥] contrast, and therefore are

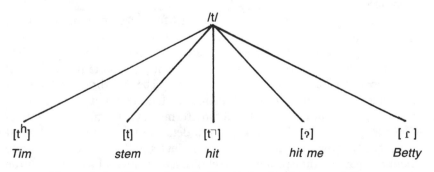

Figure 6-4.   Phonemic and phonetic levels of representation.

allophones of different phonemes, namely /t/ and /d/, respectively. On the other hand, if we substitute [t] for the [t⌐] in [hɪt⌐], we are left with the same word, *hit*. Thus, [t⌐] and [t] are in free variation, and therefore are allophones of the same phoneme, namely /t/.

There is one other possibility: namely, one in which two phones are not interchangeable because they never occur in the same environment (i.e., position within a word). Consider, for example, the phones [tʰ] and [ɾ]. These never occur in the same context; [tʰ] always occurs before a stressed vowel and [ɾ] always occurs before an unstressed vowel. Thus, in the word *tatter* /tǽtər/ (an accent mark indicates stress), the first /t/ is always [tʰ] and the second /t/ is always [ɾ]. Note that if we try to substitute one phone for the other, we get something that is not even pronounceable in English, namely *[ɾǽtʰər]. Two such phones that never occur in the same context are said to be in **complementary distribution** and are allophones of the same phoneme. In this case, [tʰ] and [ɾ] are allophones of /t/.

In sum, if two phones **contrast** (i.e., if substituting one for the other causes a change in meaning), they are allophones of *different* phonemes. On the other hand, if two phones are either in **free variation** (i.e., if substituting one for the other does not cause a change in meaning) or in **complementary distribution** (i.e., if they never occur in the same environment), they are allophones of the *same* phoneme.

Let's now return to the main topic of this section—levels of representation. We started off this chapter by talking about two levels of representation in phonology: One is the level of the actual physical production of speech, which is achieved by pushing air through the vocal tract; the other is the psychological level where the continuous speech stream is organized in terms of percepts or segments. Later, in the first part of this section, we subdivided the psychological level into two further levels of representation, namely phonemic and phonetic. Let's now flesh this system out further by seeing how modern phonological theory is organized in terms of levels.

Phonological theory recognizes at least four levels of representation: **systematic phonemic, classical phonemic, systematic phonetic**, and **physical phonetic**. (The classical phonemic level corresponds to the one we called "phonemic" in our earlier discussion, and the systematic phonetic level corresponds to the one we called "phonetic.") The first three levels consist of segments defined in terms of distinctive features, and are related by phonological rules, also stated in terms of distinctive features. (Phonological rules will be taken up in detail in the next section.) Most importantly, however, all three of these levels and the rules that relate them are part of the speaker's psychological or mental system. On the other hand, the fourth level, the physical phonetic level, constitutes a

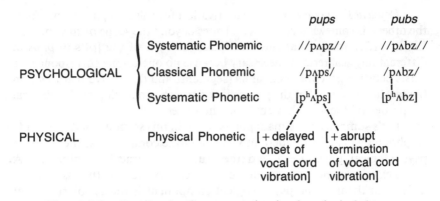

Figure 6–5.   Four levels of representation in phonological theory.

physical or physiological description of physical speech production or the resulting acoustic signal. This level may be described in terms of the physical dimensions of speech production or in terms of the physical properties of the acoustic signal. Thus, there are two related, but distinct, components of phonology relevant to this discussion: *psychological* (the systematic phonemic, classical phonemic, and systematic phonetic levels) and *physical* (the physical phonetic level).

These four levels are illustrated in Figure 6–5, in terms of the English words *pups* and *pubs*. The relevant distinctions between levels are indicated by dotted lines. These four levels of representation are posited in order to account for a range of phenomena.

Systematic Phonemic Level. The description of the final segments in *pups* and *pubs* as //z// accounts for the fact that speakers of English treat both of these segments as instances of the same morpheme, namely the plural morpheme; thus, they are represented identically on this level of representation. Double slashes are used to indicate systematic phonemes.

Classical Phonemic Level. The description of the same two segments (i.e., the final segments in *pups* and *pubs*) as /s/ and /z/, respectively, accounts for the fact that these two segments contrast. Note, for example, that the substitution of [z] for [s] in *Sue* [su] results in a different word, namely *zoo* [zu]. Thus, [s] and [z] are allophones of different classical phonemes, namely /s/ and /z/, respectively. Single slashes are used to indicate classical phonemes.

Systematic Phonetic Level. The description of the two instances of the classical phoneme /p/ in *pups* as [pʰ] and [p], respectively, accounts for the fact that speakers of English treat instances of /p/ in varying contexts as different. That is, the first /p/ in *pups* is aspirated ([pʰ]), but the second is not ([p]). Brackets are used to indicate systematic phones.

Physical Phonetic Level. The motivation for this level, as distinct from the others, is somewhat complex and goes beyond the scope of this chapter. Let it suffice to say that the description of each of the [p]'s in *pups* in different physical terms is necessary because no one-to-one correspondence exists between psychological units (segments and distinctive features), on the one hand, and either the properties of speech production or the physical properties of the speech signal, on the other.

Let's summarize the main points made in this section. First, the study of phonology can be divided into two separate components: the study of psychological phenomena and the study of physical phenomena. A complex relation holds between the two, yet they are nonetheless distinct, at least in theory. The psychological component is the set of rules that serves as input to the physical production system; the physical component is the production system itself. Second, phonologists have posited four levels of representation: systematic phonemic, classical phonemic, systematic phonetic, and physical phonetic. These levels are postulated for one simple reason: In order to account for phonological phenomena, it is necessary to treat two items as the same on one level and different on another.

In particular, on the systematic phonemic level all instances of a single morpheme are represented by identical systematic phonemes. For example, the final segments in *pups* and *pubs* are both instances of the morpheme {PLU}, so they are both represented as //z//. (Note that there is nothing magic about //z//; we could just as well have used //s//. The point is that both segments are represented by one symbol.) On the classical phonemic level, each segment that contrasts (in the sense defined earlier) with at least one other segment is represented by a different classical phoneme. For example, the final segments in *pups* and *pubs* contrast (as in *Sue* and *zoo*), so they are represented as /s/ and /z/, respectively. On the systematic phonetic level, the contextual variants of each classical phoneme are represented by different systematic phones (or allophones). For example, the first /p/ in *pups* is aspirated but the second is not, so the former is represented as [pʰ] and the latter as [p]. Finally, the physical phonetic level describes the actual production of speech in purely physical terms.

Although the previous discussion was necessary for an appreciation of phonology as a whole, the two levels of phonological representation most often of interest to professionals outside of linguistics proper are the classical phonemic and the systematic phonetic. Thus, for the remainder of this chapter, our discussion will be restricted to these two levels, which I will refer to as the *phonemic* and *phonetic*, respectively. The main point to keep in mind, however, is that these two levels and the units that comprise them (i.e., phonemes and phones) are psychological, not physical.

PHONOLOGICAL RULES

Because levels of phonological representation are not always identical to one another, part of phonology consists of rules that essentially translate segments on one level into segments on another level. Let's now look at some common phonological rules or processes in English, working from the data to the rules themselves.

Aspiration

Let's begin with a phonological process that we have already discussed informally, namely Aspiration. Consider the following English words, each of which is accompanied by its phonemic and phonetic representations.

sip	/síp/	[síp]
appear	/əpír/	[əpʰír]
pepper	/pépər/	[pʰépər]
space	/spés/	[spés]
papaya	/pəpáɪyə/	[pəpʰáɪyə]

In these data, /p/ has two allophones, [pʰ] and [p]. Our task is to determine under what conditions (i.e., in what environments) /p/ becomes [pʰ]. We might begin by trying to determine what all of the occurrences of [pʰ] have in common. One thing we observe is that all instances of [pʰ] occur immediately before a stressed vowel. Thus we can hypothesize the following rule: /p/ becomes [pʰ] when it occurs before a stressed vowel. This rule, however, will not account for the fact that the [p] in *space* [spés] is not aspirated, even though the following [é] is stressed. Since our rule is not 100 percent accurate, we will have to revise it. We might ask how the [p] in *space* is different from the [pʰ]'s in *appear* [əpʰír], *pepper* [pʰépər], and *papaya* [pəpʰáɪyə]. Note that the [pʰ]'s in *appear, pepper,* and *papaya,* in addition to preceding a stressed vowel, also begin a syllable, whereas the [p] in *space* does not. Now we are in a position to hypothesize a revised version of our rule: /p/ becomes [pʰ] when it both begins a syllable and is followed by a stressed vowel. This rule accurately predicts those cases where /p/ becomes [pʰ]; and, by exclusion, it also predicts where /p/ becomes [p].

We might leave our Aspiration Rule as it stands, in a simple prose statement: /p/ becomes aspirated when it begins a syllable and is followed by a stressed vowel. However, since informal prose statements can often be (unintentionally) vague or ambiguous, phonologists have adopted the practice of stating rules in formal notation. The standard notation for writing phonological rules is as follows.

$$W \rightarrow X/Y \_ Z$$

This rule states that segment W becomes segment X when it follows Y and precedes Z. (Read the arrow as "becomes" and the slash as "in the following environment.")

The next step is to formalize our Aspiration Rule using this format. Before doing so, however, we need some way of indicating a syllable boundary. One symbol that is often used for this purpose is $. Now we can formalize our rule as follows.

$$/p/ \rightarrow [+\text{ASPIRATED}]/\$ \_\_\_ \quad \begin{matrix} V \\ [+\text{STRESS}] \end{matrix}$$

This rule states that the phoneme /p/ becomes aspirated when it begins a syllable (i.e., when there is a syllable boundary to its left) and is followed by a stressed vowel (V). There are several variations on this notation; for example, you might also see this rule written as follows.

$$/p/ \rightarrow [p^h]/\$ \_\_\_ \acute{V}$$

The two notations mean exactly the same thing.

Before leaving this example, it is worthwhile to point out that if we were to go beyond the data on which this rule is based and include examples containing the allophones of /t/ and /k/ as well as those of /p/, we would see that /p/, /t/, and /k/ all become aspirated under identical conditions, namely when they begin a syllable and are followed by a stressed vowel. Since /p/, /t/, and /k/ constitute the set of voiceless stops in English, we could state the Aspiration Rule for them all as follows.

$$\begin{bmatrix} +\text{STOP} \\ -\text{VOICE} \end{bmatrix} \rightarrow [+\text{ASPIRATED}]/\$ \_\_\_ \quad \begin{matrix} V \\ [+\text{STRESS}] \end{matrix}$$

Note the advantage of stating the rule in terms of distinctive features rather than segments. If we were to use segments, then we would miss the generalization that this rule applies not to /p/, /t/, and /k/ individually, but rather to the intersection of their common properties: [+STOP] and [−VOICE].

Vowel Lengthening

Consider the following English words, each of which is accompanied by its phonemic and phonetic representations.

heat	/hit/	[hit]
seize	/siz/	[si:z]
keel	/kil/	[kʰi:l]
leaf	/lif/	[lif]
heed	/hid/	[hi:d]
cease	/sis/	[sis]
leave	/liv/	[li:v]

In these data, /i/ has two allophones, [i] and [i:] (a colon after a vowel indicates that it is lengthened). Once again, our task is to determine under what conditions /i/ becomes [i:]. We might begin by hypothesizing that some property of the consonant to the *left* of the vowel causes it to lengthen. This hypothesis, however, must clearly be wrong. Consider, for example, *seize* [si:z] and *cease* [sis]. The former has a long vowel and the latter has a short vowel, yet in both cases the vowel is preceded by [s]. Thus, the consonant to the left of the vowel obviously has no effect upon the length of the vowel, since here the same consonant precedes both a long vowel and a short vowel.

Alternatively, we might hypothesize that some property of the consonant to the *right* of the vowel causes it to lengthen. Here we have more luck. Note that the vowels in *heat, leaf,* and *cease* are short, and each one is followed by a voiceless consonant ([t], [f], and [s] are [−VOICE]). In contrast, note that the vowels in *heed, leave, seize,* and *keel* are long and each one is followed by a voiced consonant ([d], [v], [z], and [l] are [+VOICE]). Now we are in a position to propose a rule: /i/ becomes [i:] when it precedes a voiced consonant. This rule accurately accounts for our data. It predicts exactly those cases where /i/ becomes [i:] and, by exclusion, it also predicts where /i/ becomes [i].

Let's go one step further and formalize our rule as follows.

$$/i/ \rightarrow [+LONG]/ \underline{\quad} \begin{array}{c} C \\ [+VOICE] \end{array}$$

This rule states that the phoneme /i/ becomes lengthened when it precedes a voiced consonant (C). As in our Aspiration Rule discussed earlier, there are variations on this notation. You might also see this rule written as follows.

$$/i/ \rightarrow [i:]/ \underline{\quad} \begin{array}{c} C \\ [+VOICE] \end{array}$$

In addition, if we were to go beyond the data on which we have based this rule and include examples containing allophones of the other vowels in English, we would see that *all* vowels become lengthened under the same conditions, namely when they precede a voiced consonant. Thus, we can state the Vowel Lengthening Rule as follows.

$$V \rightarrow [+LONG]/ \underline{\quad} \begin{array}{c} C \\ [+VOICE] \end{array}$$

Once again, we can see that phonological rules apply to *classes* of segments (e.g., vowels) rather than to individual segments (e.g., /i/, /e/, /æ/, and so on).

Vowel Nasalization

Consider the following English words, each of which is accompanied by its phonemic and phonetic representations.

map	/mæp/	[mæp]
pan	/pæn/	[pæ̃n]
pad	/pæd/	[pæd]
Pam	/pæm/	[pæ̃m]
gnat	/næt/	[næt]
pang	/pæŋ/	[pæ̃ŋ]

In these data, /æ/ has two allophones, [æ] and [æ̃]. (A tilde over a vowel indicates that it is nasalized. That is, a word containing a nasalized vowel is perceived as being pronounced with the velum lowered during the vowel.) As before, our task is to determine under what conditions /æ/ becomes [æ̃]. Before getting started, however, note that the vowels in *pan, pad, Pam,* and *pang* should be long (i.e., [æ:]), since they each precede a voiced consonant; yet the phonetic transcription does not indicate this. Pay this no mind; it is common practice in phonology to ignore phonetic details irrelevant to the particular task at hand. In this case, vowel lengthening has nothing to do with vowel nasalization, so it has been ignored. Likewise, the aspiration notation in this data has been omitted, since aspiration has nothing to do with vowel nasalization.

Let's now return to the problem of determining under what conditions /æ/ becomes [æ̃]. First of all, we might assume, naturally enough, that since English has no nasalized vowel phonemes, a phonetically nasalized vowel is the result of being adjacent to a nasal consonant, /m/, /n/, or /ŋ/. Thus, our task is simplified. Is it the preceding or the following nasal consonant that is causing the vowel to become nasalized? The answer is straightforward. Since *map* [mæp] and *gnat* [næt] both contain a preceding nasal consonant but no nasalized vowel, vowel nasalization must not be caused by a preceding nasal consonant. On the other hand, since *pan* [pæ̃n], *Pam* [pæ̃m], and *pang* [pæ̃ŋ] each contain a nasalized vowel followed by a nasal consonant, it must be the following nasal consonant that is causing the vowel nasalization. We are now in a position to propose a rule: /æ/ becomes [æ̃] when it is followed by a nasal consonant. This rule accurately predicts exactly the cases where /æ/ becomes [æ̃]; and, by exclusion, it also predicts where /æ/ becomes [æ].

We can formalize this rule as follows.

$$/æ/ \rightarrow [+\text{NASAL}]/ \underline{\quad} \quad \begin{matrix} C \\ [+\text{NASAL}] \end{matrix}$$

Or, alternatively, as follows.

$$/æ/ \rightarrow [æ̃]/ \underline{\quad} \quad \begin{matrix} C \\ [+\text{NASAL}] \end{matrix}$$

Once again, if we wanted to go beyond the data on which our rule is based, we would see that *all* vowels in English become nasalized when they precede a nasal consonant. Thus, we could state the Vowel Nasalization Rule for English as follows.

$$V \rightarrow [+NASAL]/ \_\_\_ \quad \begin{matrix} C \\ [+NASAL] \end{matrix}$$

Again, we see that phonological rules apply to classes of segments, rather than to individual segments.

Flapping

Consider the following English words, each of which is accompanied by its phonemic and phonetic representations.

ride	/ráɪd/	[ráɪd]
dire	/dáɪr/	[dáɪr]
rider	/ráɪdər/	[ráɪɾər]
write	/ráɪt/	[ráɪt]
tire	/táɪr/	[táɪr]
writer	/ráɪtər/	[ráɪɾər]
lender	/léndər/	[léndər]
Easter	/ístər/	[ístər]
attack	/ətǽk/	[ətǽk]
adobe	/ədóbi/	[ədóbi]

In these data, both /t/ and /d/ become [ɾ] (an alveolar flap) under certain circumstances. Our task is to determine under what conditions /t/ and /d/ become [ɾ]. We might begin by noting that /t/ and /d/ never become [ɾ] when they begin or end a word. Thus, the relevant alveolar stops (/t/ and /d/) must be those that occur somewhere in the middle of the word. This narrows the field to *rider, writer, lender, Easter, attack,* and *adobe.* Of these, only the alveolar stops in *rider* and *writer* become [ɾ]. What is different about the environment of /t/ and /d/ in these words? First of all, they occur between vowels. (Compare *lender* and *Easter,* where the stop occurs between a consonant and a vowel.) Second, the vowel to the left is stressed and that to the right is unstressed. (Compare *attack* and *adobe,* where the vowel to the left of the stop is unstressed and that to the right is stressed.) Now we are in a position to propose a rule: /t/ and /d/ become [ɾ] when they occur between two vowels, the first of which is stressed and the second of which is unstressed. This rule accurately accounts for all of the [ɾ]'s in our data. That is, it predicts exactly those cases where /t/ and /d/ become [ɾ]; and, by exclusion, it also predicts where they do not become [ɾ].

The Flapping Rule, in turn, can be formalized as follows.

$$\begin{bmatrix} +\text{STOP} \\ +\text{ALVEOLAR} \end{bmatrix} \rightarrow [\text{ɾ}]/ \underset{[+\text{STRESS}]}{\text{V}} \underline{\qquad} \underset{[-\text{STRESS}]}{\text{V}}$$

As usual, there are variations on this notation. You might also see this rule written as follows.

$$\left. \begin{array}{c} /\text{t}/ \\ /\text{d}/ \end{array} \right\} \rightarrow [\text{ɾ}]/\acute{\text{V}} \underline{\qquad} \breve{\text{V}}$$

A breve (˘) above a vowel indicates that it is unstressed.

Nasal Deletion

Consider the following English words, each of which is accompanied by its phonemic and phonetic representations.

can	/kæn/	[kæ̃n]
cad	/kæd/	[kæd]
canned	/kænd/	[kæ̃nd]
cat	/kæt/	[kæt]
can't	/kænt/	[kæ̃t]

In these data, two phonological rules apply. First, the Vowel Nasalization Rule applies in *can* [kæ̃n], *canned* [kæ̃nd], and *can't* [kæ̃t]. Second, a rule deleting a nasal consonant applies, so that *can't* /kænt/ becomes [kæ̃t]. What we need to do is determine (a) under what conditions Nasal Deletion applies, and (b) in what order Vowel Nasalization and Nasal Deletion must apply.

Consider first the Nasal Deletion Rule itself. Note that the /n/ in *can't* is deleted, but that in *can* and *canned* is not. How can we differentiate the /n/ in *can't* from that in *can* and *canned*? One difference is that the /n/ in *can't* is followed by a /t/, while the /n/ in the other two words is not. We are now in a position to propose a rule: Delete /n/ when it precedes /t/. This rule accounts for the absence of [n] in *can't*; and, by exclusion, it also accounts for the presence of [n] in *can* and *canned*.

We can formalize this rule as follows.

$$/\text{n}/ \rightarrow \emptyset/ \underline{\qquad} /\text{t}/$$

The symbol ∅ indicates the null set; thus, the rule reads: /n/ is deleted (i.e., "becomes nothing") when it occurs before a /t/. As in our other cases, if we were to go beyond the data on which we have based this rule, we would see that *any* nasal (/m,n,ŋ/) is deleted in English when it occurs before *any* voiceless stop (/p,t,k/). Thus, we can state the Nasal Deletion Rule for English as follows.

$$\begin{array}{c} \text{C} \\ [+\text{NASAL}] \end{array} \rightarrow \emptyset / \underline{\quad} \begin{bmatrix} +\text{STOP} \\ -\text{VOICE} \end{bmatrix}$$

This brings us to our second question. To transform a phonemic form such as *can't* /kænt/ into the phonetic form [kæt], which rule must apply first: Nasal Deletion or Vowel Nasalization? The most straightforward way of answering this question is to try both orders. The one that accurately maps the phonemic representation into the phonetic representation is correct. First, let's try Nasal Deletion before Vowel Nasalization, as illustrated in the following diagram.

Phonemic Level	/kænt/
Nasal Deletion	kæt
Vowel Nasalization	cannot apply
Phonetic Level	[kæt]

This ordering is obviously wrong; it yields [kaet], which is the phonetic representation of *cat*, not *can't*. The problem is that the nasal /n/ must be present at the point at which Vowel Nasalization applies. In this case, Nasal Deletion has removed the /n/ before Vowel Nasalization has had a chance to apply, thus blocking the application of the Vowel Nasalization Rule.

Now let's try Vowel Nasalization before Nasal Deletion, as follows.

Phonemic Level	/kænt/
Vowel Nasalization	kæ̃nt
Nasal Deletion	kæ̃t
Phonetic Level	[kæ̃t]

This ordering is correct; it yields [kæ̃t], which is the phonetic representation of *can't*. In this case, the /n/ is present to trigger Vowel Nasalization. After Vowel Nasalization applies, the /n/ is deleted via Nasal Deletion. Thus, the correct ordering between the two rules is Vowel Nasalization first and then Nasal Deletion.

Thus, in this section we have seen that phonological rules are necessary for mapping (or translating) one level of phonological representation into another. Moreover, we have seen that more than one such rule may apply in this mapping process, in which case the rules may have to apply in a particular order. Before leaving this section, however, let's return to one of the forms in our last example: *can't*. Our discussion of this form assumed the following phonemic and phonetic representations.

Phonemic	/kænt/
Phonetic	[kæ̃t]

We then proposed two phonological rules, Vowel Nasalization and Nasal Deletion, to account for the relationship between these two levels of representation.

What I want to focus on now is the claim that there is no phonetic nasal segment in *can't* [kæt]. In other words, what evidence do we have for assuming that the nasal segment /n/ in *can't* is deleted phonetically? There is one approach to this question that linguists characteristically do *not* take, namely inspection of the physical speech signal itself. Under this approach, we might make a recording of a speaker uttering the word *can't* and then make a spectrogram (i.e., voiceprint) of the utterance. A spectrogram is essentially a picture of the acoustic characteristics of an utterance. Since nasals typically display certain acoustic properties (the details of which need not concern us here), we might look at the spectrogram and try to determine if these specific acoustic properties are present. If they are, then we might conclude that the nasal segment has *not* been deleted; if they are not, then we might conclude that the nasal segment *has* been deleted. A number of researchers have tried this approach and have not come to any unanimous conclusions. Sometimes physical evidence of the nasal segment is found; other times it is not. This state of affairs, however, should not come as too much of a surprise. As we have already seen, segments are psychological units which a speaker imposes on the speech signal; they are not part of the physical speech signal itself.

Linguists, on the other hand, would approach the problem from an entirely different perspective, namely by examining the hypothesized psychological system itself. That is, linguists would decide the question by comparing what they could explain by assuming the nasal *has* been deleted to what they could explain by assuming the nasal has *not* been deleted. To see how this line of reasoning works, consider the following English words: *caddy, catty, candy,* and *canty.* (*Canty* means 'cheerful' and can be pronounced exactly like the phrase *can't he.*) Each of these words is given in the following chart, along with its phonemic and phonetic representations.

caddy	/kǽdi/	[kǽɾi]
catty	/kǽti/	[kǽɾi]
candy	/kǽndi/	[kǽndi]
canty	/kǽnti/	[kǽɾi]

Note, first, that the /d/ and /t/ in *caddy* and *catty*, respectively, become [ɾ]'s. This, of course, is predicted by our Flapping Rule, which states that an alveolar stop which occurs between a stressed vowel and an unstressed vowel becomes a flap. Note, second, that the /d/ in *candy* does not become [ɾ]. (To check this claim, try to pronounce *candy* with a flap; it comes out sounding like *canty*.) This, too, is predicted by our Flapping Rule: Since the /d/ in *candy* does not occur between two vowels (but rather between a consonant /n/ and a vowel /i/), it does not become [ɾ] but instead remains [d] on the phonetic level of representation. So far, so good.

Now, however, note that the /t/ in *canty* does become [ɾ]. (This is not to say that the word *must* be pronounced with a flap—certainly [kǽnti] is possible—only that it *may* be pronounced with a flap.) This fact has no transparent explanation within the system of rules we have set up. That is, the /t/ in *canty* occurs between a nasal /n/ and a vowel /i/ on the phonemic level of representation. Thus, the Flapping Rule should not be able to apply to /kǽnti/. This leaves us with an unexplained fact: the /d/ in *candy* does not become [ɾ], but the /t/ in *canty* does!

One way out of this bind is to *assume* that the phonology of English contains a rule of Nasal Deletion which deletes nasal consonants before voiceless stops. Once we make this assumption, then we have a ready explanation for the flap in *canty* but not in *candy*. The mapping between the phonemic representation and the phonetic representation for these two words is given here.

	canty	*candy*
Phonemic Level	/kǽnti/	/kǽndi/
Vowel Nasalization	kǽnti	kǽndi
Nasal Deletion	kǽti	cannot apply
Flapping	kǽɾi	cannot apply
Phonetic Level	[kǽɾi]	[kǽndi]

Since Nasal Deletion cannot apply to *candy* (Nasal Deletion applies only when the nasal consonant precedes a voiceless stop), there is no way that Flapping can apply.

It is important to understand that this difference in behavior between *candy* and *canty* is not just an isolated example in English. There are numerous parallel cases where Flapping can apply to /t/ after a nasal consonant but not to /d/: for example, *Mindy* [mĩndi], *minty* [mĩɾi]; *candor* [kǽndər], *canter* [kǽɾər]; *pander* [pǽndər], *panter* [pǽɾər] 'one who pants'; *plunder* [plʌ̃ndər], *punter* [pʌ̃ɾər]; *bandy* [bǽndi], *panty* [pǽɾi]; and so on.

SUMMARY

Let's review what we have done. We started with five observations about the pronunciation of words. However, we had no unified explanation for these phenomena. Thus, we constructed a theory of phonology to account for our original observations. This theory is based (indirectly) upon the physiology of the vocal tract and makes use of such concepts as segment, distinctive feature, allophonic variation, levels of representation (including systematic phonemic, classical phonemic, systematic phonetic, and physical phonetic), and phonological rules. These theoretical constructs were developed by linguists in order to help explain the observations in (1–5). This theory may turn out to be incorrect in part, but it is the best working hypothesis of the internal structure of phonology that we have at the present time.

In addition, it is important to understand that there is more to the study of phonology than we have covered in this one short chapter. However, you have now been exposed to the basic ideas in the field; if you want to learn more about the subject, consult the readings at the end of this chapter. Also, you may want to check your understanding of the material in this chapter by working through the exercises that follow.

EXERCISES

(1) Give the English phonemic symbol that corresponds to each of the following articulatory descriptions.
  (a) low front spread lax vowel
  (b) voiced velar nasal
  (c) voiced interdental fricative
  (d) high back round lax vowel
  (e) voiced palatal glide

(2) Give the English phonemes that correspond to the following feature specifications.
  (a) $\begin{bmatrix} - \text{BACK} \\ + \text{TENSE} \end{bmatrix}$
  (b) $\begin{bmatrix} + \text{FRICATIVE} \\ - \text{VOICE} \end{bmatrix}$
  (c) $\begin{bmatrix} + \text{BILABIAL} \\ + \text{VOICE} \end{bmatrix}$
  (d) $[+ \text{GLIDE}]$
  (e) $\begin{bmatrix} + \text{BACK} \\ + \text{ROUND} \end{bmatrix}$

(3) Write the following English words in phonemic transcription.
  (a) *thrush*
  (b) *breathe*
  (c) *they*
  (d) *fox*
  (e) *choose*

(4) Identify the following English words.
  (a) [æt̚]
  (b) [sǽɾərn]
  (c) [ǰɔːz]

(d) [ətʰɛ́:nčɔ̃:n]
(e) [óʔmi:l]

(5) In English, the phoneme /g/ has two allophones: the voiced velar stop [g] and the voiced palatal stop [ɟ]. Based on the following phonetic representations, (a) determine the conditions under which /g/ becomes [ɟ]; and then (b) try to formalize the rule using the notation developed in this chapter.

god	[ga:d]	*gone*	[gɔ̃:n]
geese	[ɟis]	*gain*	[ɟẽ:n]
ghoul	[gu:l]	*good*	[gʊ:d]
gab	[ɟæ:b]	*gear*	[ɟɪ:r]

(6) Like /g/, the phoneme /k/ in English exhibits exactly the same sort of allophonic variation between [k] (velar) and [c] (palatal): [c] occurs before /i,ɪ,e,ɛ,æ/ and [k] occurs before other vowels. (a) State the rules for the allophones of both /k/ and /g/ and (b) put the rule into formal notation.

(7) Consider the following data from Droolingua, a hypothetical language attributed to employees of the Pentagon. There are no voiced stop phonemes in Droolingua, only voiceless ones. Each one has three allophones: a voiceless stop, a voiceless aspirated stop, and a voiced stop.

[pʰi:k]	'cornflake'
[padan]	'Mr. Shekel'
[loban]	'oil of olay'
[piga]	'bleat'
[su:bu]	'Waring blender'
[tʰa:p]	'larvae'
[kʰa:got]	'wooden teeth'
[kap]	'McNeese State University'
[pibu]	'cortex'
[setnok]	'variorum edition'
[kʰu:dan]	'friends of the library'
[lupnot]	'special hat'
[tuknes]	'cheese food'

(a) Under what conditions does a stop become aspirated?
(b) Formalize the rule in (a).
(c) Under what conditions does a stop become voiced?
(d) Formalize the rule in (c).

ANSWERS TO EXERCISES

The following answers are in some cases not the only possible ones. Discussion of other possible answers is part of the exercises.

(1) (a) /æ/   (d) /ʊ/
    (b) /ŋ/   (e) /y/
    (c) /ð/

(2) (a) /i,e/   (d) /w,y/
    (b) /f,θ,s,š,h/   (e) /u,ʊ,o,ɔ/
    (c) /b,m,w/

(3) (a) /θrʌš/   (d) /faks/
    (b) /brið/   (e) /čuz/
    (c) /ðe/

(4) (a) *aunt* or *ant*   (d) *attention*
    (b) *Saturn*   (e) *oatmeal*
    (c) *jaws*

(5) (a) /g/ becomes [ɟ] when it is followed by a front vowel. (Note: /g/, a velar segment, becomes "fronted" to a palatal segment when it is followed by a "front" vowel.)

    (b)
$$\begin{bmatrix} +\text{STOP} \\ +\text{VELAR} \\ +\text{VOICE} \end{bmatrix} \rightarrow [+\text{PALATAL}]/ \_\_ \quad \begin{matrix} V \\ [-\text{BACK}] \end{matrix}$$

(6) (a) Velar stops become palatal stops when they occur before front vowels.

    (b)
$$\begin{bmatrix} +\text{STOP} \\ +\text{VELAR} \end{bmatrix} \rightarrow [+\text{PALATAL}]/ \_\_ \quad \begin{matrix} V \\ [-\text{BACK}] \end{matrix}$$

(7) (a) Stops become aspirated when they occur before a long vowel.

    (b) $[+\text{STOP}] \rightarrow [+\text{ASPIRATED}]/ \_\_ \quad \begin{matrix} V \\ [+\text{LONG}] \end{matrix}$

    (c) Stops become voiced when they occur between two vowels.

    (d) $[+\text{STOP}] \rightarrow [+\text{VOICE}]/V \_\_ V$

SUPPLEMENTARY READINGS

Primary

1. Chomsky, N., and Halle, M. (1968). *The sound pattern of English*. New York: Harper and Row.
2. Jakobson, R., Fant, G., and Halle, M. (1963). *Preliminaries to speech analysis*. Cambridge, MA: MIT Press.

Secondary

3. Hyman, L. (1975). *Phonology: Theory and analysis*. New York: Holt, Rinehart and Winston.
4. Schane, S. (1973). *Generative phonology*. Englewood Cliffs, NJ: Prentice-Hall.
5. Schane, S., and Bendixen, B. (1978). *Workbook in generative phonology*. Englewood Cliffs, NJ: Prentice-Hall.
6. Sommerstein, A. (1977). *Modern phonology*. London: Edward Arnold.
7. Wolfram, W., and Johnson, R. (1982). *Phonological analysis: Focus on American English*. Washington, DC: Center for Applied Linguistics.

You are now prepared to read all of the secondary works. However, it may be best to approach them in the following order. Wolfram and Johnson (7) is a recent introductory text dealing solely with American English. Schane (4) and the accompanying workbook (5) provide an excellent introduction to "doing" phonology; they deal primarily with non-English data. Hyman (3) provides, among other things, a brief history of phonological theory. Sommerstein (6) contains a survey of different theories of phonology. The primary works are more difficult and are now mainly of historical interest.

Chapter 7

Language Variation

Language variation is the study of those features of a language that differ systematically as we compare different groups of speakers or the same speaker in different situations. Rather than comparing features of two different languages (say, English and French), the field of language variation is concerned with **regional** varieties of the same language (say, a comparison of English as spoken by natives of Mississippi and natives of Massachusetts); **social** varieties of the same language (say, the English of upper middle class New Yorkers compared to that of lower working class New Yorkers); and **stylistic** varieties of the same language (say, how a given speaker uses language during a job interview compared to a casual conversation with a close friend). In this chapter we will look at some examples of these three types of variation: regional, social, and stylistic.

Within each of these categories, we can further note several sources of linguistic variation. Consider the following observations.

(1) In some parts of the United States, a large container used to carry water is called a *pail*; in other parts, the same item is called a *bucket*.

(2) In some regions of the United States, the word *greasy* is pronounced with medial [s]; in others it is pronounced with a [z].

(3) Among some groups in the United States, words such as *this*, *that*, *these*, and *those* are pronounced with initial [ð]: among others, they are pronounced with initial [d].

(4) For some groups of English speakers in the United States, a sentence such as *He walks home every day* would be formed as *He walk home every day*.

(5) For certain groups of speakers in the United States, the question *What is it?* would be formed as *What it is?*

(6) A person being interviewed for a job might say *In which department will I be working?* The same speaker, in a more informal situation, might say *Which department will I be working in?*

Observations (1) and (2) illustrate the fact that particular lexical items (i.e., vocabulary) and phonological forms are associated with specific geographical areas of the United States. Observations (3), (4), and (5) illustrate the fact that particular phonological, morphological, and syntactic forms are associated with specific social groups. Observation (6) illustrates the fact that any one speaker has at his or her command a variety of styles appropriate for a variety of situations.

All of these phenomena essentially involve language variation, in that they reflect the way language varies regionally, socially, and stylistically. Moreover, we will assume that the phenomena in observations (1–6) are governed by a system of principles. What we will do now is try to elucidate the linguistic categories and rules that will account for these phenomena. Bear in mind that what follows is a theory designed to explain the data in observations (1–6).

LANGUAGE UNIVERSALS, LANGUAGES, DIALECTS, AND IDIOLECTS

In Chapters 3 through 6, we have looked at language from the perspective of different components of the grammar—semantics, syntax, morphology, and phonology. From another perspective, the study of linguistics can be divided into a different set of domains, depending on what group of speakers we are looking at. One such domain is **language universals**, those properties (i.e., categories and rules) that all human languages, past and present, have in common. For example, all known languages make use of the categories noun and verb. Another domain concerns the properties of a particular **language** (e.g., Classical Latin, Old Norse, Modern English, and so forth). Still another domain is a **dialect**, a systematic variety of a language specific to a particular region or social class (e.g., American English, British English, Southern American English, Black English Vernacular, and so on). A final domain is the **idiolect**, the specific linguistic system of a particular speaker (e.g., the linguistic system of Mary Richards, Lou Grant, or Ted Baxter). All but the last of these domains are of primary interest to linguists, although different linguists tend to focus on different domains. The reason that most linguists are not especially interested in idiolects is that individual variations from speaker to speaker are thought to be idiosyncratic rather than systematic. Figure 7-1 summarizes the relationship among these different domains.

Since the topic of this chapter is language variation and since one domain of language variation is a dialect, we can start by differentiating a dialect from a language. One useful rule of thumb is that different languages are not mutually intelligible, whereas different dialects generally are. So, for example, if you are a monolingual speaker of English and

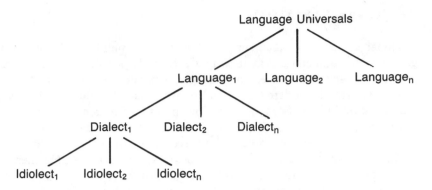

Figure 7-1.   Domains of language study, by groups of speakers.

you encounter a monolingual speaker of Norwegian, the two of you will have a great deal of difficulty communicating through language alone, since English and Norwegian are two different languages. On the other hand, if you are a native of Texas and you encounter a native of Boston, the similarities between your linguistic systems will far outweigh any differences; and you will have (relatively) little trouble communicating with each other, since Texan and Bostonian represent two different dialects of the same language. The relationship between languages and dialects is schematized in Figure 7-2.

One point that must be made at the outset of our discussion is that a dialect is an abstraction, a theoretical construct hypothesized by linguists to account for subsystems of regularities within a particular language. Informally, we might say that each subsystem is a dialect. It must be kept in mind, however, that in reality every native speaker of a language speaks his or her own idiolect, one shading into the other. When a significant number of idiolects share a common set of features not shared by other idiolects, then we might say that this group of idiolects forms a dialect.

Let's now take a look at three types of variation within a language: **regional variation** (or regional dialects), **social variation** (or social dialects—typically referred to as standard or nonstandard dialects), and **stylistic variation.**

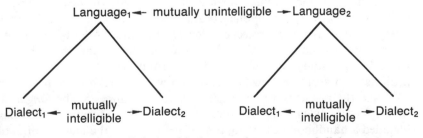

Figure 7-2.   Relationship between languages and dialects.

REGIONAL VARIATION

Regional varieties of a language result from a number of political, geographical, and cultural factors. First, the early population of an area leaves its linguistic heritage. For example, a paper napkin is sometimes called a *serviette* in modern Canadian English, because of the early French settlement of Quebec. Second, migration routes tend to demarcate dialect boundaries. For example, if you were to look at a regional dialect map of the United States, you would see three major dialect areas running horizontally from the east coast to the Mississippi River: Northern, Midland, and Southern. This is because the eastern coast was colonized by settlers from different parts of England, and when they began to migrate they moved west, rather than north or south. Third, political and ecclesiastical divisions contribute to regional dialect differences. For example, the equivalent of a county in Louisiana is called a *parish* even today, because of the early influence of the Catholic Church. Fourth, physical geographical boundaries can contribute to regional dialects. For example, the language variety known as Gullah or Sea Island Creole has not been absorbed into mainstream American English, because the speakers of this dialect live on islands off the coast of South Carolina and are geographically segregated from speakers on the mainland. In short, regional varieties of a language are primarily a function of settlement history and physical geography.

The study of regional varieties of a language, at least in the modern Western tradition, began in 19th-century Europe. By the early 20th century, the last volume of Joseph Wright's *English Dialect Dictionary* had been published, and regional dialect atlases had been begun or completed for Germany, France, and Italy by investigators working largely independently of one another. A dialect atlas is essentially a series of maps on which the geographical distribution of particular linguistic features is plotted.

Following the lead of the Europeans, a group of American linguists met in 1889 and established the American Dialect Society. Their original intention was to develop an American dialect dictionary modelled on Wright's. Over the next several decades, however, the nature of their regional investigations caused them to shift the focus of their work from a dialect dictionary to a dialect atlas. Consequently, in 1928 they inaugurated a large-scale project entitled The Linguistic Atlas of the United States and Canada (LAUSC) under the direction of Hans Kurath. The work for this study was subdivided into a number of smaller regional projects. Work on the New England area was carried out from 1931 to 1933 and the results were published in several volumes as the *Linguistic Atlas of New England (LANE)* from 1939 to 1943. The format of this atlas included a handbook describing the informants and the method of data collection and a series of maps, each indicating the geographical distribution of one or more dialect features. For example, one map showed the distribution of the terms *cottage cheese*, *pot cheese*, *sour-milk cheese*, and *Dutch cheese* throughout New England.

Fieldwork on the Middle and South Atlantic States was begun in 1933 and completed in 1949. (World War II interrupted the collection of data.) From this fieldwork came a number of important studies. In 1949 Kurath published *A Word Geography of the Eastern United States*. Based upon the patterning of regional vocabulary differences, Kurath divided the eastern coast into three major regional dialect areas: Northern, Midland, and Southern. In 1953 E. Bagby Atwood published *A Survey of Verb Forms in the Eastern United States*, and in 1961 Kurath and Raven McDavid published *The Pronunciation of English in the Atlantic States*.

These derivative works aside, however, the publication of the regional atlases has been slow and sporadic since the end of World War II. Even though countless hours of fieldwork have been invested in the Middle and South Atlantic States, the North Central States, and the Gulf States, most of the results still await publication. In fact, the only other atlas project that has been published in complete and final form since *LANE* is the *Linguistic Atlas of the Upper Midwest*, which was published in several volumes between 1973 and 1976.

A number of factors account for the slow progress of the LAUSC since World War II. First, a study of this magnitude (i.e., covering the entire United States and Canada) required a vast number of fieldworkers—an interview with a single informant could take days. Consequently, it would be difficult to get enough trained fieldworkers willing to dedicate themselves to this type of undertaking. Second, because of the large number of workers involved, they sometimes varied greatly in their training for this task; some fieldworkers were experienced linguists, while others might be doing it simply for summer employment. Finally, the fieldworkers sometimes used widely different methods for collecting data, making their results difficult to compare. For example, suppose the task were to determine if a particular informant used the term *pail* or *bucket* to refer to a device for carrying water from a well. One fieldworker might simply wait for the informant to use one of these forms spontaneously, which, of course, might take days. A second fieldworker might point to a pail or bucket and ask the informant, "What do you call this?" A third fieldworker might lead the informant even more by suggesting a term; for example, "Do you ever call this a *pail*?" Thus, a single fieldworker studying a single informant might collect vastly different data, depending upon the method used. The point is that any project covering more than half a century (1931 to the present), more than 3,500,000 square miles (the area of the United States alone), and involving hundreds of fieldworkers and thousands of informants is fraught with inherent logistical problems.

In addition to these specific factors, there were more general problems faced by proponents of the LAUSC. First, the Depression and World War II cost them financial support and personnel. Money and manpower were channeled away from pure research into applied areas more directly concerned with the war effort. Second, regional dialect areas become less well defined as we move away from the east coast. As you will recall, American regional dialectology was modelled on the European studies, which dealt with relatively immobile populations and relatively small and well-defined dialect areas. North America, on the other hand, is vast in comparison to Europe; and the population, especially since World War II, has become increasingly mobile. Under such circumstances, massive regional studies become difficult, if not completely impossible. Finally, the arrival of Chomsky's generative grammar in 1957 attracted the attention of many younger linguists. Consequently, the study of regional dialects has experienced competition for people entering the linguistics profession.

Having briefly gone over some of these background issues, let's now take a look at a representative sampling of some of the lexical and phonological dialect characteristics of North America.

Regional Lexical Variation

The following are some of the more prominent regional lexical (i.e., vocabulary) differences in North American English, along with a rough geographical distribution for each one: *pail* (North), *bucket* (South); *bag* (North), *sack* (South); *faucet* (North), *spigot* (South); quarter *of* four (North), quarter *till* four (South); *dove* (North), *dived* (South); *chesterfield* (Canada), *sofa* (United States); *serviette* (Canada), *napkin* (United States); and *eh?* (Canada), *huh?* (United States). Frederic Cassidy, in his research for the *Dictionary of American Regional English*, found thousands of examples of more exotic regionalisms: for instance, *eaceworm* 'earthworm' (Rhode Island); *democrat bug* 'box-elder bug' (Kansas and Iowa, Republican strongholds!); *snoose* 'snuff' (Wisconsin and Minnesota); *hooftie* 'hippie' (Pennsylvania; from *hooft* 'hip' in Pennsylvania German); *black Christmas* 'Christmas without snow' (Alaska); and *peach-limb tea* 'a whipping administered to a child' (Arkansas).

Regional Phonological Variation

The following are classic examples of regional phonological variation.

Linking [r]. This feature, which is associated with eastern New England and New York City, refers to a phenomenon whereby a vowel-vowel sequence between words is "linked" with an [r]. For example, consider a phrase like *That idea is crazy*. Note that *idea* [aɪdíə] ends with a vowel, and the following word *is* [ɪz] begins with a vowel. For a speaker whose dialect contains the "linking [r]" feature, this phrase would be pronounced as if *idea* ended in an [r] (*idear*). Speakers of this dialect presumably have a rule in their phonological systems which inserts an [r] between a word ending in a vowel and another word beginning with a vowel, as follows.

$$\varepsilon \rightarrow [r]/V \, \# \underline{\quad} \# \, V \quad (\# \text{ indicates a word boundary})$$

In contrast, this rule predicts that the "linking [r]" would not appear in the phrase *That idea sounds crazy*, since there are no vowel-vowel sequences between words (*idea* ends in a vowel, but *sounds* begins with a consonant).

Vowel Neutralization before Nasals.   For many speakers of Southern dialects, the phonemes /I/ and /ɛ/ are both represented phonetically as [I] before a nasal consonant. This process, whereby two segments lose their contrast in a particular phonetical environment, is known as **neutralization**. (The Flapping Rule discussed in Chapter 6, where /t/ and /d/ are both represented phonologically as a flap under certain conditions, is another example of neutralization.) So, for example, the words *pen* and *pin* would both be represented phonetically as [pʰĩn] for speakers of this dialect. Such speakers apparently have a rule in their phonological systems which changes /ɛ/ to [I] before a nasal consonant, as follows.

$$/\varepsilon/ \rightarrow [I]/ \underline{\quad} \quad \begin{array}{c} C \\ [+\text{NASAL}] \end{array}$$

Thus, for speakers of this regional dialect, the pairs *ten-tin* and *hem-him* are phonetically identical. On the other hand, the words *pet* and *pit* would be represented phonetically as [pʰɛt] and [pʰɪt], respectively, since no nasal occurs after the vowels in these words. Likewise, *net* and *knit* would be represented phonetically as [nɛt] and [nɪt], respectively, since the nasal in each of these words comes before, rather than after, the vowel.

Before leaving this rule of Vowel Neutralization, let me give you a concrete example which illustrates the practical effects of such dialect differences. During the summer of 1985, I was visiting the National Zoo in Washington, D.C., which attracts tourists from all over the country. Because this zoo displays the famous pandas Hsing-Hsing and Ling-Ling, it predictably sells quite a lot of "panda paraphernalia"—shirts, postcards, and so on. I was standing near a novelty shop when a man approached the clerk and asked for a "panda [pʰĩn]." The clerk brought him a panda *pin* (i.e., a button designed to be worn on a shirt). The man promptly said, "No, I want a [pʰĩn], like a fountain pen," and the clerk responded, "Oh, you want a [pʰɛ̃n]." Finally, the man got what he wanted: a *pen* decorated with panda pictures. However, neither the man nor the clerk, it appeared, ever did understand the cause of the confusion. We, on the other hand, can explain this interchange by assuming a rule of Vowel Neutralization, which is a feature of Southern dialects but not of others. The man (presumably from the South) pronounced *pen* as [pʰĭn], which the clerk (presumably not from the South) interpreted as *pin*.

Other Regional Phonological Features.   There are many examples of phonological variation too numerous to discuss in detail here. The following, however, constitute a representative sample: *greasy* [s] (North), [z] (South); *root* [ʊ] (North), [u] (South); *bottle* [baʔəl] (New York City); *wash* [warš] (Washington, D.C. area); *cot* and *caught* [a] (Pennsylvania); *shone* [ɔ] (Canada); and *out* [əʊ] (Canada, eastern Virginia, and South Carolina).

Several additional points should be made before leaving this section on regional variation. First, regional dialects, at least in North America, differ primarily in terms of vocabulary and pronunciation (i.e., lexically and phonologically). As we will see in the next section, social dialects differ primarily in terms of pronunciation, word formation, and sentence structure (i.e., phonologically, morphologically, and syntactically). Second, many of the regional dialect differences detected by fieldworkers in the 1930's and 1940's are not as clear-cut as they once were. As a result, you may have noticed that some of the dialect features ascribed to your particular area of the country do not match the way you speak. For example, you may say *faucet* (Northern) rather than *spigot* (Southern), but you're from Alabama! This should come as no great surprise; as we've already seen, the mobility of the American population since World War II has blurred, if not obliterated, what were earlier distinct limits on a particular dialect feature. Third, as we discussed earlier, a dialect is a theoretical construct devised by linguists to account for certain linguistic patterns. That is, a dialect boundary exists solely by virtue of the fact that the limits of a number of different dialect features coincide there. For example, the fact that the boundaries of *bucket*, *sack*, *spigot*, *dived*, and so on coincided (at least formerly) constitutes evidence for hypothesizing a Southern dialect area. A dialect area does not (and in fact, cannot) exist apart from these individual dialect features.

SOCIAL VARIATION

In the preceding section we discussed data drawn from studies in regional dialectology. While many researchers still maintain an interest in this field, much research in language variation has shifted, over the past 25 years or so, to a field known as **sociolinguistics**. Among the phenomena of concern to this field is the interrelationship between the socioeconomic status of a group of speakers and the characteristics of the dialect they speak. For example, working class New Yorkers "drop their r's" (i.e., delete post-vocalic [r]) in words like *forty-four* more often than middle class New Yorkers do. It would be misleading, however, to say that regional dialectology and sociolinguistics are mutually exclusive fields of study. On the contrary, researchers in regional dialectology often include socioeconomic information about their informants (e.g., age and education). Likewise, researchers in sociolinguistics must often take into account regional influences on the social dialects they are studying. Nevertheless, we can draw a few generalizations about why research in language variation has expanded from regional dialectology to include sociolinguistics, and about the different types of phenomena that sociolinguistics emphasizes.

Several trends developed in the United States during the late 1950's and early 1960's that focused more and more attention on social variation. First, since regional dialectologists had categorized information all along according to such social variables as age and education, it was a natural step for linguists to become interested in social variables for their own sake. The one person who did the most to bring sociolinguistics to prominence was William Labov. His doctoral dissertation, which was completed in the mid 1960's, dealt with the social stratification of English in New York City. In particular, Labov correlated several different phonological variables (e.g., the deletion of post-vocalic [r]) with different social classes (i.e., upper middle, lower middle, upper working, and lower working). Among his innovations was the use of a pre-existing sociological classification system for his informants. That is, he used a model of social stratification developed independently within the field of sociology, whereas most regional dialectologists had classified their informants using more or less subjective criteria. Moreover, he attempted to collect data from four different styles of speech: casual, careful, reading, and formal. Finally, he tried to use the results of his studies to develop both linguistic and sociological theory, whereas many regional dialectologists were working without any particular attention to fundamental issues in linguistic theory.

Second, linguists found it impossible to deal with language variation without acknowledging the fact that listeners judge a speaker according to the characteristics of the speaker's dialect. For example, someone who says *I ain't working this afternoon* may be judged as inferior to another person who says *I'm not working this afternoon*. Thus arose an interest in **standard** and **nonstandard** dialects. It is no simple matter to define the difference between a standard and a nonstandard variety of language. However, for our purposes, we can define a standard dialect as one that draws no negative attention to itself; that is, educated people would not judge a person speaking such a dialect as socially inferior, lacking education, and so forth. On the other hand, a nonstandard dialect does draw negative attention to itself; that is, educated people might judge the speaker of such a dialect as socially inferior, lacking education, and so on. A nonstandard dialect can thus be characterized as having **socially marked** forms, such as *ain't* in the example cited earlier.

It is important to understand that identifying a dialect as standard or nonstandard is a sociological judgment, not a linguistic judgment. If we say that Dialect X is nonstandard, we are saying that the educated members of the society in which X is spoken judge the speakers of X as inferior in some way, based on certain linguistic characteristics of X. We are not, however, saying that X is inferior linguistically in the sense that it is cruder, less well developed, and so forth than the standard. All dialects of all natural languages are absolutely rule governed and systematic. None is more or less developed than another; all are equally complex.

Let's look at a concrete example of the difference between a sociological and a linguistic judgment. Consider the reflexive pronouns in the following sentences.

(7a)   John fed *himself*.
(7b)   John fed *hisself*.
(7c)   John fed *heself*.

First of all, observe that (7a) and (7b) are used by speakers of English, but (7c) isn't. In other words, (7a) and (7b) are part of English, but (7c) isn't. This is a linguistic fact. Second, the pronominal forms in (7a) and (7b) are used by different groups of speakers. That is, they belong to different dialects. This, too, is a linguistic fact. Third, the utterance of sentence (7a) goes unnoticed by educated speakers of the language; it draws no negative attention to the speaker; it is unremarkable. On the other hand, the utterance of (7b) does not go unnoticed; it does draw negative attention to the speaker; it is, in fact, remarkable. These and the judgments that follow from them (e.g., (7a) is standard, (7b) is nonstandard) are sociological facts.

Third, this interest in standard-nonstandard dialects and socially marked forms led quite naturally to an interest in Black English Vernacular (BEV), a nonstandard dialect spoken primarily by low income, inner city blacks. There were several reasons that BEV became the focus of interest in the study of nonstandard dialects. For one thing, the Civil Rights movement and the integration of the public schools brought the language differences between lower class blacks and middle class whites into noticeable contrast. This led to concerns about how best to administer public education. Also, BEV is thought to be the nonstandard dialect most different from standard English. Thus, it seemed reasonable to some linguists to begin their description of nonstandard dialects with that most distinct from standard English. In addition, the extreme interest in BEV was fueled by the controversy surrounding its origin. Some scholars maintained the traditional position that BEV was no different from that dialect spoken by poor Southern whites. Others, however, who were studying Caribbean creoles pointed out creole forms in modern-day BEV, and suggested that BEV itself developed from a creole. (A **creole** is the native language of a group of speakers which has evolved from a **pidgin**, a mixture of two existing languages brought into contact by trade or colonization.) These factors focused attention on BEV to the virtual exclusion of other nonstandard dialects of American English (for example, those of the deep South and Appalachia).

Fourth, research on nonstandard dialects in general and BEV in particular led quite naturally to its application to practical problems in mass education. The relevance of such research is obvious. For example, a teacher is less likely to be concerned with a student who uses *sack* instead of *bag* (a purely regional distinction) than with a student who uses *Can't nobody tell me what to do* instead of *Nobody can tell me what to do* (a socially marked distinction). Likewise, variations that are considered nonstandard may result in a child's being diagnosed for language therapy or failing a standardized test. For example, a student who pronounces *these* with initial [d] instead of [ð] may be judged as having an "articulation problem." (For expository purposes, I am using the term *pronounce* here and throughout as an informal substitute for "represent phonetically.") Because social variations in language are, rightly or wrongly, so strongly linked to how students are tested and evaluated, many sociolinguists have focused their efforts on communicating with teachers, testing services, and speech-language pathologists about the nature of nonstandard dialects.

Finally, while regional dialects are largely characterized by lexical variation, nonstandard dialects are more likely to be characterized by grammatical variation (i.e., variations in phonology, morphology, and syntax). Many linguists find grammatical variation of more interest than lexical variation because it tends to be more systematic and predictable. For example, given a form such as *submarine*, referring to a sandwich made on an oblong loaf of bread, no amount of linguistic theorizing would enable an observer to predict that other speakers might call the same object a *hero*, *hoagie*, *grinder*, or *poboy*! On the other hand, grammatical forms are more likely to reflect predictable variations, as we will see in the next three sections.

Nonstandard Phonological Variation

As we have seen, not all phonological variation carries social weight. For example, a speaker who pronounces *caught* as [kʰɔt] would probably not form any negative social judgments about a speaker who pronounces the same word as [kʰat], at least not on the basis of this one form. Similarly, a speaker from New England whose dialect contains the Linking [r] Rule would probably not form a social judgment about a speaker whose dialect lacks this feature. However, some phonological variation is socially marked: Some listeners form a negative social judgment of a speaker whose dialect displays certain phonological forms. Let's now look at some specific examples.

Substitution of [d] for [ð].   Consider the pronunciation of *this*, *that*, *these*, *those*, and so on with initial [d] instead of [ð]. From a social perspective, a listener may associate such forms with speakers from, say, working class sections of New York City. If the listener holds this group in low social esteem, he or she may label such forms as "bad" or "incorrect" English. As pointed out earlier, however, it is essential to try to separate social judgments from linguistic ones. Let's concentrate on examining such forms from a linguistic standpoint: that is, with the purpose of discovering, from a phonological perspective, *why* these particular forms are used by some speakers.

First, in what sense can the pronunciation of *these* as [diz] be said to constitute a predictable and systematic phonological variation? In order to answer this question, we can begin by comparing the descriptions of the phonemes /ð/ and /d/. The phoneme /ð/ is a voiced interdental fricative; /d/ is a voiced alveolar stop. Intuitively, it would seem more plausible for a substitution to occur between similar segments than between dissimilar segments. At first glance, it may seem that /ð/ and /d/ have little in common, since they differ in place and manner of articulation. On the other hand, both segments have in common the fact that they are voiced consonants. Note, moreover, that although /ð/ and /d/ differ in their places of articulation, the places of articulation are very close. In fact, it might be said that /d/ is one of the "closest" voiced consonants to /ð/. (To confirm this, consult the consonant chart in Chapter 6.) Therefore, the place of articulation contrast between these two segments is not so great as it may initially seem.

But what about the contrast in the manner of articulation? In order to understand why a dialect might substitute [d], a stop, for [ð], a fricative, some additional background is required. Specifically, there are several pieces of evidence that might be used to support the claim that stops are more "natural" than fricatives, especially interdental fricatives such as the phoneme /ð/. One such piece of evidence comes from language acquisition, which includes the study of the order in which children acquire linguistic forms. Evidence from this field suggests that children acquire stops before they acquire fricatives, indicating that stops are somehow more "basic" consonants than fricatives. A second piece of evidence comes from language change, the study of how languages evolve over time, from one generation of speakers to the next. As a rule, the likelihood of finding a language which had alveolar stops in its consonants and then later added interdental fricatives is much greater than that of finding a language which had interdental fricatives in its consonant inventory and then later added stops. A third, related piece of evidence that alveolar stops are more natural than interdental fricatives is the fact that languages without interdental fricatives are relatively easy to find—French, German, and some dialects of Spanish are a few examples—whereas languages without at least one alveolar stop are extremely rare. All of these facts, then, support the hypothesis that a dialect which substitutes a stop such as [d] for a fricative such as [ð] is following a "natural" linguistic trend. (Having gone through this argument, try to determine, as an exercise, why words such as *think* and *throw* might be pronounced with initial [t] rather than [θ] in some dialects of American English.)

    Consonant Cluster Reduction.   A consonant cluster is a series of at least two consonants within the same syllable; for example, *iced* /aɪst/ contains the consonant cluster /st/. Consonant Cluster Reduction, in turn, is a phonological rule that reduces a consonant cluster by deleting one of the consonants. More specifically, the second member of a consonant cluster (typically a stop) is deleted at the end of a word if the following word starts with a consonant. Thus, for example, *iced tea* /aɪst ti/, which contains a consonant cluster /st/ followed by another consonant /t/, would become [aɪs ti] by the rule of Consonant Cluster Reduction. Note that *iced tea* is, not surprisingly, often spelled *ice tea*. Moreover, such reduction occurs in the running speech even of speakers of standard dialects. This can be confirmed through introspection—try saying *iced tea* at a normal rate of speech—or by listening to another person say it at a normal rate of speech. It is very difficult to enunciate the final [t] of *iced* without pausing between words, thereby creating an artificial speaking style.

    As we have seen, Consonant Cluster Reduction is a phonological process that occurs in all varieties of English, both standard and nonstandard. Very often, however, socially marked forms result from phonological processes which are part of the system for *all* speakers of a language. In particular, many types of phonological variation are not socially marked when they occur in speech, and may in fact go unnoticed until, for example, they result in a nonstandard spelling. Moreover, a socially marked form often results from extending the environment of a rule that applies in the standard dialect, so that the rule applies in contexts where it did not previously apply.

    In order to see how such things occur, let's first consider how Consonant Cluster Reduction can influence a speaker's written English. Consider the sentence *He pushed the car* /hi pʊšt ðə kar/. Note that *pushed* ends in a consonant cluster /št/ and the next word starts with a consonant

/ð/; thus Consonant Cluster Reduction can apply and delete the /t/. We have argued that the deletion of the final /t/ on *pushed* would not be socially marked if this sentence were uttered at a normal speaking rate. However, assume that a speaker is attempting to produce a written version of these words based (at least partially) on how they are pronounced. Due to the influence of Consonant Cluster Reduction, it would not be unusual for the written version to take the form *He push the car*. First, notice that *push* now fails to conform to standard spelling. Second, notice that when *pushed* becomes *push*, Consonant Cluster Reduction deletes not just a segment (/t/) but also the segment which represents the past tense suffix for regular verbs (usually represented in spelling as -*ed*). It is not difficult to imagine a case in which a teacher without some familiarity with phonological processes might wrongly conclude that this writer "lacks the concept" of past tense. (Such misguided evaluations are, unfortunately, quite common; Labov's "Academic Ignorance and Black Intelligence" cites numerous examples.) As we have seen, however, the nonstandard spelling actually has a straightforward phonological explanation.

So far we have discussed one source of nonstandard phonological forms: A phonological rule of standard English, which goes unnoticed in speech, serves to create socially marked forms in spelling. A second source for nonstandard phonological forms is the extension of a rule in standard English so that it applies in more contexts than it formerly did. Let's return to our example of *pushed the car*. The rules that deletes the /t/ can be stated informally as follows: Delete the second member of a word-final consonant cluster when the following word begins with a consonant. This rule, in turn, can be formalized as follows:

$$C \rightarrow \emptyset / C \_\!\_ \# C$$

This rule would delete the /t/ in *pushed the car* (since the cluster /št/ is followed by a word beginning with a consonant, /ð/), but it would not delete the /t/ in *pushed a car* (since the cluster /št/ is followed by a word beginning with a vowel, /ə/).

There are, however, nonstandard dialects of English in which *both* of the forms just mentioned would undergo Consonant Cluster Reduction. This can be explained by hypothesizing that the nonstandard dialect has generalized the Consonant Cluster Reduction Rule so that it deletes the second member of a word-final consonant cluster, regardless of what kind of segment begins the next word. This rule can be formalized as follows:

$$C \rightarrow \emptyset / C \_\!\_ \#$$

This rule in the nonstandard dialect applies in exactly the same cases as the rule in the standard dialect. However, it also applies in contexts that the original rule does not, namely where the consonant cluster is followed by a word beginning with a vowel (e.g., *He pushed a car* ➤ *He push a car*) or where the consonant cluster is followed by nothing at all (e.g., *He got pushed* ➝ *He got push*).

Before leaving this example, let me try to clarify two points of potential confusion. First, the Consonant Cluster Reduction Rule in standard English is more general than the version we have just discussed. For example, it can apply within a single word as well as across the boundary between two words, as in *asked* /æskt/ ➝ [æst]. I have restricted our discussion to a particular version of the rule solely for expository purposes. Second, I have presented the standard and nonstandard rules of Consonant Cluster Reduction as if all speakers have one or the other. In reality, the situation is more complex. All speakers of American English can apply Consonant Cluster Reduction before a word beginning with a consonant; moreover, all speakers have the *potential* for applying Consonant Cluster Reduction before a word beginning with a vowel or when nothing at all follows. The more often the rule is applied under the latter circumstances, the more socially marked the dialect. Thus, Consonant Cluster Reduction illustrates the principle discussed earlier, namely that a dialect is an abstraction, a generalization. The fact is that everyone's language (i.e., idiolect) is slightly different from everyone else's. A dialect is simply a grouping of idiolects that share certain characteristics (such as the frequency of Consonant Cluster Reduction before a word beginning with a vowel).

Other Nonstandard Phonological Features.   There are many examples of socially marked phonological variation too numerous to detail here; the following, however, constitute a representative sample. One is the substitution of [t] for [k] and vice-versa: [kemark] for *K-Mart*, [krɛdɪk] for *credit*, [rɪsk] for *wrist*, [ot] for *oak*, [dɛst] for *desk*, and so on. The segments [t] and [k] are very similar acoustically, especially when they occur before another consonant, as in *K-Mart Plaza*. A speaker who is only semiliterate (i.e., unfamiliar with the spelling of a word) might understandably perceive a word like *K-Mart* as ending in the phoneme /k/. As an aside, it is interesting how dependent we are upon our knowledge of spelling. When we are introduced to someone whose name is difficult for us to pronounce, we often ask how the name is spelled. Since so many proper names are unfamiliar (e.g., Mikhail Baryshnikov, the ballet dancer), we try to get a "fix" on their phonological representation; one way to do this is by associating each name with its spelling.

Another example of nonstandard phonological variation is the substitution of [f] for [θ]: [maʊf] for *mouth*, [smɪf] for *Smith*, and so on. Like [t] and [k], [f] and [θ] are very similar acoustically. Moreover, the phoneme /f/ is much more common among the world's languages than is /θ/. Thus, a semiliterate speaker is likely to perceive the final segment in *Smith* as the more common /f/ than the less common /θ/. However, such a misinterpretation is not restricted to semiliterates. LSU's football stadium has been nicknamed *Death Valley* (presumably out of wishful optimism for the "death" of the opposing team); the nickname, however, has been misperceived by some as *Deaf Valley*. I am told by those who call it this that the name is due to the "deafening" noise during football games.

A final example of socially marked phonological variation is the devoicing of a word-final stop: [kIlt] for *killed*, [əholt] for *ahold*, [hɛt] for *head*, and so on. The phonological rule of Final Devoicing, whereby a voiced stop phonemically (e.g., /b,d,g/ in English) becomes the corresponding voiceless stop phonetically ([p,t,k]), is quite common among the world's languages. This rule applies (in one form or another) in both German and Russian, and has applied selectively to English earlier in its history, as can be seen in the pairs *spilled/spilt*, *dreamed/dreamt*, *learned/learnt*, *burned/burnt*, and so on.

Nonstandard Morphological Variation

Morphological variation refers to differences in word formation, especially those related to the inflection of nouns and verbs. Whereas many phonological processes are common to all spoken dialects of English, variations in morphology tend to be restricted to particular social dialects. In general, morphological variation is more socially marked in speech than is phonological variation. However, morphological variation, like phonological variation, is also predictable and systematic. In fact, nonstandard morphological forms often reflect more regular treatments of the noun and verb systems of English than their standard counterparts do, as we will see in the following examples.

Reflexive Pronouns.   One example of nonstandard morphological variation was given in the exercises for Chapter 5. In one exercise, we observed that some nonstandard dialects of English use the following system of reflexive pronouns.

	SINGULAR	PLURAL
1st person	myself	ourselves
2nd person	yourself	yourselves
3rd person	herself/hisself	theirselves

This system is identical to the standard English system, with two exceptions: The third person singular form *hisself* is used, instead of the standard English form *himself*; and the third person plural form *theirselves* is used, instead of the standard English form *themselves*.

Again, if we set aside any social judgments that we may have about the nonstandard forms, we can see that these forms are highly systematic from a linguistic perspective (and, in fact, are more predictable than the standard English forms *himself* and *themselves*.) Note that the first and second person reflexive pronouns have as their base a possessive pronoun: *my*, *our*, or *your*. (The third person singular feminine form, *herself*, can be interpreted as either possessive + *self* or objective + *self*.) In other words, given the first and second person forms, the principle for forming a reflexive pronoun in English appears to be something like the following: Add -*self* or -*selves* to the possessive form. Following this rule would give us *hisself* and *theirselves* for the third person forms. Therefore, from a linguistic perspective, the nonstandard forms *hisself* and *theirselves* are actually more systematic than the standard forms *himself* and *themselves*. The reflexive pronoun system illustrates quite pointedly the fact that nonstandard dialects exhibit systematic morphological variation.

Omission of Final -s *on Verbs.*   Consider the sentence *He walk home every day*. We can begin by comparing this sentence to its standard English counterpart, *He walks home every day*. At this point, there appear to be two potential ways of analyzing the nonstandard form, *walk* for *walks*. It might be argued that the -*s* in *walks* has been deleted by Consonant Cluster Reduction, a phonological process. This hypothesis is supported by the fact that the /s/ in *walks* /wɔks/ is word final. However, we have stated the generalization that Consonant Cluster Reduction tends to be restricted to stop consonants, and /s/ is a fricative rather than a stop. Since deletion of a fricative would violate the pattern typically associated with Consonant Cluster Reduction, the deletion of the -*s* in *walks* does not appear to result from this phonological rule.

A second way to account for the nonstandard form *walk* is to hypothesize that a morpheme has been deleted, namely the {PRES} inflection that occurs in standard English as -*s* on the third person singular form of present tense verbs. The obvious question that arises is: Why is this morpheme omitted in some nonstandard dialects? To see why, let's look at the standard English system for the inflection of present tense verbs.

	SINGULAR	PLURAL
1st person	I walk	We walk
2nd person	You walk	You walk
3rd person	He/she walk	They walk

Upon examining the standard English system, we can see immediately that most present tense verbs have no overt manifestation of {PRES}. If we substitute the nonstandard forms (*He/she walk*) for the corresponding standard forms, we come out with a perfectly regular system, as illustrated here.

	SINGULAR	PLURAL
1st person	I walk	We walk
2nd person	You walk	You walk
3rd person	He/she walk	They walk

This regularization of the third person present tense verb forms generalizes to all main verbs and auxiliaries in some nonstandard dialects of English, as in, for example, *He do* for *He does*; *He don't* for *He doesn't*; and *He have* for *He has*.

   Other Nonstandard Morphological Features.   Once again, more examples exist than can be detailed here. The following, however, are representative. One feature is the use of nonstandard past tense and past participial verb forms: for example, *see, seed*, or *seen* for *saw*; *come* for *came*; and *rid* for *rode*. (Atwood's *Survey of Verb Forms* is filled with such examples, owing primarily to older and relatively uneducated informants.) Another feature is the omission of *-s* on plural nouns (the morpheme {PLU}) and possessive NP's (the morpheme {POSS}): for example, *girl* for both *girls* and *girl's*. It is significant that in BEV the *-s* morphemes representing {PRES}, {POSS}, and {PLU} are omitted with different frequencies. That is, {PRES} is omitted more frequently than {POSS}, and {POSS} is omitted more frequently than {PLU}. This indicates that the omission of *-s* is morphological rather than phonological. If it were phonological, all three morphemes would be omitted with equal frequency, since they are phonologically identical.

   Another nonstandard morphological feature is the generalization of one inflected form of *be* to all forms. Note that, unlike other present tense verbs in English, which have a predominant form (without *-s*) and an exceptional form (with *-s*), *be* has three forms, all of which appear to be exceptional: *am, are*, and *is*. Thus, speakers of some nonstandard dialects regularize all present tense forms of *be* to one single form: for example, *I is, You is, We is*, and *They is*. Note that when this happens *be* is no longer an "irregular" verb (i.e., one with exceptional forms). The point is that nonstandard morphological variations, like nonstandard phonological variations, tend to reflect a highly systematic treatment of English.

Nonstandard Syntactic Variation

Like morphological variations, syntactic variations tend to be more socially marked than phonological variations, some of which are regional as well as social. Let's take a look at some specific nonstandard syntactic constructions.

   Inversion in wh-*Interrogatives.*   In some nonstandard dialects of English, an interrogative such as *What is it?* may be formed as *What it is?* In order to demonstrate the relation between these two syntactic forms, we will need to make use of several concepts discussed in Chapter 5 (Syntax), namely underlying structure, surface structure, and transformation. With these concepts at hand, we can begin by analyzing the **derivation** of the standard English form *What is it?*; that is, by making some observations about the transformations that relate its underlying and surface structures.

Let us assume that, in the underlying structure of this interrogative, we have a sequence of elements like the following:

it - is - what

Note that this underlying structure differs from the surface form in two ways. First, the subject NP (*it*) is in initial position in the underlying structure, but follows the verb (*is*) on the surface. Second, the *wh*-word (*what*) is in final position in the underlying structure, but in initial position in the surface form. In order to account for these differences between the underlying and surface structures, we will postulate that each of these changes—the inversion of the subject-verb sequence *it is* to *is it* and the movement of the *wh*-word to initial position—constitutes a transformation. We can state the first of these transformations, Subject-Verb Inversion, informally as follows: If a subject NP is followed by a form of the verb *to be*, invert the subject NP and the verb form when forming an interrogative. The second transformation, *wh*-Movement, can be stated informally as it was in Chapter 5: Move the *wh*-word to initial position. Applying each of these transformations to the underlying structure yields the standard English form *What is it?*, as shown in the following derivation.

Underlying structure:	it - is - what
Subject-Verb Inversion:	is - it - what
wh-Movement:	what - is - it
	What is it?

So far, so good: We have provided an account of the standard English structure. However, how can we account for the nonstandard English structure, *What it is?* Let's make the initial assumption that this form has the same underlying structure as its standard counterpart:

it - is - what

What transformational rules are needed in order to go from this underlying structure to the surface form *What it is?* Only one: *wh*-Movement. Applying this transformation to the underlying structure would yield the surface form *What it is?*

Let's compare the standard and nonstandard derivations side by side. As we have seen, the difference between them can be explained by assuming that Subject-Verb Inversion applies in the standard derivation but not in the nonstandard derivation. This situation is summarized here.

	STANDARD ENGLISH	NONSTANDARD ENGLISH
Underlying structure:	it - is - what	it - is - what
Subject-Verb Inversion:	is - it - what	does not apply
wh-Movement:	what - is - it	what - it - is
	What is it?	*What it is?*

At this point, it should be clear that the nonstandard derivation omits a step—Subject-Verb Inversion—that appears in the standard derivation. This should not be interpreted to mean that the nonstandard derivation is "deficient" or "incomplete" in some way. Rather, a dialect containing this nonstandard feature is perfectly rule governed and differs from standard English in a systematic and predictable way.

Double Negatives. Let's now take a look at the infamous double negative construction, exemplified by sentences such as *I don't have no money* (cf. standard English *I don't have any money*). This construction is significant not so much because it is socially marked (which of course it is in Modern English), but because of the faulty reasoning usually associated with its prohibition.

Every school child is familiar with the following rule: Double negatives are incorrect because two negatives make a positive. This statement of the rule can largely be traced to a highly influential book written by Robert Lowth in 1762, *A Short Introduction to English Grammar*. Lowth's work was one of many similar collections of "do's and don't's" about the English language which appeared during the 18th-century prescriptive grammar movement. Unfortunately, many of these proclamations were based on personal prejudices against certain structures (for example, Jonathan Swift objected to verb forms such as /dɪstárbd/ instead of /dɪstárbəd/ for *disturbed*) and on the notion that new forms (including words such as *banter, bully,* and *mob*) would corrupt the language. Moreover, many leaders of this movement believed that English should emulate models such as Greek and Latin, which were perceived as more authoritative and stable than English.

Lowth's prohibition against double negatives illustrates this latter tendency, in that it was an attempt to model English after mathematics: "Two Negatives in English destroy one another, or are equivalent to an Affirmative." Here Lowth was apparently analogizing from the fact that the product of two negative numbers is a positive number: for example, $(-2) \times (-2) = 4$. Interestingly enough, Lowth could likewise have *defended* the double negative by analogy to mathematics, and might just as well have argued that the sum of two negative numbers is itself a negative number: that is, two negatives reinforce, rather than cancel, each other. The point is that Lowth proclaimed the double negative in English to be "illogical" not because it violates our linguistic system, but because it violates a principle from another system—mathematics.

If Lowth's reasoning were correct, we would expect certain things to follow from it. First, we would expect a sentence such as *I don't have no money* to mean 'I have some money.' Contrary to Lowth's prediction, however, this sentence means 'I don't have any money,' as any native speaker of English will be quick to point out. Second, we would expect human languages in general to shun double negative constructions. This, however, is not the case. If we turn to the present-day forms of languages other than English, we find that double negatives appear as a matter of course. For example, the standard English sentence *I don't want anything*, which contains one negative (the contracted form of *not*), has as its Spanish equivalent *No quiero nada*, where both *no* and *nada* indicate negation. Thus, there is nothing inherently deviant about the double negative construction. Moreover, if we look back at earlier stages of the English language, we find double negatives in the language of quite a few highly esteemed writers. The double negatives in the following passages have been italicized.

> Old English (King Alfred, the *Orosius*, ca. 880–890): "*ne* bið ðær *nænig* ealo gebrowen mid Estum" (literally "not is there not-any ale brewed among Estonians"; Modern English "no ale is brewed among the Estonians").
>
> Middle English (Chaucer, the *Canterbury Tales*, ca. 1390): "he that is irous and wrooth, he *ne* may *nat* wel deme" (literally "he that is angry and wrathful, he not may not well judge"; Modern English "he cannot judge well").
>
> Early Modern English (Shakespeare, *2 Henry IV*, ca. 1600): "There's *never none* of these demure boys come to any proof."

From a historical perspective, then, it is difficult to say that the double negative construction was either socially or linguistically marked in earlier forms of English.

If, then, Lowth's analysis of double negatives is inaccurate, what actually led to the socially marked status of double negatives in Modern English? Without going into excessive detail, here's what seems to have happened. In Old English, the double negative construction was obligatory, as it is in Modern Spanish. That is, the Old English equivalent of *I don't have no money* would have been grammatical, and the equivalent of *I don't have any money* would have been ungrammatical. By Shakespeare's time, the double negative construction had become optional. That is, the Early Modern English equivalents of *I don't have no money* and *I don't have any money* existed side by side, both fully grammatical. Apparently, however, the single negative construction somehow became associated with educated speakers, while the double negative became associated with uneducated speakers. This, of course, eventually led to the double negative construction being socially marked in Modern English. The point to keep in mind, however, is that sociolinguistic phenomena are a function of the interaction of linguistic and sociological forces; mathematical and logical systems have no bearing on them whatsoever.

Other Nonstandard Syntactic Features. There are, of course, many other socially marked syntactic constructions too numerous to detail here. The following, however, constitute a representative sample. One such feature is the deletion of an inflected form of *be*. For example, *He is my brother* becomes *He my brother*. Fasold, in his 1972 work *Tense Marking in Black English*, makes the point that BEV contains sentences with inflected *be* and invariant *be* side by side but with systematically different meanings, as illustrated here.

Permanent condition: He *is* my brother.
Temporary condition: He *be* my brother (when he needs money).

Furthermore, it appears that only an inflected form of *be* is subject to this rule of *be*-Deletion. (Actually, if this is the case, the rule should probably be renamed *am/are/is*-Deletion!) Along these lines, Labov has determined that BEV speakers can delete an inflected form of *be* only where standard English can contract. Thus, in standard English *be* can be contracted in a construction such as *It is his* → *It's his*, but not in *That's what it is* → **That's what it's*. Similarly, in BEV *be* can be deleted in *It is his* → *It his*, but not in *That's what it is* → **That's what it.*

Another nonstandard syntactic feature involves the treatment of main verb *be* in sentences such as *Do they be sick?* In standard English, Subject-Verb Inversion (SVI) applies to auxiliaries to form an interrogative: *John has seen Mary* → *Has John seen Mary?* On the other hand, SVI never applies to main verbs: *John saw Mary* → **Saw John Mary?* Instead, when there is no auxiliary verb, a form of *do* is inserted to take the place of the missing auxiliary: *John saw Mary* → *John did see Mary* (via *do*-Insertion) → *Did John see Mary?* (via SVI). Thus, standard English has a general rule for forming interrogatives: SVI applies to auxiliaries but not to main verbs; when there is no overt auxiliary, insert a form of *do*. There is, however, a major exception to this rule in standard English: Main verb *be* behaves like an auxiliary rather than a main verb. For example, *They are sick* → *Are they sick?*

Now consider what form we would get if main verb *be* behaved like all other main verbs, that is, not undergoing SVI and consequently triggering the insertion of *do*: *They be sick* → *They do be sick* (via *do*-

Insertion) ➛ *Do they be sick?* (via SVI). This is the nonstandard counterpart of standard English *Are they sick?* In this case, the nonstandard dialect has regularized an exception in standard English, namely the treatment of main verb *be*. The nonstandard dialect treats main verb *be* exactly like all other main verbs.

Another socially marked syntactic feature involves moving a negative auxiliary to sentence-initial position when the subject is an indefinite NP (e.g., *everyone, nobody,* and so on), as in *Everybody can't win* ➛ *Can't everybody win.* Standard English has a similar Negative Fronting Rule, which moves a negative adverbial to sentence-initial position and has the effect of triggering SVI: *I have never had such a good time* ➛ *Never I have had such a good time* (via Negative Fronting) ➛ *Never have I had such a good time* (via SVI). Once again, we can see both the similarities and the systematic differences between standard and nonstandard dialects of English.

To summarize this section, socially marked grammatical variations are often highly systematic from a linguistic perspective. That is, they often reflect predictable variations of standard English forms and are by no means "illogical" or "incorrect" from the standpoint of how language actually works. Any negative judgments that we may have about nonstandard forms are based more on our social biases about the speakers who use them than on their linguistic structure.

Does this mean that linguists take an "anything goes" attitude toward language? That is, do linguists advocate the use of double negatives and other socially marked forms? I cannot speak for all linguists, of course, but my own point of view is that social judgments are just as real as linguistic judgments. That is, a form like *What it is?* is likely to elicit a negative social judgment from many listeners, despite their ability to understand the meaning of the sentence. It would be foolhardy to pretend that such social judgments are nonexistent or unimportant. On the other hand, it would be just as misguided to claim that a structure like *What it is?* constitutes an illogical or inferior linguistic form. I believe that anyone who is in the business of teaching language and evaluating the language of others should understand the distinction between social and linguistic judgments, as well as the underlying regularity of many socially marked forms.

Before leaving this section, however, I want to clarify two points of potential confusion. First, in our discussion of regional and social dialects, we treated these two areas as mutually exclusive. This is a convenient compartmentalization for thinking and talking about language variation, but in actual practice the situation is more complex. Let's consider an example of how a regional feature might become socially marked. In most regional dialects outside the Midwest, the word *anymore* must occur after a negative word when it appears in a declarative sentence, as in *She sure isn't happy anymore.* However, this restriction on *anymore* has been lifted in the Midwest, so that *anymore* can occur in positive as well as negative declaratives, as in *She sure is happy anymore.* This "positive *anymore*" construction is completely unmarked in the Midwest; but consider what might happen when a Midwesterner moves to an area of the country, say, the deep South, which does not have this feature. Here the "positive *anymore*" construction will be marked and the newcomer may be perceived as speaking a nonstandard variety of English, especially if he or she is from a lower socioeconomic class.

Second, in our discussion of socially marked features, I have avoided (at least in most cases) labelling them as characteristic of BEV or some other nonstandard dialect. I have done this because quite a bit of controversy has arisen during the last 20 years over the claim that BEV has certain unique forms found in no other nonstandard dialects. Rather than get into this controversy, I will simply refer you to the readings at the end of the chapter, some of which treat this issue in detail.

STYLISTIC VARIATION

Earlier in this chapter, we looked at linguistic features that vary from one group to the next. In this section, we will look at stylistic variation—that is, systematic variations in the language of any one speaker, depending upon the occasion and the participants in the interchange. Different styles or **registers** range from extremely formal to quite informal.

An analogy can be drawn between stylistic variation in language and variation in dress. For example, if I go on a job interview for a teaching position—a fairly formal encounter with an unfamiliar audience—I am likely to wear a dark suit, a conservative tie, and black dress shoes. If I get the job, however, it is unlikely that I will continue to dress in this same manner while teaching from day to day. Rather, I am likely to dress more informally, perhaps in a sweater, trousers, and loafers. And, if I go to a backyard barbecue at the home of one of my colleagues, I am likely to wear shorts, a tee-shirt, and tennis shoes.

Although my manner of dress changes according to the situation and the participants, these changes have in common the fact that they reflect what is appropriate for my role in each situation, the activities I expect to participate in, and the impression I want to make on the other participants. In this regard, my navy blue suit is not "better" than my Bermuda shorts in any absolute sense. Rather, the suit is more appropriate for the job interview, while the Bermuda shorts are more appropriate for the backyard barbecue. (Anyone who has ever looked into a closetful of clothes and declared, "I don't have a thing to wear" is actually saying, "I don't have anything to wear that is appropriate for this particular occasion.'') Moreover, variations in dress are largely automatic; that is, they do not require a lot of conscious thought. For example, while I might decide to wear sandals instead of tennis shoes to the barbecue, it would never occur to me to wear the sandals on my hands. Likewise, while I may have to make a conscious decision about which suit to wear to the job interview, the decision to wear some suit is relatively unconscious. In other words, we move from one style to another without giving it a lot of conscious thought, so long as we are familiar with the conventions of each style.

A similar set of observations can be made about stylistic variation in language. First of all, linguistic style is a matter of what is **appropriate**. Like variation in our manner of dress, stylistic variations in language cannot be judged as appropriate or not without reference to the participants in the interchange (i.e., speaker and listener or reader and writer). For example, you would never speak to a 5 year old child, an intimate friend, and an ethics professor using the same style of speech. Note that using the term *eleemosynary* 'charitable' would probably be inappropriate for the child and the friend, while using *number one* 'urinate' would probably be inappropriate for the friend and the professor. Moreover, stylistic variations in language are largely automatic, in that we do not normally have to stop and think about which style to shift into next. For example, even though many Americans are given to peppering their conversations with ''four-letter words'' occasionally, very few speakers have to consciously suppress such forms when they are talking to their mother, the president of their company, or a store clerk. In short, shifting styles is essentially automatic and unconscious, and is governed by the concept of appropriateness.

It would be misleading, however, to suggest that stylistic varieties of a language are either discrete or well understood. Even though it is fairly easy for an observer to determine when two styles are different, it is sometimes difficult to define a clear-cut set of linguistic styles or the specific characteristics of each style. The best we can do is identify the relative formality of a particular form (i.e., state the circumstances in which it would be appropriate) and determine the type of variation it represents: lexical, phonological, morphological, or syntactic. With these points in mind, let's take a look at some different types of stylistic variation.

Stylistic Lexical Variation

One rather obvious stylistic dimension that speakers vary from one situation to another is vocabulary. When speaking or writing in a more formal register, our word choice may lean toward polysyllabic words rather than their shorter equivalents. For example, someone writing a letter of application for a job may close with a phrase like *Thank you for your consideration.* In more informal correspondence, the same person may use *Thanks for your time* to express the same idea. In the same way, a person may use connectives such as *however* and *therefore* in a more formal register, and use *but* and *so* in a less formal one. (Note that I have used the relatively formal connective *thus* at numerous points throughout this book, yet I would virtually never use this term in an informal conversation—it's simply inappropriate for that context.) Similarly, idiomatic expressions such as *let the cat out of the bag, kick the bucket, make the grade,* and *give me a break* are also characteristic of more informal registers. Likewise, words borrowed from Latin and Greek tend to be more formal than native Germanic lexical items: for example, *canine* (from Latin) rather than *dog; thermal* (from Greek) rather than *heat; dental* (from Latin) rather than *tooth;* and (not surprisingly) *lexical* (from Greek) rather than *word.*

Stylistic Phonological Variation

The application (or nonapplication) of various phonological rules also correlates with changes in register. In particular, neutralization rules (i.e., those that reduce two different phonemes to the same phone) tend to be suppressed in formal styles of speaking. For example, the Flapping Rule, which reduces both /t/ and /d/ to [ɾ], may be suppressed, so that *latter* is pronounced [lætər] and *ladder* is pronounced [lædər] (rather than both being pronounced [lærər]). Likewise, Consonant Cluster Reduction may be suppressed, so that *soft drink* is pronounced [sɔft drĭŋk] (rather than [sɔf drĭŋk]). Similarly, English has a rule of Vowel Neutralization that reduces all unstressed vowels to [ə], so that *affect* /æfékt/ and *effect* /ifékt/ are both ordinarily pronounced [əfékt]; speakers often suppress this rule in very formal registers.

The suppression of these neutralization rules in informal settings, however, can have unintended effects. I have a colleague whom I first encountered in an informal conversation in the hallway. After listening to him speak for a few minutes, I inferred that he was not a native speaker of English, since non-native speakers often fail to apply neutralization rules. Later, after I learned this fellow was a native of Chicago, I realized what had given me my initial impression: He systematically (and quite unnaturally) suppressed rules like Flapping, Consonant Cluster Reduction, and Vowel Neutralization in *all* styles of speech.

These examples illustrate two points worth emphasizing. First, pronunciations characterized by phonological neutralization do not reflect "careless" speech; on the contrary, they reflect a style of speech appropriate for informal registers. Second, it is easy to make the mistake of thinking that informal styles are appropriate only for informal occasions, but that formal styles are appropriate for all occasions. The latter half of this proposition is false, as we have seen from the example of my colleague from Chicago. Using a formal register in casual situations is just as inappropriate as using a casual style on formal occasions.

Most stylistic phonological variations do not manifest themselves directly in writing. For example, *effect* is spelled only one way regardless of whether it is pronounced with [i] or [ə]. A few phonological variations, however, can effect an alternate spelling: for example, *gonna* for *going to*, *wanna* for *want to*, *'em* for *them*, and so on. More typical of alternate spellings, however, are those that do not reflect variations in pronunciation: for example, *thru* for *through*, *nite* for *night*, and *rime* for *rhyme*. Obviously, of course, alternate spellings of either variety are appropriate only in extremely informal settings: postcards to friends, notes on the refrigerator, and so forth.

Stylistic Morphological Variation

The formation of words can also exhibit stylistic variation. One of the features most commonly associated with more informal registers is contraction: for example, *I'm* for *I am* and *you're* for *you are*. Note, however, that contraction of a lexical NP (e.g., *John'll* for *John will*) seems to be more informal than contraction of a pronoun (e.g., *he'll* for *he will*). Moreover, contraction in speech is characteristic of all but the most formal styles. For example, even when speaking, say, to the president of your company, you might be more likely to say *I'll do it immediately* rather than *I will do it immediately*. In fact, most people would have to concentrate very carefully in order to block contraction in speech.

Another morphological characteristic of informal registers is the use of shortened forms: for example, *psych* for *psychology*, *econ* for *economics*, and *comp lit* for *comparative literature*. Note that in an academic treatise on compulsive behavior you might find the term *sports fanatic*, but in the sports section of the newspaper you would see *sports fan*. Once again, contracted and shortened forms are no more "careless" than their lengthier counterparts; rather, they are perfectly appropriate in more informal speech and writing.

Stylistic Syntactic Variation

Changes in syntax may also occur as a function of changes in register. For example, a speaker in a job interview might ask *In which department will I be working?* Having gotten the job, however, the same speaker might ask a colleague *Which department do you work in?* Notice that in shifting from a more formal to a more informal register, the speaker has placed the preposition *in* at the end of the clause, rather than at its beginning. The more formal structure, with *in* in initial position, may reflect the speaker's awareness of a prescriptive rule: Don't end a sentence with a preposition. This prohibition originated with the 18th-century prescriptive grammarians; it was based on an attempt to model English after Latin, a language in which prepositions cannot appear in sentence-final position. In fact, the word *preposition* comes from a combination of Latin morphemes meaning 'put before (NP's).' Likewise, the use of *whom* for *who* in the objective case is characteristic of more formal styles. These two variables (moving a preposition to initial position and substituting *whom* for *who*) interact to form a continuum from casual to formal: for example, *Who do you work for?* → *Whom do you work for?* → *For whom do you work?*

Another syntactic characteristic of informal styles is deletion in interrogatives. Such deletion forms another continuum from relatively formal to more informal: for example, *Do you want another drink?* → *You want another drink?* → *Want another drink?* The rule here seems to be (a) delete the auxiliary (in this case *do*) and (b) delete *you*. It is clear, however, that these deletions are absolutely rule governed, since the subject *you* cannot be deleted unless the auxiliary has been deleted (cf. **Do want another drink?*). Once again, the more informal syntactic constructions discussed in this section do not constitute "careless," "sloppy," or "incorrect" English. The key to their use is appropriateness. Imagine, for example, that you knock on a friend's door and a voice from inside asks *Who's there?* You respond with *It is I* (rather than *It's me*). The use of this extremely formal construction (with a nominative case pronoun following an uncontracted form of *be*) is clearly inappropriate in this case.

We could enumerate many other examples of stylistic variation, but space is limited. Before closing this section, however, I want to make one final point concerning the central concept of appropriateness. All of the examples we have covered in this section on stylistic variation involve standard English. The only difference between, say, *Who did you speak to?* and *To whom did you speak?* is a matter of register. There are times, however, when the use of even nonstandard forms is appropriate. For example, a black adolescent from the inner city would in all likelihood be ostracized by his friends on the street if he were to address them in standard English, no matter how informal the style. He would be better off speaking BEV under such circumstances, because anything else would be inappropriate. Roger Shuy, a well known sociolinguist, has told a similar story about his own experiences. While in college, he got a summer job working on a loading dock in his home town. At first, he was shunned by his coworkers, lower working class men who worked on the dock year round. The fact that he was excluded from their circle bothered him and pretty soon he figured out the problem: He was speaking standard English, which was inappropriate in this situation. Once he started using some nonstandard forms (e.g., *ain't, he don't, me and him went,* etc.), he was accepted into the group.

SUMMARY

Let's review what we have covered in this chapter. We began with six observations about language variation. However, we had no transparent explanation for these phenomena. Thus, we constructed a (partial) theory of variation to account for our six observations. This theory makes use of such concepts as regional, social, and stylistic variation; dialect; social markedness; standard and nonstandard forms; register; and appropriateness. We have also seen that any variety of language can differ from another in terms of its lexicon, phonology, morphology, and syntax. Perhaps most importantly, we have seen that language variation is highly systematic.

As usual, I want to point out that there is much more to the study of language variation than what has been presented in this one short chapter. However, you have now been exposed to some of the basic ideas in the field; if you want to learn more, the readings at the end of the chapter will introduce you to additional information about language variation. In the meantime, the following exercises can be used to check your understanding of the principles we have covered.

EXERCISES

(1) One of the rules of prescriptive grammar states that the nominative case of a pronoun should be used after a form of main verb *be*: hence, *It is I, That is he,* and so on. However, most speakers, at least in an informal register, tend to use the objective case of a pronoun in these structures: *It's me, That's him.* Given the following data (where an asterisk marks an ungrammatical structure), what general principle do speakers appear to be following when they use the objective case pronoun following *be* instead of the nominative case?

    (ai)   The girl hit him.
    (aii)   *The girl hit he.

    (bi)   Please call me.
    (bii)   *Please call I.

    (ci)   I don't know her.
    (cii)   *I don't know she.

(2) Some nonstandard forms actually fill gaps or regularize exceptions in the standard English system, as was the case with *hisself* and *theirselves*. Now consider another case: All but one of the following phrases can be contracted in two different ways; the exceptional case has only one contracted form.

(i)   I am not
(ii) We are not
(iii) You are not
(iv) He/she is not
(v)   They are not

(a) Which phrase has only one contracted form in standard English?
(b) By analogy with the other four phrases, how would the "missing" contracted form for this phrase be constructed? Give a phonological representation for this form.
(c) Assume, first, that two consecutive nasals cannot occur in the same syllable in English (e.g., *mnemonic* is represented phonemically as /nimanɪk/) and, second, that in some dialects of English the vowel before a nasal is raised (e.g., *can't* is pronounced as [kʰẽt] rather than as [kʰæt]). Apply these principles to the form you constructed for (b). What nonstandard form seems to fill the role of the "missing" contracted form?

(3) Based on exercise (2), it appears that *ain't* fills a gap in the standard English system by providing an alternative contracted form for the phrase *I am not*. However, the use of *ain't* is not restricted to the first person subject in nonstandard dialects. Given the following data, in what sense is the nonstandard system more regular than the standard one?

STANDARD SYSTEM		NONSTANDARD SYSTEM	
(no form)	we aren't	I ain't	we ain't
you aren't	you aren't	you ain't	you ain't
he/she/it isn't	they aren't	he/she/it ain't	they ain't

(4) The phonetic representations of words such as *greasy* and *Mrs.* contrast for some Northern and Southern speakers in the United States as follows.

NORTHERN	SOUTHERN
[grisi]	[grizi]
[mɪsɪz]	[mɪzɪz]

What systematic contrast occurs between the Northern and Southern dialects? How does the phonological environment account for the Southern forms?

(5) When a speaker attempts to emulate a stylistic register that he or she is not completely familiar with, a phenomenon known as **structural**

hypercorrection may result. This term describes the use of a structure associated with a more formal register in a linguistic environment where it is not typically used. Now consider the following data.
(i)   To whom should I speak?
(ii) Whom did you see?
(iii) Whom is taking you to dinner?

(a) Which sentence illustrates structural hypercorrection?
(b) What principle has the speaker of these sentences apparently learned?
(c) What principle has the speaker failed to learn?

(6) In one of her comedy routines, Lily Tomlin introduced the character of Ernestine, a rather obnoxious telephone operator. A typical utterance from Ernestine might be *Is this the party to whom I was just speaking to?*
(a) How would you render this utterance in a more informal style?
(b) Which forms and constructions does Tomlin use to help characterize Ernestine's personality?

(7) Consider the following sentence: *That is not where they are now.* What form would this sentence take if the *be*-Deletion Rule were to apply to it?

(8) Consider the following paragraph.
"Muffy pulled out her overnight case. She plan to go to her frien's house the nex day. She had been there before. She walked a mile to get there. She wish she did not have to walk all the way."

Weasel Podowski handed in this composition to his English teacher, Miss Moveable Feast. Miss Feast, who is a friend of yours, claims that Weasel has no sense of time, because he makes so many "tense errors." You realize Miss Feast's mistake.
(a) What part of Weasel's grammatical system is responsible for these errors?
(b) Write a rule (in formal notation) that accounts for these errors.

ANSWERS TO EXERCISES

The following answers are, in some cases, not the only possible ones. Discussion of other possibilities is part of the exercises.

(1) After other verbs in English (e.g., *hit*, *call*, and *like*), the objective case of a pronoun is used; the nominative case results in an ungrammatical sentence. Speakers who use the objective case pronoun after a form of main verb *be* are following the general pattern

associated with all other verbs. They are essentially regularizing an exception.

(2) (a) Two contracted forms are readily apparent for phrases (ii-v)— *We're not-We aren't*, and so on. Phrase (i), though, has only one contracted form in standard English, *I'm not*, and so violates the overall pattern for contracting phrases of this type.

   (b) On analogy with phrases (ii-v), the "missing" form for (i) would be *amn't* ([ǽmnt]).

   (c) Deleting one of the nasals in [ǽmnt] and raising the vowel from [æ] to [e] would yield [ēnt] = *ain't*.

(3) The nonstandard system is more regular in that it uses one contracted negative verb form (*ain't*) for all persons and numbers, whereas the standard system uses two (*aren't* and *isn't*), which vary according to person and number.

(4) In the Northern forms, [s] (a voiceless consonant) appears between vowels; in the Southern forms, however, [z] (a voiced consonant) appears. The occurrence of [z] for [s] in the South may arise from the fact that the surrounding segments are vowels, which are also voiced. This type of rule, in which a segment becomes more like a neighboring segment in some way, is called an **assimilation** rule. Which of the rules covered in Chapter 6 (Phonology) is an assimilation rule?

(5) (a) Sentence (iii).

   (b) Substitute *whom* for *who*, regardless of its function.

   (c) *Whom* can only substitute for *who* when it is an object of a verb or preposition. Note, incidentally, that the only environment in which *who* cannot occur in standard English is when it immediately follows a preposition: **To who did you speak* (cf. *Who did you speak to?*).

(6) (a) Something like *Is this the person I was just speaking to?*

   (b) By using overly formal forms (*the party*) and constructions (*to whom*), Tomlin characterizes Ernestine as somewhat self-important. Note that the two occurrences of the preposition *to* (one fronted and the other not fronted) suggest that Ernestine doesn't have complete mastery of the formal style "to which she aspires to."

(7) *That not where they are now.* Note: *are* can't undergo deletion, since it can't be contracted with *they* in this sentence.

(8) (a) phonology

   (b) C → ∅/C __ C

SUPPLEMENTARY READINGS

1. Cassidy, F. (1981). DARE. *National Forum* (Summer), 36–37.
2. Cassidy, F. (1985). *Dictionary of American regional English*. Cambridge, MA: Harvard University Press.
3. Dillard, J. (1972). *Black English: Its history and usage in the United States*. New York: Random House.
4. Fasold, R. (1981). The relation between black and white speech in the south. *American Speech, 56,* 163–189.
5. Fasold, R. (1984). The *sociolinguistics of society*. New York: Blackwell.
6. Labov, W. (1972). Academic ignorance and black intelligence. *The Atlantic* (June), 59–67.
7. McDavid, R. I. (1958). The dialects of American English. In W. N. Francis (Ed.), *The structure of American English* (pp. 480–543). New York: Ronald Press.
8. Trudgill, P. (1974). *Sociolinguistics: An introduction*. Harmondsworth, England: Penguin.
9. Wolfram, W. (1981). Varieties of American English. In C. Ferguson and S. Heath (Eds.), *Language in the USA* (pp. 44-68). Cambridge, England: Cambridge University Press.
10. Wolfram, W., and Fasold, R. (1974). *The study of social dialects in American English*. Englewood Cliffs, NJ: Prentice-Hall.

You are now prepared to read all of these works. Wolfram (9) is a well-organized introduction to language variation in America. McDavid (7) is an accessible overview of early regional dialectology in the United States. Cassidy (1) provides a brief sampling of the expressions found in his dictionary of American regionalisms. Cassidy (2) is the result of 20 years of research and contains over 12,000 regional expressions found in the United States. This volume, which is the first of five, covers only those regional terms beginning with the letters A, B, and C. Trudgill (8) and Wolfram and Fasold (10) are good introductions to the field of sociolinguistics. Fasold (5) is a recent and thorough text covering the sociology of language (where linguistic factors are brought to bear on the study of society) as opposed to sociolinguistics (where social factors are brought to bear on the study of linguistics). Dillard (3) is a thorough account of the purported creole origins of BEV. Labov (6) is a brief popular discussion of the issues involved in the relationship between BEV and education. Fasold (4) is a comparison of nonstandard forms peculiar to BEV and those found in dialects spoken by Southern whites.

Chapter 8

Language Acquisition

Language acquisition is the study of how human beings acquire a grammar: a set of semantic, syntactic, morphological, and phonological categories and rules which underlie their ability to speak and understand the language to which they are exposed. For example, a normal child born to English-speaking parents in the United States obviously is not born knowing English. By the age of 5, however, the child can speak and understand English with relative facility. Language acquisition is the study of how this transformation takes place—from a mental state in which the child does not possess a grammar of a particular language to a mental state in which the child does. As defined here, language acquisition does not include the process by which a person (typically an adolescent or an adult) learns a language other than his or her native tongue. This process is called second language acquisition and will not be discussed in this chapter. Keeping this distinction in mind, let's consider some observations we can make about the acquisition of a first language.

(1) A child acquiring English might form the plural of *foot* first as *foots*, then as *feets*, then as *feetses*, and finally as *feet*.
(2) A child acquiring English might form an interrogative such as *Why can't I go?* as *Why I can't go?*
(3) All normal children acquire a language, but not all children learn to read and write.
(4) Many children gain a fairly sophisticated facility with language before they master tasks such as tying their shoes, telling time, or adding numbers.

Observation (1) illustrates the fact that language is acquired in stages. Observation (2) illustrates the fact that language is not acquired through simple imitation (adults don't say *Why I can't go?*, so the child cannot simply be mimicking the adult). Instead, the child infers a system of rules (i.e., a grammar) for forming sentences, based upon the samples of the language to which he or she is exposed. Observation (3) illustrates the hypothesis that human beings are genetically programmed to acquire a language. That is, children do not *learn* a language in the way they learn to read and write, through conscious effort and instruction; rather they *acquire* a language in the same way they acquire the ability to walk, effortlessly and without instruction. Observation (4) illustrates the hypothesis that language acquisition is subserved by a mental faculty designed specifically and solely for that purpose. In other words, language acquisition is not thought to be a function of intelligence or general intellectual abilities.

All of these phenomena have something directly to do with language acquisition, the way we acquire the grammar of our first language. As usual, we will assume that the phenomena in observations (1–4) are systematic; that is, they are governed by a system of principles. What we will now try to do is construct a set of concepts that will account for these phenomena. Keep in mind that what follows is a theory designed to account for the data in observations (1–4).

PRELINGUISTIC STAGES

In the first year of life, infants go through three stages generally thought to have nothing directly to do with the acquisition of a language. The **crying** stage lasts from birth to around 2 months. The **cooing** stage, characterized by vowel-like sounds, lasts from about 2 months to 5 months. And the **babbling** stage, characterized by syllable-like consonant-vowel sounds, lasts from about 5 months to 12 months. Note that these sounds are described as language-*like*; they are not thought to be either an early form of language or necessary prerequisites to language acquisition. For example, even babies born deaf babble as infants, but they cease after about 6 months of life. The fact that deaf babies babble along with hearing infants suggests that such stages do not constitute "practice" for language acquisition. However, the linguistic status of these stages is still best regarded as an open question, for the present time.

If, however, language-like behaviors such as cooing and babbling are not actually "practice" for language acquisition, what are they? One reasonable hypothesis is that they are simply genetically determined stages that the human organism goes through on its way to maturation. In fact, there is evidence that much of what appears to be "practice" for a specific skill is actually just a genetically encoded stage and may not be necessary for the acquisition of that particular skill. For example, young birds go through a stage of flapping their wings before they actually begin to fly.

Years ago a scientist named Grohmann decided to test the hypothesis that this wing-flapping behavior is "practice" for flying. He studied two groups of newly hatched pigeons. One group (the control group), he simply left alone. The other group (the experimental group), he encased in open-ended tubes that restrained the young pigeons from flapping their wings. Otherwise, both groups were allowed complete freedom to follow the dictates of nature. After several weeks, the control group, which were allowed to flap, quite naturally began to fly. At this point, Grohmann removed the tubes from the experimental group and they too immediately began to fly, just as well as the control group. The point, of course, is that wing-flapping does not appear to be "practice" for flying at all; rather, it seems to be a genetically encoded stage in maturation. Likewise, cooing and babbling do not appear to be "practice" for language acquisition.

This is not to say that nothing goes on during the first year of life that has to do with language acquisition. For example, infants generally exhibit the beginnings of comprehension at around 9 months. Also, intonational patterns emerge late in the first year. Likewise, infants begin to exhibit meaningful gestures around 9 to 10 months, which has been interpreted by some linguists as an early stage in the acquisition of pragmatics.

LINGUISTIC STAGES

In this section, we will look at the stages of language acquisition from the perspective of the four components of grammar: phonology, morphology, syntax, and semantics, in that order. However, before getting into details, I want to clarify several potential points of confusion.

First, in acquiring language, children go through more or less the same stages at more or less the same time. These stages, however, represent general trends, and every child does not follow them in lock-step fashion. For example, a child will typically acquire stops (e.g., /p,b,t,d,g,k/ in English) before liquids (e.g., /l,r/ in English). This does not mean, however, that every normal child will acquire all of the stops, completely and correctly, before any of the liquids. Likewise, a child will typically acquire grammatical morphemes (e.g., inflectional affixes, prepositions, articles, and so on in English) by the age of 5. Again, this does not mean that no normal child will acquire them earlier or later; rather, it is simply a general pattern.

Second, in this chapter we will deal solely with the acquisition of English. However, the principles discussed here typically apply, where they are relevant, to the acquisition of other first languages as well. For example, children tend to correctly interpret complex sentences in which the order of the clauses reflects the order of events before they correctly interpret sentences in which this ordering relation does not hold. As a result, a child exposed to English will typically be able to correctly interpret *John ate before he came home* before he or she is able to interpret *Before John came home, he ate*. This general principle, however, seems to apply to children acquiring any first language.

Third, it is much more difficult to draw inferences about first-language acquisition than it is to study almost any other area of linguistics. This is because language acquisition is the only area of linguistics that requires investigators to deal with immature informants (i.e., infants and children). One problem for investigators is interpreting the structure underlying a child's utterance. For example, a child acquiring English may utter *wear shirt no* rather than, for example, *I don't want to wear that shirt*. Is such an utterance a structured sentence or just an unstructured string of words? Is *wear shirt* a verb-object construction or just a memorized phrase? Is the placement of *no* at the end of the utterance the result of a rule or simply an afterthought? It is often impossible to answer such questions conclusively. Another problem is that investigators cannot question a child like they can an adult speaker. For example, a linguist can ask an adult informant such questions as *Is sentence X an acceptable sentence in English?* and *Are sentences X and Y paraphrases of each other?* In the example just mentioned, however, it would be quite difficult (to say the least) to elicit from the child whether *wear shirt no* and *no wear shirt* are equivalent in meaning.

Thus, a primary concern for anyone studying language acquisition is to avoid overinterpreting a child's productions. Let's consider an actual example from the literature. In "The Acquisition of Language," Breyne Moskowitz cites an interchange between Ronald Scollon, a language acquisition researcher at the University of Hawaii, and a 19 month old girl named Brenda.

> Brenda: [kʰa] (4 times)
> Scollon: What?
> Brenda: Go. Go.
> Scollon: (undecipherable)
> Brenda: [baɪš] (9 times)
> Scollon: What? Oh, bicycle? Is that what you said?
> Brenda: [na]
> Scollon: No?
> Brenda: Not.
> Scollon: No. I got it wrong.

Now consider how Moskowitz interprets this interchange: "Brenda was not yet able to combine two words syntactically to express 'Hearing that

car reminds me that we went on the bus yesterday. No, not on a bicycle.'
She could express that concept, however, by combining words
sequentially'' (p. 91). However, when we compare Brenda's productions
to Moskowitz's interpretation, it is clear that Moskowitz may be attributing
more linguistic structure to Brenda's utterances than they actually have.
In short, keep in mind the inherent problems involved in using infants
and children as informants.

Acquisition of Phonology

Let's take a look at some representative examples of the stages a child
goes through in acquiring the phonology of his or her language.

Vowels. Children exposed to English tend to acquire first /a/ and
then /i,u/. This sequence follows from two principles. First, extreme values
in this system tend to be acquired before intermediate values. In this
instance, the child is filling in the end points of the vowel triangle as shown
in Figure 8-1. (For reference, see the vowel chart in Chapter 6.) Note that
/a,i,u/ are maximally distinct from each other: /i/ and /u/ are maximally
distinct from each other along the horizontal dimension [±BACK]; and
both /i/ and /u/, in turn, are maximally distinct from /a/ along the vertical
dimensions [±HIGH] and [±LOW]. Second, children typically acquire
segments common among the world's languages before they acquire those
that are relatively rare. For example, /a/ is universal (i.e., it occurs in
all languages) and /i,u/ are nearly universal (i.e., they occur in the vast
majority of languages). Thus, the interaction of both principles predicts
that /a,i,u/ will be acquired early, and the other intermediate vowels will
come later. Note that here and throughout, when I say that a child *acquires*
such-and-such a segment, I don't mean simply that he or she produces
a sound that an adult observer perceives as that segment. Rather, I mean
that the child has actually incorporated that segment into his or her

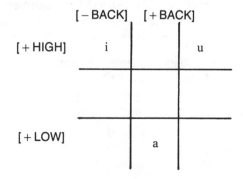

Figure 8-1. The child's first vowels.

phonological system. Such a judgment, of course, requires interpretation by the analyst—which, as we saw in the last section, is a tricky business.

Consonants. Children exposed to English tend to acquire /p,b,m/ first and then /t/. This sequence follows from several principles. First, **place of articulation** tends to be acquired from the front of the mouth to the back. That is, labials are generally acquired before dentals and alveolars, which in turn are acquired before palatals and velars. (For reference, consult the consonant chart in Chapter 6.) Thus, for example, in English the labial stop /p/ would be expected to appear before the alveolar /t/, which in turn would appear before the velar /k/. Second, **manner of articulation** tends to be acquired from most consonant-like to least consonant-like. That is, consonants are generally acquired in this order: stops, nasals, fricatives, affricates, and liquids. Thus, among the alveolar consonants in English, we would expect /t,d/ before /n/; /n/ before /s,z/; and /s,z/ before /l/. The interaction of both principles predicts that /p,b,m/ and then /t/ will be acquired early and the other consonants will come later. These principles are schematized in Figure 8-2.

Let's now consider some of the forms predicted by the interaction of the principles governing the acquisition of vowels and consonants. Variations on *ma* /ma/ and *pa* /pa/ are extremely widespread as early forms for male and female parents, respectively. This is no accident: As we have just seen, /m,p,a/ are all acquired very early. Another predictable form is Dennis the Menace's *telebision* (with a /b/) for *television* (with a /v/). Even though Dennis is a fiction of Hank Ketchum's imagination, this example is based on fact. Our principles governing child phonology predict that the stop /b/, which is acquired early, will substitute for the fricative /v/, which is acquired somewhat later. Note, incidentally, that our theory predicts that /b/ alone (not just any stop) will substitute for /v/. The phoneme /b/ is the only stop in English that agrees with /v/ in both place of articulation ([+LABIAL]) and voicing ([+VOICE]).

Likewise, these principles are often reflected in adult perceptions of child productions which become "lexicalized" into proper names. One child, for example, referred to his mother with a form perceived as

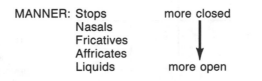

PLACE: Labial—Dental/Alveolar—Palatal/Velar
more front ⟶ more back

MANNER: Stops   more closed
Nasals
Fricatives   ↓
Affricates
Liquids   more open

Figure 8-2. Acquisition of consonants by place and manner of articulation.

/bámbi/, presumably for *mommy* /mámi/. This child had apparently acquired /b/ and was in the process of acquiring /m/, thus substituting the voiced labial stop for the voiced labial nasal in /mámi/, which became /bámbi/. In fact, the child's family began to refer to the mother as *Bombi*. Another example is the name *Teeter* /títɛr/ from *sister* /sístər/. In this case, the child had an aunt whom the mother called *Sister*, a phenomenon common in the South. The child, who apparently had acquired the stop /t/ but not the fricative /s/, substituted /t/ for /s/, since both are [+ALVEOLAR] and [-VOICE]. This resulted in a production that the adults perceived as /títɛr/, and the aunt from then on was known in the family as *Teeter*. A final example of the same phenomenon is the proper name *Kaki* /kǽki/ (again, common in the South) from *Kathy* /kǽθi/. Children exposed to English acquire /θ/ generally quite late. (It is both a fricative and an extremely rare segment among the world's languages.) Stops, on the other hand, are acquired early; thus the voiceless stop /k/ is substituted for the voiceless fricative /θ/. The reason that /k/ (rather than some other voiceless stop) is substituted for /θ/ probably has to do with the fact that *Kathy* begins with /k/. A child's first bisyllabic words often contain syllables that begin with identical segments (e.g., *mama, papa, daddy, mommy, peepee, doodoo,* and so on).

Syllable Structure. The simplest type of syllable found among the world's languages is CV, where C = consonant and V = vowel. All languages contain words made up of CV syllables. In fact, Japanese words, with a few predictable exceptions, are all of this form: for example, *Fujiyama* and *Hasegawa*. English, however, has a quite complex syllable structure; for example, we have words like *spy* (CCV), *ask* (VCC), *spry* (CCCV), *asked* (VCCC), and even *splints* (CCCVCCC). Thus, it comes as no surprise that a child will go through several stages in acquiring the full range of syllable types in English. This acquisition generally proceeds in the following order.

(C)V	(initial C is optional)
CV	(initial C)
CVC	(final C)
CCVC	(initial cluster)
CCVCC	(final cluster)

Thus, for example, a child trying to pronounce *stoves* might proceed through the following stages: [o] or [tʰo], [tʰov], [stov], and then [stovz]. Likewise, we get [mɪk] for *milk* [mɪlk], [skǽmbəl] for *scramble* [skrǽmbəl], [dĭk] for *drink* [drĭk], and so on. Another example of a child's production becoming "lexicalized" as a new word is *tummy* /tʌmi/ for *stomach* /stʌmɪk/. Note, first, that *stomach* begins with a cluster /st/. A child who has not yet acquired clusters will reduce /st/ to /t/. (Recall that stops are generally acquired before fricatives.) Note also that the second syllable of *stomach* ends in a final consonant /k/. If the child has not yet acquired syllable-final consonants, the /k/ will be omitted, resulting in /tÁmɪ/. Finally, English has a rule that tenses a lax vowel in word-final position. (Note, for example, that *said* contains the lax vowel /ɛ/, but the tense vowel /e/ occurs in final position as in *say*.) This rule changes /ɪ/ to /i/, yielding /tÁmi/. Again, the point is that a child's acquisition of phonology is rule governed and predictable.

Acquisition of Morphology

We will now examine a few representative examples of the stages a child goes through in acquiring the morphology of his or her language. At about the age of 2, the child begins to form utterances made up of more than one word. Grammatical morphemes are generally absent at first, but are typically mastered by age 5. The class of grammatical morphemes includes inflectional and derivational affixes, among other things. (See Chapter 5 for a review of these concepts.)

Inflectional Affixes. In general, the {PRES PART} affix, spelled *-ing*, is acquired fairly early, presumably because this affix shows little phonological variation; that is, it always appears as /ɪŋ/or /ɪn/. The morphemes {PAST}, {PLU}, {POSS}, and {PRES}, on the other hand, are all acquired somewhat later, presumably because they exhibit somewhat more phonological variation. Take, for example, {PAST}, which is attached to verbs and generally spelled *-(e)d*. Note that {PAST} shows up variously as /t/ (as in *walked*), /d/ (as in *hugged*), and /əd/ (as in *added*). The rule governing this alternation is simple. If a verb ends in a voiceless segment, add the voiceless /t/; *walk* ends in the voiceless segment /k/, so {PAST} shows up as /t/. If the verb ends in a voiced segment, add the voiced /d/; *hug* ends in the voiced segment /g/, so {PAST} shows up as /d/. One exceptional case is that /əd/ is added if the verb ends in /t/ or /d/; *add* ends in /d/, so {PAST} shows up as /əd/. Note that the exceptional part of the rule is purely functional. If we were to simply add /d/ to *add*, we would get /ædd/, which is indistinguishable from the uninflected form /æd/. The insertion of /ə/, however, breaks up the two /d/'s and we get /ædəd/. Because of this phonological variation, it makes sense that a child acquiring English will take some time to infer the rules governing the various forms of {PAST}, which can be summarized as follows.

FINAL SEGMENT OF ROOT	PHONOLOGICAL FORM OF {PAST}	EXAMPLE
[−VOICE]	/t/	walk-walked
[+VOICE]	/d/	hug-hugged
/t,d/	/əd/	add-added

However, the fact that the child is inferring rules is unarguable. This can be seen by examining the formation of irregular {PAST} forms in English. For example, a child acquiring the past tense form of *go* might first use the adult form *went*. This, however, is apparently just a memorized form unrelated to *go*, since the child quickly moves to a second stage in which the past tense is formed following the rule outlined earlier, namely as *goed* /god/. Note that *go* ends in a voiced segment /o/; thus the past tense should be formed by the addition of /d/, yielding /god/. A third stage that a child often goes through is to treat *went* as an uninflected root, thus constructing the past tense by the rule discussed earlier, namely as *wented* /wéntəd/. Note that *went* ends in /t/; thus, the past tense should be formed by the addition of /əd/, yielding /wéntəd/. Finally, the child learns that *go* has an exceptional or irregular past tense form, and his or her usage begins to conform to the adult's.

The acquisition of {PLU}, generally spelled -*(e)s*, follows the same progression as that of {PAST}. The morpheme {PLU} shows up variously as /s/ (as in *ducks*), /z/ (as in *dogs*), and /əz/ (as in *hoses*). The rule governing this alternation is similar to that for {PAST}. If the noun ends in a voiceless segment, add voiceless /s/; *duck* ends in /k/, which is voiceless, so {PLU} shows up as /s/. If the noun ends in a voiced segment, add the voiced /z/; *dog* ends in /g/, which is voiced, so {PLU} shows up as /z/. An exception is that /əz/ is added if the noun ends in /s,z,š,ž,č,ǰ/; *hose* ends in /z/, so {PLU} shows up as /əz/. As was the case with {PAST}, the exceptional form of the rule is purely functional. If we were to simply add /z/ to *hose*, we would get /hozz/, which is indistinguishable from the uninflected form /hoz/. The insertion of /ə/, however, breaks up the two /z/'s and we get /hózəz/. Once again, it makes sense that a child exposed to English would take some time to infer the rules governing the various phonological forms of {PLU}, which can be summarized as follows.

FINAL SEGMENT OF ROOT	PHONOLOGICAL FORM OF {PLU}	EXAMPLE
[−VOICE]	/s/	duck-ducks
[+VOICE]	/z/	dog-dogs
/s,z,š,ž,č,ǰ/	/ə z/	hose-hoses

As with {PAST}, the fact that the child is acquiring rules is clear from examining the formation of plural forms that are irregular in English. For example, a child acquiring the plural of *foot* might first use the adult form *feet*. Once again, this seems to be simply a memorized form unrelated to *foot*, since the child moves rapidly to a second stage, in which he or she forms the plural following the rule outlined earlier, namely as *foots* /futs/. Note that *foot* ends in a voiceless segment; thus the plural should be formed by adding the voiceless segment /s/, resulting in /futs/. A third stage often follows in which the child treats *foots* or *feets* as an uninflected form, thus constructing the plural following the rule, namely as *footses* /fútsəz/ (or *feetses*). Note that *foots* (and *feets*) ends in /s/; thus the plural should be formed by adding /ə z/, yielding *footses* /fútsəz/ (or *feetses*). Finally, the child learns that *foot* is exceptional in English in that it has an irregular plural form, and his or her usage begins to conform to the adult's.

The morphemes {POSS} and {PRES}, generally spelled *-'s* and *-(e)s*, respectively, exhibit the same phonological variation as {PLU}. This is illustrated in the following chart.

	{PLU}	{POSS}	{PRES}
/s/	cats	Pat's	waits
/z/	cads	Bud's	wades
/ə z/	cases	Bess's	winces

What is interesting, however, is that these three morphemes are not acquired at the same time. Rather, a child exposed to English typically acquires them in the following order: {PLU}, {POSS}, and then {PRES}. This indicates that the child acquires them as a function of their morphological, rather than their phonological, structure. The late Roman Jakobson, a Harvard linguist, proposed a sensible explanation for this progressive acquisition. He hypothesized that a child acquires such affixes based on the size of their domain of application: The smaller the domain, the earlier the acquisition. Thus, {PLU} is acquired first because it is attached to nouns (e.g., *kids*). {POSS} is acquired next because it is attached to NP's (e.g., *the kid next door's dog*). (See Chapter 5 for a detailed discussion of this distinction.) {PRES} is acquired last because, even though it is attached to a verb, it is a function of the entire sentence. That is, the affixation of {PRES} to a verb depends on its subject, and a subject plus a verb is essentially a sentence. Only a third person singular subject takes an overt affix on a present tense verb (e.g., *The kid drinks* versus *The kids drink*). These distinctions between {PLU}, {POSS}, and {PRES} are summarized in the following diagram.

ORDER OF ACQUISITION	MORPHEME	DOMAIN
1	{PLU}	N
2	{POSS}	NP
3	{PRES}	S

Derivational Affixes.   The acquisition of derivational affixes is not as well understood as the acquisition of inflectional affixes. This is because there are many more derivational affixes in English than there are inflectional affixes. (You may recall from Chapter 5 that English has only eight inflectional affixes.) Moreover, many derivational affixes in English have been borrowed from Latin and Greek, whereas all inflectional affixes are native to English. Thus, derivational affixes are associated with more learned vocabulary, which as we might expect is acquired relatively late: for example, the word *atheistic* (from Greek) will typically come later than *ungodly* (native English). Nonetheless, we can make one generalization concerning the acquisition of derivational affixes: The more productive they are, the earlier they are acquired. A more productive affix is one that can be attached to a relatively large number of roots. For example, the *-ly* suffix, which attaches to an adjective to form the corresponding adverb, is very productive, yielding forms such as *quick-quickly*, *careful-carefully*, and *intelligent-intelligently*. Likewise, the agentive suffix *-er*, which attaches to a verb to form the corresponding noun, is quite productive: *love-lover*, *farm-farmer*, *drive-driver*, and so on. A less productive affix is one that can be attached to relatively few roots. For example, the suffix *-hood*, which typically attaches to a concrete noun to form an abstract noun, is relatively unproductive: We have *father-fatherhood* and *mother-motherhood*, but not *uncle-*unclehood*, *aunt-*aunthood*, or *cousin-*cousinhood*.

We can close this section by stating simply that a child's acquisition of morphology is for the most part systematic and rule governed, even though some domains, such as the acquisition of derivational morphology, are not well understood.

Acquisition of Syntax

Let's now look at some representative examples of the stages a child goes through in acquiring the syntax of his or her language.

Length of Utterance and Word Order.   Somewhere between the ages of 1 and 2 years, every child enters the **one-word** or **holophrastic stage**. This stage normally lasts between 3 and 9 months and is characterized by one-word utterances, where each word typically refers to some concrete object in the child's environment (e.g., *shoe, milk, eye, ball, car, Mommy, Daddy*). Around the age of 2, children typically enter the **two-word stage**, which is characterized by utterances containing a maximum of two words. These utterances are typically interpreted by adults as subject-verb (e.g., *doggie run*), verb-modifier (e.g., *push bike, sit there*), or possessor-possessed (e.g., *Mary chair*). At this stage, word order is not always consistent; thus *doggie run* might be expressed as *run doggie*, or *push bike* as *bike push*. Moreover, utterances in the two-word stage tend to omit bound and free grammatical morphemes, including auxiliary verbs. For example, an adult might say to a child, *The doggie's running.* The child's version, *doggie run*, omits the article (*the*), the auxiliary verb (*is*), and the present participle affix (*-ing*). Instead, the child's strategy appears to be one of focusing on "content" words (i.e., lexical morphemes). As a result, the absence of grammatical morphemes may result in some surface ambiguity. For example, *Mary chair* could potentially indicate possession ('Mary's chair'), a state of affairs ('Mary is in the chair'), or a request ('Put Mary in the chair'). Furthermore, the same child might use the utterance *Mary chair* at various times to convey all of these messages. However, contextual clues would typically enable a listener to interpret the intended meaning.

Next comes the **multiword stage**, which is characterized by utterances of more than two words. Roger Brown at Harvard has referred to this stage as **telegraphic speech,** since it is open ended in terms of length but generally lacks many grammatical morphemes, just like a telegram. For example, we might hear *That Mary chair* for 'That's Mary's chair,' or *Mary sit on chair* for 'Mary is sitting on the chair' or 'Mary wants to sit on the chair.' It is in this stage that word order starts to become fixed. As we would expect, the most common word orders are those acquired earliest. Thus, in English, adjective-noun order (e.g., *big boy*) and subject-verb-object order (e.g., *Mary want teddy*) are acquired relatively early. Systematic permutations found in questions, negatives, and passives generally come later.

Questions. Stages in the acquisition of questions by children acquiring English have been studied quite extensively by language acquisition researchers. As we look at these stages, keep in mind that English has two basic interrogative structures: *yes-no* interrogatives (e.g., *Has Biff seen Tammy?*) and *wh*-interrogatives (e.g., *Who has Biff seen?*). The formation of *yes-no* interrogatives involves the rule of Subject-Verb Inversion (SVI), a transformation which moves the first auxiliary verb to the left of the subject: for example, *Biff has seen Tammy* ⟶ *Has Biff seen Tammy?* The formation of *wh*-interrogatives involves two rules, SVI and *wh*-Movement (WHM). The latter transformation moves a *wh*-word to sentence-initial position: for example, *Has Biff seen who?* ⟶ *Who has Biff seen?*

A child exposed to English first signals questions simply by **intonation.** A declarative in English typically has falling intonation (⎯⎯⎯⎯⎯◥), whereas a *yes-no* interrogative has rising intonation (⎽⎽⎽⎽⎽◞). Thus, a child will first form *yes-no* interrogatives simply by adding a rising intonation contour to a declarative structure (e.g., *Daddy going* = 'Daddy is going' and *Daddy going?* = 'Is Daddy going?'). In the second stage, *wh*-interrogatives appear with the *wh*-word in sentence-initial position (e.g., *Where Daddy going?*). At this stage, *yes-no* interrogatives are still marked only by intonation (e.g., *Daddy going?*). In the third stage, *yes-no* interrogatives are formed by SVI (e.g., *Is Daddy going?*). In this stage, however, *wh*-interrogatives are formed without SVI, even though an auxiliary may be present (e.g., *Where Daddy's going?*). In the fourth stage, the child finally forms *wh*-interrogatives with both WHM and SVI (e.g., *Where's Daddy going?*). These stages may be summarized as follows.

STAGE	QUESTION TYPE	RULES	EXAMPLE
1	*yes-no*	Intonation	Daddy going?
	wh	-------------	---------------
2	*yes-no*	Intonation	Daddy going?
	wh	WHM	Where Daddy going?
3	*yes-no*	SVI	Is Daddy going?
	wh	WHM	Where Daddy's going?
4	*yes-no*	SVI	Is Daddy going?
	wh	SVI + WHM	Where's Daddy going?

Progression through these stages makes perfect sense. First, the earliest linguistic structure acquired by a child seems to be the intonation contours of the language to which he or she is exposed, regardless of what that language may be. In fact, intonation seems to be acquired by about the age of 12 months. Second, WHM is a structurally simpler rule than SVI. WHM moves any *wh*-item to sentence-initial position, regardless of category (NP, PP, ADVP, and so on). SVI, on the other hand, is less general; it moves one specific category (first auxiliary) to the left of another specific category (subject NP). Thus, it makes some sense that WHM would be acquired before SVI. Third, *yes-no* interrogatives are formed by the application of one rule (SVI), whereas *wh*-interrogatives are formed by the application of two rules (SVI and WHM). Thus, it is predictable that the adult form of *yes-no* interrogatives would appear in a child's speech before the adult form of *wh*-interrogatives.

Negatives. As was the case with questions, stages in the acquisition of negative sentence structures have been studied extensively. As we look at these stages, keep in mind that negative declarative sentences in the adult grammar are formed by putting *not* immediately to the right of the first auxiliary in the corresponding affirmative structure. For example, *Biff has seen Tammy* → *Biff has not seen Tammy*; likewise, *Biff might have seen Tammy* → *Biff might not have seen Tammy*; and so forth.

In the acquisition of negatives, the first stage that a child exposed to English goes through is to put *no* or *not* before (or sometimes after) a positive utterance; for example, *Not Daddy eat cookie* = 'Daddy can't/shouldn't/ didn't eat a cookie' (the exact meaning is dependent upon context). At this stage, the positive utterance seems to form a sort of "nucleus" and the negative word immediately precedes or follows it, but is not integrated into it. In the second stage, the negative word is incorporated into the positive utterance, typically between the subject and verb (e.g., *Daddy not eat cookie* = 'Daddy can't/shouldn't/didn't eat a cookie'). At this stage, the negative may be affixed to an auxiliary verb (typically *can't* or *don't*); however, when such forms do occur for *no* or *not*, they appear to be unanalyzed (i.e., memorized) negative forms. For example, *don't* does not seem to be a contraction of *do not* at this stage. In the third stage, the negative item typically appears first as a contraction on an auxiliary (e.g., *won't*) and finally as a free form (e.g., *will not*). At this point, the child has finally acquired the adult form; for example, *Daddy won't/will not eat a cookie*. The major characteristics of each stage can be summarized as follows.

STAGE	RULE	EXAMPLE
1	Negative in initial (occasionally final) position	Not Daddy eat cookie.
2	Negative between subject and verb	Daddy not eat cookie.
3	Negative follows first auxiliary	Daddy won't/will not eat a cookie.

Again, this progression makes sense. If the child's early positive utterances form some sort of nucleus, then we would expect their negative counterparts to be formed by simply appending a negative item before or after this nucleus. Once a child begins to analyze utterances into subject and verb, we would expect the negative item to appear between them, since this is its basic position within the adult grammar. Finally, since acquisition of the auxiliary system is relatively late (compared to major sentence constituents such as subject, object, and verb), we would expect relatively late acquisition of the adult rule for negatives, namely put *not* after the first auxiliary.

Once again, the point of this section is that a child's acquisition of syntactic categories and rules proceeds through orderly, systematic, and predictable stages.

Acquisition of Semantics

As we saw in Chapter 3, semantics is probably the most poorly understood component of grammar. Likewise, the way that children acquire semantics is also not well understood. Nonetheless, we can still draw some generalizations concerning this process. In doing so, it will be convenient to distinguish between **lexical semantics** (meanings of individual words) and **sentence semantics** (the interpretation of entire sentences). Let's look at a few representative examples within each area.

Lexical Semantics. Two fairly clear processes that children go through in acquiring the meaning of individual words are **overgeneralization** and subsequent **narrowing**. These processes can best be seen in the acquisition of concrete nouns. At first, the child will overgeneralize a word by using it to refer to more things than it does in the adult's lexicon. For example, *cookie* might be used to refer to anything round: a cookie, a cracker, a coin, a wheel, the moon, and so on. Over time, however, the meaning of *cookie* is narrowed so that it refers to only those items that an adult would call a *cookie*. Moreover, this narrowing often occurs in stages. For example, *dog* might be used at first to refer to any animal, then only to four-legged animals, then only to four-legged animals with fur, then only to relatively small four-legged animals with fur, and so on. Note, incidentally, how well this process lends itself to analysis in terms of semantic features, which we discussed in Chapter 3.

In addition, the process of overgeneralization may occur in the child's production without affecting comprehension. For example, a child may use the term *daddy* to refer to any adult male, such as Uncle Fred or the mailman. However, if asked *Where's Daddy?* with other males present, the child may correctly point to his or her father. This is not as paradoxical as it sounds. It is a general characteristic of language acquisition that comprehension outdistances production; that is, a child can perceive distinctions that he or she cannot yet produce. This principle seems to apply even in the acquisition of a second language. An adult learning a second language often reaches a point where he or she can understand someone else speaking that language but not yet speak it fluently.

Consider another systematic stage that children seem to go through. In acquiring the meaning of individual words, children will acquire so-called **basic-level terms** first. Although this concept is not well defined, researchers did some work several years ago where they found that children exposed to English tend to acquire terms like *house* before terms such as *building* or *split-level*. *House* is what is called a basic-level term, in that it is in some sense intermediate between a very general term such as *building* and a very specific term such as *split-level*. Along the same lines, children would be expected to acquire *bird* (basic-level) before *animal* (too general) or *robin* (too specific). Although the notion of "basic-level term" appeals to our intuitions, there is no precise definition of what exactly distinguishes a basic-level term from one that is not "basic."

A third principle is that children typically acquire the positive member of a pair before the negative member when acquiring the meanings of opposites. For example, when 3 year olds are presented with two sticks of different lengths, they give more correct responses to questions like *Which stick is longer?* than to *Which stick is shorter?* The difference between positive and negative terms is better defined than that between basic and nonbasic terms. The positive term within a pair of opposites is the unmarked member of the pair; that is, the one which carries the fewest presuppositions. For example, if you tell me that you just saw a new movie, I might ask *How long was it?* I would ask *How short was it?* only if you had given me some reason in advance for believing it was short. In this example, *long* is the positive term and *short* is the negative term. Likewise, we would expect a child exposed to English to acquire *tall* before *short*, *big* before *little*, *wide* before *narrow*, and *deep* before *shallow*.

Sentence Semantics.   The way a child acquires the ability to interpret sentences is not purely a semantic phenomenon; it is inextricably bound up with syntax. Even our example concerning the acquisition of positive terms depends upon the child's ability to interpret an entire sentence: *Which stick is longer?* Thus, throughout this section, keep in mind that it is virtually impossible to keep the acquisition of sentence semantics completely separate from syntax.

One interesting case is the acquisition of the ability to interpret **passive** sentences. At one time, linguists thought that children acquired their entire linguistic system (except for vocabulary) perfectly and completely by about the age of 5. More recent research, however, indicates that some structures such as passives may not be acquired fully by some children until as late as 6 to 10 years of age. Some children as old as 4 and 5 interpret passive sentences as if they were active. For instance, sentences such as *John pushed Mary* (active) and *John was pushed by Mary* (passive) are both interpreted as 'John pushed Mary.' In such cases, it appears that the child is responding to the order of the major sentence constituents (*John*, *pushed*, and *Mary*) and ignoring the grammatical morphemes (*was* and *by*). In other words, the child seems to be interpreting the first NP (*John*) as subject and the second NP (*Mary*) as object.

An interesting method has been developed for testing a child's ability to interpret such sentences. In this method a child is given a sentence and a set of toys, and is instructed to "act out" the sentence using the toys. Thus, for example, a child might be given two dolls, one "John" and the other "Mary." Then the child is presented with a sentence like *John was pushed by Mary* and asked to demonstrate what was said with the aid of the dolls. If the child acts out the sentence by having "John" push "Mary," then the experimenter concludes that the child interprets the sentence as 'John pushed Mary.'

A child exposed to English must also acquire the ability to interpret **bare infinitives**. Like the interpretation of passives, this ability may be acquired relatively late. A bare infinitive is a subordinate clause containing an infinitive verb and no overt subject (thus, the infinitive is said to be "bare"). For example, the sentence *I told you where to eat* contains a subordinate clause *where to eat*, which has no overt subject NP; thus *where to eat* is a bare infinitive clause. The strategy for interpreting the subject of such bare infinitives is called the **Minimum Distance Principle** (MDP), which can be stated as follows: Interpret the subject of a bare infinitive as the closest NP to the left. Note that our sample sentence, *I told you where to eat*, has two NP's to the left of the bare infinitive, namely *I* and *you*. The closest NP to the left of the bare infinitive is *you*. Thus, the MDP states that the subject of the bare infinitive *where to eat* will be the closest NP to the left, *you*. This is exactly how speakers of English interpret this sentence: 'I told you where *you* should eat,' not 'I told you where *I* should eat.' In general, the MDP seems to work fairly well in the interpretation of English.

There are, however, exceptions. Consider, for example, the analogous sentence *I asked you where to eat*. The MDP predicts that the subject of the bare infinitive *where to eat* should be the closest NP to the left, *you*. This, however, is not the way speakers of English generally interpret this sentence. For most speakers, it is interpreted as 'I asked you where *I* should eat' rather than 'I asked where *you* should eat.' Not surprisingly, Carol Chomsky, who has done research on children's interpretation of such structures, found that children acquiring English are able to interpret sentences that conform to the MDP before they are able to interpret those that don't. Consequently, a child will typically go through a stage in which *I told you where to eat* will be correctly interpreted as 'I told you where *you* should eat,' but *I asked you where to eat* will be incorrectly interpreted as 'I asked you where *you* should eat.' As an informal exercise, try to determine which of the following sentences would be correctly interpreted first by a child acquiring English: *I promised Mary to go* or *I persuaded Mary to go*.

A final ability that children acquire in systematic stages involves the interpretation of sentences linked by temporal connectives. Eve Clark of Stanford University has studied children's interpretation of sentences linked by *before* and *after*. Consider, for example, the following synonymous sentences: *He came home before he ate lunch*, *Before he ate lunch he came home*, *He ate lunch after he came home*, and *After he came home he ate lunch*. Clark found that children typically go through four different stages in their interpretation of such sentences. In the first stage, they interpret all the sentences according to **order of mention**: that is, the event reported in the first clause is interpreted as happening before the event reported in the second clause. Thus, *He came home before he ate lunch* will be interpreted correctly ('First he came home, then he ate lunch'), but *Before he ate lunch he came home* will be interpreted incorrectly ('First he ate lunch, then he came home'). In the second stage, children interpret all sentences containing *before* correctly; however, they continue to interpret sentences containing *after* according to the order-of-mention strategy. Thus, *After he came home he ate lunch* will be interpreted correctly ('First he came home, then he ate lunch'), but *He ate lunch after he came home* will be interpreted incorrectly ('First he ate lunch, then he came home'). In the third stage, they interpret both *before* and *after* as 'before.' Thus, *Before he ate lunch he came home* will be interpreted correctly ('First he came home, then he ate lunch'), but *After he came home he ate lunch* will be interpreted incorrectly ('First he ate lunch, then he came home'). In the fourth and final stage, the children interpret all four sentence types correctly; that is, *before* as 'before' and *after* as 'after.' This progression is summarized in the following diagram.

STAGES

(I)   All sentences interpreted via order of mention (i.e., event in first clause happened first; event in second clause happened second).

(II)   *Before* interpreted correctly; *after* interpreted via order of mention.

(III)   *Before* and *after* interpreted as 'before.'

(IV)   All sentences interpreted correctly.

EXAMPLES

Stages (+ = correct; 0 = incorrect)

	I	II	III	IV
He came home *before* he ate lunch.	+	+	+	+
Before he ate lunch he came home.	0	+	+	+
He ate lunch *after* he came home.	0	0	0	+
After he came home he ate lunch.	+	+	0	+

One further point to note in this example is that children interpret more sentences correctly at stage II than at stage III. This illustrates the fact that a child acquiring a native language may appear to be regressing at certain points in his or her development. However, once language acquisition is seen as a series of rule governed and systematic stages, it is clear that the child is not regressing at all, but simply revising his or her set of rules. Note the parallel between this example and the acquisition of the plural of *foot*, discussed earlier: *feet* ⟶ *foots/feets* ⟶ *footses/feetses* ⟶ *feet*. The child appears to be regressing, but actually is simply acquiring a rule.

After this discussion of the acquisition of phonology, morphology, syntax, and semantics, one point should be clear. A child's acquisition of a first language involves more than simply imitating and memorizing samples of the language to which he or she is exposed. Rather, it involves constructing a grammar of the language. This grammar, in turn, is a system composed of categories and rules which essentially constitute a definition of that language. Moreover, this grammar is acquired in stages, each of which more and more closely resembles the adult system.

ISSUES IN LANGUAGE ACQUISITION

In the first half of this chapter, we looked at some representative stages a child goes through in acquiring a first language, or, more specifically, a grammar of that language. In other words, we have considered how a child passes from an initial mental state (presumably having no grammar) through intermediate states until he or she reaches a final mental state (possessing a grammar more or less equivalent to an adult's). One thing we have not dealt with so far is the **initial state**; we have simply assumed that it is "blank," having no grammar at all. It turns out, however, that within the field of linguistics in general and language acquisition in particular, there has been quite a bit of controversy about this initial state. In the second half of this chapter we will briefly discuss some of the positions that various researchers hold concerning this initial state. It is important to keep in mind, however, that there is a great deal of controversy and very little direct evidence bearing upon the properties of the human organism as it begins its task of language acquisition.

Nativism and Empiricism

In general terms, there are basically two schools of thought on the nature of the initial mental state. On one side, we have what might be called **nativism**. Extreme nativism (as I am defining it here) would hold that human beings are born with all of the knowledge in their minds that they will eventually have as adults. With respect to language, this position would hold that a child is born knowing a language and this knowledge manifests itself during the first few years of life. On the other side, we have what might be called **empiricism**. Extreme empiricism (as I am defining it here) would hold that human beings are born with none of the knowledge in their minds that they will have as adults. With respect to language, this position would hold that a child is born with no linguistic knowledge whatsoever and that all language ability is somehow learned throughout life by making associations among events in the environment. As you can see, these two positions are mutually exclusive.

It is fairly easy to see that the extreme nativist position cannot be correct. If human beings were born knowing, say, English, it would be impossible to explain the fact that the vast majority of people in the world do not acquire English as a first language. The same, of course, could be said of Russian, Chinese, or any other language. On the other hand, it is not quite as easy to see that the extreme empiricist position is wrong, as indeed it is. The problem with this view is that it would be impossible to explain how human beings ever acquire a language at all (or for that matter, any knowledge whatsoever). If human beings are born with absolutely nothing in their minds, how can they make even the simplest "associations" among events in their environment? Consequently, it should come as no surprise that no serious researcher today could hold either of these extreme positions. Rather, students of language and language acquisition generally hold positions somewhere between these two extremes. Again, in oversimplified terms, we might say that most researchers hold a position of either modified nativism or modified empiricism. Since, as we have seen, no one holds the extreme views in actual practice, from now on I will refer to the modified positions as **nativism** and **empiricism**, respectively.

The nativist position (sometimes referred to as **mentalism**) focuses on the fact that much of human behavior is **biologically determined**. That is, much of our behavior is a function of the fact that we are human beings and our genes are structured in characteristic ways. Our ability to walk is an example of biologically determined behavior: We do not learn to walk, no one teaches us to walk; as normal human beings, we simply **acquire** the ability to walk because such ability is dictated by our genes. To use one of Chomsky's favorite examples, we do not "learn" to have arms any more than birds "learn" to have wings; rather, different species develop different attributes as a function of their different genetic structures.

With respect to language acquisition, the person most often associated with nativism is Chomsky. Quite simply, Chomsky holds the view that human beings are born already "knowing" something about the structure of human language. That is, human beings, by virtue of their characteristic genetic structure, are born in an initial mental state in which particular properties of human language are already specified. Candidates for these linguistic properties of the initial state would be those characteristics common to all human languages: for example, the fact that the phonology of every human language appears to operate in terms of segments, distinctive features, levels of representation, and phonological rules. In other words, according to this view, human beings are born with part of their grammar already in place. For example, they "know" that whatever language they are exposed to, they will have to organize the phonological component for that language in terms of segments, distinctive features, levels of representation, and phonological rules. It would probably not be too far wrong to say that the nativist position is a dominant (although certainly not exclusive) view of language acquisition among American linguists today. We will discuss the motivation for this position in more detail later on.

On the other hand, the empiricist position (sometimes referred to as **behaviorism**) focuses on the fact that much of human behavior is **culturally determined**. That is, much of our behavior is a function of specific environmental factors. The ability to write (among literate societies) is an example of culturally determined behavior. We **learn** to write by going through specific training; we do not simply acquire this ability spontaneously and naturally the same way we learn to walk. Witness the fact that all normal human beings learn to walk, just as they all acquire a first language; there are entire cultures, however, which do not use any writing system at all. A more transparent example of culturally determined knowledge would be learning the rules of, say, football. This game is played by two teams of 11 players each, on a field 100 yards long, and so on and so forth. (Note, incidentally, that in Canada the game is played with 12 players on each team on a field 110 yards long.) Knowledge of the game of football is obviously culturally determined. Human beings are clearly not born with any sort of knowledge of football. Instead, the rules of the game must be learned in the same way we learn to tie our shoes or to drive on the proper side of the road: by conscious attention, specific training, and trial and error.

With respect to language acquisition, the person most often associated with empiricism is B. F. Skinner. In 1957, Skinner published *Verbal Behavior*, in which he set out his views in detail. In greatly oversimplified terms, Skinner believes that language is learned essentially through vaguely defined powers of "association" and that human linguistic communication is a stimulus-response chain. That is, a stimulus in a person's environment causes him or her to speak (a response). In turn, this utterance (now a stimulus) causes another person to speak (a response), and so on. Under this view, the initial state has some innate structure (perhaps general powers of association and abstraction), but not much. Moreover, this view holds that language is not necessarily a human-specific capacity. That is, adherents to this position would not automatically assume that human languages are qualitatively different from animal communication systems (e.g., those found among bees, dolphins, and chimpanzees). However, since empiricism has been largely discredited within linguistics (see, for example, Chomsky's review of *Verbal Behavior*), at least in its present form and for the present time, there is little point in pursuing it here.

The main points of these two views are summarized in Figure 8-3. Keep in mind, however, that this represents a greatly oversimplified view. In reality, there are probably as many different views, representing points between what we have been calling nativism and empiricism, as there are people who have thought about the subject. Moreover, the controversy

NATIVISM	EMPIRICISM
—Mentalism	—Behaviorism
—Chomsky	—Skinner
—Mind has more innate structure	—Mind has less innate structure
—Language acquisition is primarily biologically determined	—Language acquisition is primarily culturally determined
—Language is acquired	—Language is learned

Figure 8–3. Nativism versus empiricism.

surrounding these views is still very much alive; Chomsky's position is by no means universally held.

Language-Specific and General Cognitive Capacities

In the last section we discussed the nature of the initial mental state that humans bring to the task of language acquisition. We saw that nativists believe that the initial state already contains a great deal of genetically predetermined structure. On the other hand, we saw that empiricists believe the initial state to contain very little predetermined structure. Even though both positions disagree on how much structure the human mind comes equipped with, they agree that there must be at least some innate structure in the initial state.

This in turn brings us to another question: Is any of this innate structure specifically designed to facilitate language acquisition? In other words, does the initial state contain **language-specific capacities** or does it contain only **general cognitive capacities**? Chomsky makes it quite clear that he believes the initial state to contain language-specific information. For example, the phonologies of all languages are organized in terms of segments, distinctive features, levels of representation, and phonological rules. In contrast, others who have addressed this question, most notably the late French psychologist Jean Piaget, have held that the initial state does not contain language-specific information. Rather, language acquisition results from the interaction of various general cognitive capacities, such as memory, intelligence, motivation, and so on. If these "general cognitive capacities" sound vague, it is because they are. The state of the human mind as it enters the world is very poorly understood. This question of what kind of innate structure (i.e., language-specific versus general) is even harder to debate than that of how much structure (i.e., nativism versus empiricism). Thus, rather than pursue the controversy, let's turn to what I believe is the most clearly articulated position on the subject, namely Chomsky's.

Chomsky's Position

As we have seen, Chomsky is essentially a nativist. He is convinced that human beings are born with a very rich fabric of mental structure already in place. Moreover, he is convinced that part of this mental structure is language-specific in nature. Chomsky has arrived at this position through what we might call a "what else" argument. That is, he starts with a number of observations about language and language acquisition and argues that the simplest way to explain them is to assume that human beings are born with a certain amount of language-specific knowledge already in place. Let's now consider some of the observations that have lead Chomsky to this conclusion.

The Complexity of Acquired Structures.   As we have seen throughout this chapter (indeed, throughout this entire book), the acquisition of a language is essentially the acquisition of a grammar: that is, a set of categories and rules for characterizing all and only the sentences of that language. By hypothesis, the semantic component consists of knowledge organized in terms of sense relations (e.g., anomaly, hyponymy, etc.), reference relations (e.g., anaphora, coreference, etc.), and logical relations (e.g., entailment and presupposition). The syntactic component consists of knowledge organized in terms of categories (e.g., NP, VP, etc.), constituent structure (i.e., bracketing of categories into higher units), and transformations (e.g., WHM, SVI, etc.). The morphological component consists of knowledge organized in terms of different types of morphemes (e.g., lexical or grammatical, free or bound, and inflectional or derivational). The phonological component consists of knowledge organized in terms of segments, distinctive features, levels of representation, and phonological rules. If this is a reasonably accurate representation of a grammar, then the final state achieved by a human being (i.e., an adult grammar) is exceedingly complex. From Chomsky's point of view, it is difficult to explain how human beings acquire such a complex system, unless we assume that they are genetically predisposed to do so.

Fixed Onset and Development.   As we have seen in the first half of this chapter, the acquisition of language begins at about the same time for all normal children (i.e., it has a "fixed onset") and progresses through predictable stages, regardless of each child's particular environment or the specific language to which he or she is exposed. For example, a child typically acquires the intonational patterns of a language around the end of his or her first year. The significance of this "fixed onset and development" can best be appreciated by considering the fact that efforts to speed up language acquisition are generally in vain. Specific studies have found that it is generally impossible to "teach" a child a detail of language until the child is ready to acquire it spontaneously. A case often cited in the literature concerns a little boy who told his mother *Nobody don't like me.* She tried to correct this double negative by responding with *Nobody likes me.* They repeated this interchange eight times, until the boy finally said *Oh! Nobody don't likes me.* Presumably, the boy eventually acquired the adult rule for forming negatives as well as the {PRES} morpheme, but only when he reached the appropriate stage of development.

In order to appreciate the systematic and uniform progression of language acquisition, it is useful to consider the errors children do not make in acquiring their native language. For example, part of the experience of a child exposed to English might be utterances such as *She is cooking dinner* and *Is she cooking dinner?* From these and many other such examples, a child might be expected to form a rule for forming interrogatives as follows: Move the first occurrence of *is* to the beginning of the sentence. However, this rule would predict that at some stage in the child's acquisition of English syntax, he or she would make an error of the following sort. Given a sentence with two occurrences of *is* (e.g., *The spoon she is using is broken*), the child would form the interrogative by moving the first occurrence of *is* to the beginning of the sentence. This would yield **Is the spoon she using is broken?* rather than the correct form *Is the spoon she is using broken?*

The significant point is that children acquiring English (or any other language with such a rule) seem never to make such mistakes. It appears that children are constrained from forming a syntactic rule which is independent of structure; that is, a rule of the form: Move the first, second, or *n*th word to, say, the beginning of the utterance. Rather, all syntactic rules for all languages seem to be structure-dependent; that is, they must be framed in structural terms, with reference to units such as NP, auxiliary, subject, main clause, and so forth. In our example, the rule would be something like the following: Move the first occurrence of *is* following the subject NP of the main clause to initial position of that clause. Thus, in our sample structure, the rule would identify and move the occurrence of *is* in the main clause, while completely ignoring the occurrence of *is* in the subordinate clause. Details of this analysis aside, Chomsky argues that it is difficult to account for the uniform onset and quite narrowly constrained development of language, unless we assume that children are genetically predisposed to acquire a grammar that meets certain predetermined criteria.

Rapidity of Acquisition. A child acquires his or her first language in remarkably rapid fashion. Even though some structures are acquired later than researchers had originally thought, the fact remains that a normal child acquires the majority of his or her grammar by about 5 years of age. This is amazing when you consider the nonlinguistic tasks that many children do not master until later (e.g., tying their shoes, telling time, learning the basic conventions of etiquette, throwing a ball, snapping their fingers, riding a bicycle, and so on). Moreover, the rapidity of first language acquisition is brought into relief by considering the painstaking labor involved in learning a second language as an adult. Approximately half of the Americans who attend college are required at some time in their careers to take a foreign language. Very few, however, ever actually gain facility in it.

Such facts suggest a genetic predisposition among humans that begins to dissipate around the age of puberty and falls off dramatically at the onset of adulthood. This view is supported by the fact that children who are exposed to two languages seem to acquire both of them with equal ease and rapidity. Another piece of evidence comes from Genie, a girl discovered in Los Angeles in 1971 at the age of 13. Genie had been deprived since infancy of exposure to language; that is, she had reached puberty without being exposed to language. Subsequent attempts to teach English to Genie indicated that, although she was intelligent, she was unable to acquire English in the same way as a normal child or as completely. (See Susan Curtiss's book, *Genie*.) Once again, in Chomsky's view, it is difficult to explain both the rapidity of language acquisition and the rapid decline in this ability, unless we assume that language acquisition is part of a human being's genetically programmed biological development.

Features Common to All Languages. On the face of things, it appears that human languages are wildly divergent. English and Japanese, for example, seem so different that it would be hard to find anything that they have in common. In fact, as recently as the late 1950's, many linguists believed that languages could differ without limit and in unpredictable ways. If, however, we look below the surface, we find that human languages are remarkably similar. As we discussed earlier, the grammars of all languages can be characterized in terms of four components—semantics, syntax, morphology, and phonology—each of which is organized in terms of the same types of categories and rules. These similarities, of course, could reflect the fact that all of this apparatus is part of a theory consciously constructed by linguists. In other words, grammars of languages share these components and subcomponents because linguists analyze languages in terms of them; that is, linguists find what they are looking for. However, if we accept as inevitable the fact that theorists in any field must necessarily look at the subject through a theory of their own construction, languages still exhibit certain common properties that are by no means logically necessary. You may recall from the beginning of Chapter 7 that such common properties are called **language universals**.

During the past 25 years an enormous number of language universals have been proposed. Consider just a few examples. From the standpoint of phonology, all languages have at least one voiceless stop (e.g., /p,t,k/ in English), but not all languages have a voiced stop (e.g., /b,d,g/). Likewise, all languages have the vowel /a/ (and the vast majority contain /i,u/), but not all languages have /ɛ/ and /ɔ/. Similarly, all languages have syllables of the form CV, but not all languages have syllables of the form VC. From the standpoint of morphology, if a language has both derivational and inflectional suffixes (as in English), then the derivational suffix will precede the inflectional suffix (e.g., *drivers* versus **driveser*, discussed in Chapter 5). Likewise, if a language inflects nouns for gender (i.e., masculine and feminine), it always inflects them for number (i.e., singular and plural). In Spanish, for example, nouns are inflected for gender, as in *hermano* 'brother' versus *hermana* 'sister' (*-o* = masculine, *-a* = feminine). Thus, nouns in Spanish are necessarily inflected for number, as in *hermano* 'brother' versus *hermanos* 'brothers'. On the other hand, a language that inflects for number does not necessarily inflect for gender. In English, for example, nouns are inflected for number, as in *brother* versus *brothers*, but not for gender. From the standpoint of syntax, if a language moves *wh*-items (e.g., *who*, *what*, etc. in English), it moves them leftward to clause-initial position, never rightward to clause-final position. Similarly, in simple declarative sentences, the vast majority of languages (approximately 99 percent) order the subject before the object. And the list goes on and on.

Even though some of these universals are absolute (i.e., all languages have property X) and others are implicational (i.e., if a language has property X, then it will also have property Y), the fact is that none of these universals are logically necessary. For example, there is no logical reason that inflectional suffixes must follow derivational suffixes. It is perfectly possible to imagine a human language in which the opposite situation holds. Likewise, there is no logical reason that languages move *wh*-items to the left; they could just as easily move them to the right. And so on and so forth. Chomsky's view is once again straightforward: It is difficult to explain the vast number of common (but not logically necessary) features among languages, unless we assume that such properties are specified by the genetically determined initial state.

Independent of Instruction. A normal child acquires the bulk of his or her first language before ever starting school; thus, it is clear that teachers do not "teach" a child language. Indeed, children who never attend school in their lives acquire language. Likewise, parents do not "teach" their children language. In fact, most parents have no conscious knowledge of the rules of their language. What parent (other than one who has studied syntax) would be able to state, say, the rule of Subject-Verb Inversion? Even for those few adults who have conscious knowledge of (some of) the rules of their own language, it is hard to imagine how they could convey such information to a child. Consider an extremely simple example, often cited by Chomsky. Every native speaker of English knows that in the sentence *Bob proved that he is incompetent*, the pronoun *he* can refer either to Bob or to someone else. Likewise, every such speaker knows that in the sentence *Bob proved him to be incompetent*, the pronoun *him* must refer to someone other than Bob. The point is that this knowledge is clear-cut and acquired without training; yet imagine trying to explain the principle involved here to a 5 or even a 10 year old child!

Moreover, much of our grammatical knowledge is acquired without appropriate experience; that is, we know things about our language for which we apparently have no relevant experience. A favorite example of Chomsky's involves what he calls **parasitic gaps**. In such constructions, a pronoun can be omitted without affecting the interpretation of the sentence—for example, *Who did you insult by ignoring him?* versus *Who did you insult by ignoring?* (Most speakers prefer one or the other of these sentences, but the point is that both of them are perfectly interpretable and can be interpreted as identical in meaning.) These parasitic gap constructions, however, are extremely rare in English. Compare, for example, the sentences *Who insulted Bob by ignoring him?* and **Who insulted Bob by ignoring?* In this pair, which is the typical case in English, the pronoun *him* cannot be optionally omitted. Chomsky's point is that constructions containing parasitic gaps are so uncommon that it is unlikely that a child would ever be exposed to one while acquiring the syntax of English. Nevertheless, all native speakers of English know exactly under what circumstances a pronoun may and may not be omitted, and they apparently know this without training and without relevant experience.

From Chomsky's point of view, it is difficult to explain the fact that humans acquire such subtle grammatical distinctions without training and experience, unless we assume that the basic grammatical principles that underlie these distinctions are biologically determined and present in the initial state.

Independent of Intelligence and Motivation. It is significant that the acquisition of a first language does not seem to be a direct function of intelligence. The individual with an IQ of 70 acquires the grammar of the language to which he or she is exposed just as the individual with an IQ of 125 does. Even children with Down's syndrome acquire a grammar. Likewise, language acquisition does not seem to be a function of motivation. Normal children do not "try" to acquire language; they do not have to work at it; they simply acquire it—effortlessly and spontaneously. In fact, it is impossible to interrupt or retard language acquisition short of isolating the child from language completely (as in the case of Genie mentioned earlier). Again, from Chomsky's perspective it is virtually impossible to explain the fact that language acquisition is independent of intelligence and motivation, unless we assume that it is a biologically determined process.

Since there has been so much controversy and misunderstanding over this line of reasoning, let me reiterate this argument in point form. Chomsky first makes the following observations.

(a) The final state achieved (i.e., an adult grammar) is extremely complex.
(b) Language acquisition is characterized by a fixed onset and uniform stages of development.

(c) Language acquisition is comparatively rapid (i.e., it is accomplished almost totally by age 5 or 6).
(d) All languages have numerous features in common—features which are not the product of logical necessity.
(e) Human language is not taught.
(f) Language acquisition is independent of intelligence and motivation.

Chomsky then concludes that these observations are difficult (if not impossible) to explain, unless we make the following assumptions. First, human beings acquire a language because they are genetically programmed to do so. Second, this genetic endowment contains (among other things) language-specific capacities, present at birth. The only requirement for language acquisition external to the individual is exposure to a human language. In other words, language acquisition is both biologically and culturally determined. The biologically determined linguistic capacities present in the initial state interact with the culturally determined experience of the child (i.e., the particular language spoken around the child) to set off the acquisition of a human language.

This position, of course, may turn out to be either totally or partially incorrect. And, in fact, there is widespread controversy over its details. It is, however, the most clearly articulated and (for me, at least) the most convincing theory presently available to explain observations (a-f).

SUMMARY

Let's review what we have done. We started with four observations about the acquisition of a first language. However, we had no ready explanation for these phenomena. Thus, we constructed a (partial) theory of language acquisition to account for our original observations. This theory makes use of such concepts as prelinguistic and linguistic stages, the latter of which constitute grammars (i.e., systems of categories and rules) that more and more closely correspond to the adult's. We have also seen that the acquisition of language can be subdivided into the acquisition of phonology, morphology, syntax, and semantics. Moreover, we have looked at some of the fundamental philosophical issues surrounding language acquisition. These issues reflect two positions regarding the initial mental state of the human organism: nativism (more innate structure) and empiricism (less innate structure). Furthermore, controversy exists over whether the initial state contains language-specific capacities or only general cognitive capacities.

As usual, it is worth pointing out that there is much more to the study of language acquisition than what has been presented in this one short chapter. However, you have now been exposed to some of the basic ideas in the field; if you want to learn more about the subject, see the readings at the end of this chapter. In the meantime, the following exercises may be beneficial in checking your understanding of the material in this chapter.

EXERCISES

(1) For each set of structures (a-g), which construction would children exposed to English be most likely to acquire first?
   (a) /ɪ/   /a/   /æ/
   (b) /k/   /t/   /p/
   (c) /t/   /s/   /r/
   (d) VC   CV   CVC
   (e) {POSS}   {PRES}   {PLU}
   (f) SVI   WHM   Intonation
   (g) *not*   *can't*   *cannot*

(2) True/False
   (a) In forming interrogative structures, a child exposed to English generally acquires WHM before SVI.
   (b) Intelligence seems to play a major role in a child's ability to acquire a language.
   (c) It will generally take a child longer to acquire Japanese than to acquire English.
   (d) It is generally impossible for a parent to speed up the process of language acquisition.
   (e) A child exposed to English typically acquires uncontracted negatives before contracted negatives.
   (f) To support the empiricist point of view, a researcher would be more likely to cite second language acquisition by an adult rather than first language acquisition by a child.
   (g) The babbling stage seems to be a necessary prerequisite for normal language acquisition.
   (h) Before a child exposed to English has acquired the ability to interpret passives, he or she would be likely to interpret *Tommy petted Bozo* and *Bozo was petted by Tommy* as having different meanings.
   (i) A child exposed to English would be likely to acquire the meaning of *old* before *young*.

(3) Consider the following interchange between 4 year old Muffin and her mother.
   Muffin: Why you don't eat?
   Mother: What?
   Muffin: Why don't you eat?
   These data illustrate that Muffin is in the process of acquiring a particular syntactic rule of English. Which one?

(4) A child exposed to English might go through the following stages in acquiring the rule for forming the past tense of verbs. At which stage

has the child actually acquired a *rule* similar to that in the adult grammar?
Stage I: *eat*
Stage II: *ate*
Stage III: *eated*
Stage IV: *ate*

(5) Assume a child is acquiring English. Which of the following representations of *stick* would be most likely to appear first: [tʰɪk] or [stɪ]?

(6) Moskowitz, a language acquisition specialist, claims that "In constructing a grammar children have only a limited amount of information available to them, namely the language they hear spoken around them." Chomsky would say that Moskowitz is not entirely correct. What additional information would he claim that the child brings to the task of language acquisition?

(7) A child acquiring English who says *feetses* for *feet* has apparently misanalyzed the base form to which the {PLU} suffix is attached. What is the base of *feetses* for this child?

ANSWERS TO EXERCISES

The following answers are, in some cases, not the only possible ones. Discussion of other possible answers is part of the exercises.

(1) (a) /a/   (e) {PLU}
     (b) /p/   (f) Intonation
     (c) /t/   (g) *not*
     (d) CV

(2) (a) T   (f) T
     (b) F   (g) F
     (c) F   (h) T
     (d) T   (i) T
     (e) F

(3) SVI

(4) Stage III

(5) [tʰɪk]

(6) Genetically encoded universal properties of language (sometimes called **universal grammar**).

(7) *feets*

SUPPLEMENTARY READINGS

Primary

1. Chomsky, N. (1959). A review of B. F. Skinner's *Verbal Behavior. Language, 35,* 26–58.
2. Chomsky, N. (1980). *Rules and representations.* New York: Columbia University Press.
3. Curtiss, S. (1977). *Genie: A psycholinguistic study of a modern-day "wild child."* New York: Academic Press.
4. Lightfoot, D. (1982). *The language lottery.* Cambridge, MA: MIT Press.
5. Newmeyer, F. (1983). *Grammatical theory.* Chicago: University of Chicago Press.
6. Skinner, B. F. (1957). *Verbal behavior.* New York: Appleton-Century-Crofts.

Secondary

7. Chomsky, N. (1983). Interview. *Omni* (November), 113–118, 171–174.
8. Clark, H., and Clark, E. (1977). *Psychology and language* (Chapters 8–10). New York: Harcourt Brace Jovanovich.
9. Lenneberg, E. (1964). The capacity for language acquisition. In J. Katz and J. Fodor (Eds.), *The structure of language* (pp. 579–603). Englewood Cliffs, NJ: Prentice-Hall.
10. Moskowitz, B. A. (1979). The acquisition of language. *Scientific American* (November), 82–96.

You are now prepared to read all of the secondary works. Clark and Clark (8) and Moskowitz (10) provide good discussions of the stages a child goes through in acquiring a language. Lenneberg (9) distinguishes between biologically determined and culturally determined behavior, and discusses the characteristics of each. Chomsky (7) provides a straightforward rendering of his views on the biological basis of language acquisition.

An introductory course in linguistics is probably necessary to fully appreciate the primary works. Chomsky (2), Lightfoot (4), and Newmeyer (5) are excellent discussions of the view Chomsky sets out in (7). Curtiss (3) is a classic study in the effects of depriving a child of linguistic stimuli. Skinner (6) and Chomsky (1), however, are difficult going and are now primarily of historical interest. The former is the classic statement of the empiricist view of language, and the latter is Chomsky's detailed rejection of it.

Chapter 9

The Neurology of Language

The **neurology of language**, also known as **neurolinguistics**, is the study of the brain structures that a person must possess in order to process language. It might help in understanding the focus of this field to review the subjects we have covered in this book. The study of language can be broken down into **pragmatics**—how language is used to communicate; **grammar** proper (syntax, semantics, morphology, and phonology)—the internal structure of language; **language variation**—the forms of a language that vary according to region, social class, and style; and **language acquisition**—the initial mental state of human beings and the stages they go through in acquiring their first language. Each of these subdisciplines of linguistics deals with a particular aspect of the psychological system of categories and rules that human beings employ to characterize and use their knowledge of their own native language. In the neurology of language, the particular focus is on the brain structures necessary for normal language processing.

Within this general scheme of how neurolinguistics fits into the study of language, let's consider some observations we can make about the neurology of language.

(1) Damage to the brain can affect a person's ability to process language; damage to the heart, lungs, liver, or kidneys (short of killing the person) does not.

(2) Damage to the left side of the brain is more likely to cause language processing difficulties (e.g., being able to hear speech but unable to comprehend it) than is damage to the right side of the brain.

(3) Damage to the anterior (front) part of the brain is more likely to affect the production of linguistic stimuli through speaking and writing. Damage to the posterior (rear) part of the brain is more likely to affect the comprehension of linguistic stimuli through listening and reading.

(4) In addition to causing language processing difficulties, brain damage may disrupt a person's ability to comprehend sensations (e.g., to recognize a common object such as an orange), to carry out voluntary actions such as licking the lips on command, or to speak distinctly.

Observation (1) illustrates the fact that the physical organ underlying the ability to process language is the brain; in particular, brain damage can result in a language-specific dysfunction called **aphasia**. Observation (2) illustrates the fact that most human beings process language in the left cerebral hemisphere. This reflects the fact that human brains exhibit **hemispherical specialization**: The left hemisphere controls one set of abilities, among them language processing, while the right controls other abilities, such as orientation in space and visuospatial processing. Observation (3) illustrates the fact that different parts of each hemisphere control different mental functions. This is sometimes referred to as **localization of function**. Thus, damage to the left anterior part of the brain is likely to interfere with language production, whereas damage to the left posterior part of the brain is likely to interfere with language comprehension. Observation (4) illustrates the fact that, in addition to causing a language dysfunction (aphasia), brain damage may disrupt a person's ability to comprehend sensations (**agnosia**), to perform voluntary actions (**apraxia**), or to produce articulate speech (**dysarthria**).

Before getting into the details of neurolinguistics, let me address three points concerning the nature of research in this field. First, a common method of investigating the neurology of language is through observing the effects of a breakdown in the neurological system; that is, through observing patients who have a language dysfunction and who have suffered brain damage from a stroke, a tumor, or some type of trauma. Damage to the brain, or to any organ, is called a lesion. A stroke causes a lesion by shutting off the blood supply, and thus the oxygen supply, to some part of the brain. A stroke can result from various causes, such as an embolus (a blood clot or air bubble that blocks an artery in the brain) or an aneurism (a weak spot in an artery which ruptures and diverts blood away from a particular part of the brain). A tumor causes damage by putting pressure on part of the brain from the inside, in effect ''squeezing'' the brain between the tumor itself and the skull. A trauma to the brain is caused by some sort of external force, such as a blow to the head.

Of these three types of damage, stroke damage is typically of more interest to the neurolinguist than damage caused by tumor or trauma. This is because a stroke is capable of damaging a very specific and localized part of the brain, whereas damage caused by tumor or trauma tends to be more global, affecting a greater part of the brain. For example, a tumor in the left rear of the brain may push the entire exterior of the brain against the skull, causing global rather than localized damage. Similarly, a trauma to the left side of the head may damage the right side of the brain as the brain comes in contact with the right side of the skull. In short, then, one major avenue of inquiry that neurolinguists use is pathology, in particular lesions caused by strokes.

Second, neurolinguistics is basically a correlational and statistical enterprise. It is correlational in that the linguist tries to find correspondences between particular language functions and particular parts of the brain. The neurolinguist draws inferences of the following type: Patients 1, 3, and 5 all have had strokes in area A of the brain and all exhibit language dysfunction Y; patients 2, 4, and 6 all have had strokes in area B of the brain and all exhibit language dysfunction Z; therefore, it appears that brain area A controls language function Y and that brain area B controls language function Z. Neurolinguistics is statistical in that the linguist cannot draw absolute correlations between a particular part of the brain and a particular language dysfunction for all human beings. For example, in a sample of 10 patients with damage to brain part A, only 8 may exhibit language dysfunction Y. On the basis of these data, the neurolinguist would be able to hypothesize that there is an 80 percent probability that damage to brain part A will lead to language dysfunction Y. In short, then, neurolinguists essentially make statistical correlations between localized brain damage and particular language processing deficits.

Third, as was the case with language acquisition, the research methods used in neurolinguistics have some inherent difficulties. As we have just seen, one main avenue for studying neurolinguistics is through pathology—that is, through studying patients with brain damage. Obviously, however, the neurolinguist cannot inflict damage on a normal subject in order to see what happens, but instead must wait for a suitable subject to come along. Moreover, the patient must have relatively localized brain damage and must also exhibit fairly specific behavioral abnormalities. If the brain damage is global or if the behavioral abnormalities are too general, the analyst will have difficulty correlating a particular area of the brain with a particular behavioral deficit. In short, the neurolinguist is constrained to some extent by having to draw inferences on the basis of what nature provides.

In order to convey a better understanding of how research in neurolinguistics is carried out, this chapter is divided into four major areas: the anatomy of the central nervous system; a survey of some of the major figures who have added to our understanding of language and brain; a discussion of the different functions performed by each of the cerebral hemispheres; and a survey of brain disorders affecting language in particular, and expression and comprehension in general.

ANATOMY OF THE NERVOUS SYSTEM

The basic unit of the nervous system is the **neuron**; there are about 12 billion neurons in the nervous system. Each neuron is made up of three parts: a **cell body**; an **axon**, which transmits nervous impulses away from the cell body; and **dendrites**, which receive impulses coming in to the cell body. The point at which the nervous impulse passes from the axon of one neuron to the dendrites of another is called a **synapse**. Thus, neurons communicate with each other by transmitting information through this complex of axons, dendrites, and synapses.

The part of the nervous system that is of primary interest to neurolinguists is the **central nervous system** (CNS), which is made up of the brain and the spinal cord. The diagram of the CNS in Figure 9–1 illustrates the major landmarks which will be of interest to us as we go through this chapter.

The **spinal cord** (1) transmits messages between the brain and the peripheral nervous system extending throughout the rest of the body. The spinal cord transmits the message from the brain that says, for example, to cross your right leg over your left. The spinal cord, however, plays no role in language processing. The **lower brain stem** (2) consists of the **medulla oblongata** and the **pons**. These structures serve essentially as a bridge between the spinal cord and the higher brain stem. (In fact, *pons* is the Latin word for 'bridge.') Damage to the lower brain stem can cause a speech disorder known as **dysarthria**. This is not a language deficit, but rather the inability to produce articulate speech.

The **higher brain stem** (3) consists of the **thalamus** and **midbrain**. These structures control involuntary regulatory functions such as breathing, heart rate, and body temperature. These functions are "involuntary" in the sense that they are not subject to conscious control; for example, a person does not have to "think" in order to maintain a body temperature of 98.6° F. In addition, the thalamus receives all incoming sensory stimuli (except for the sense of smell) and transmits each stimulus to the part of the brain where it is integrated. In essence, then, the thalamus is a sort of relay station which evaluates an incoming stimulus for modality (i.e., vision, hearing, taste, etc.) and sends it to the part of the brain which processes that type of stimulus.

The **cerebellum** (4), which lies to the rear of the brain stem, controls equilibrium. Damage to the cerebellum results in nonlinguistic dysfunctions such as **dysmetria** and **ataxia**. Dysmetria describes the phenomena of "undershoot" and "overshoot." For example, if a person reaches for a glass from a table but "overshoots" or goes beyond the glass, this may indicate damage to the cerebellum. Ataxia, on the other hand, describes a lack of muscular coordination during voluntary movements. The cerebellum plays no known role in language processing.

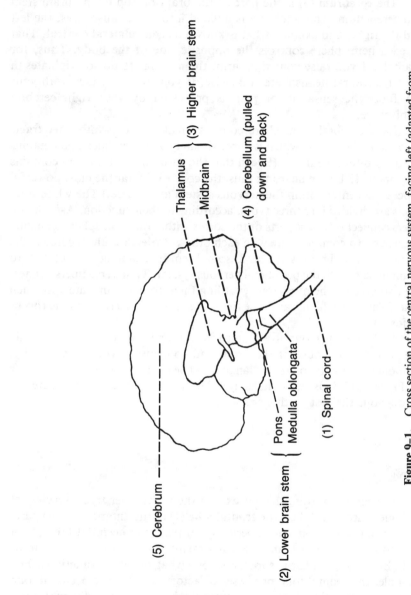

Figure 9–1. Cross section of the central nervous system, facing left (adapted from Penfield and Roberts, 1959, p. 15).

(3) Higher brain stem

Thalamus
Midbrain

(4) Cerebellum (pulled down and back)

(5) Cerebrum

Pons
Medulla oblongata

(2) Lower brain stem

(1) Spinal cord

The **cerebrum** (5) is the part of the brain on top of the brain stem and cerebellum. The cerebrum is divided into two hemispheres, the left and the right, and exhibits what is known as **contralateral control**. That is, each hemisphere controls the opposite side of the body. Thus, for example, if you raise your right arm, the message to do so originates in the left cerebral hemisphere. Likewise, if you step on a tack with your left foot, the sensation of pain is processed by your right cerebral hemisphere.

Each cerebral hemisphere consists of a mass of **white fiber tracts** covered by the **cortex**, which is approximately 0.25 inch thick and contains about 10 billion neurons. (Recall that the entire nervous system contains only about 12 billion neurons; thus, the cortex is by far the most powerful processing center within the nervous system as a whole.) The white fiber tracts are divided into three types, according to their function. **Association fibers** connect different parts of the cortex within one hemisphere, enabling these parts to communicate with each other. **Projection fibers** connect the cortex to the brain stem and spinal cord, enabling the cortex to communicate with the peripheral nervous system. **Transverse fibers** connect the two cerebral hemispheres, enabling them to communicate with each other. The 200 million transverse fibers are known collectively as the **corpus callosum**.

Let's now turn our attention to the cortex itself, which is essentially the central storehouse of the brain and controls all voluntary activity, including the ability to process language. The diagram of the human cortex in Figure 9–2 illustrates the major landmarks which we will refer to throughout the rest of this chapter.

Lobes

The cerebrum (i.e., the cortex and the white fiber tracts serving it) is divided into four lobes: the **frontal lobe** (1) in the anterior (front) part; the **parietal lobe** (2) in the superior (top) part; the **occipital lobe** (3) in the posterior (back) part; and the **temporal lobe** (4) in the inferior (bottom) part. Each lobe, in turn, subserves somewhat different functions. For example, the frontal lobe processes olfactory stimuli, the occipital lobe processes visual stimuli, and the temporal lobe processes auditory stimuli. Each cerebral hemisphere has these lobes, so we can speak of the left temporal lobe, the right occipital lobe, and so on. We will see later on that the left frontal and temporal lobes house the major language processing centers for most humans.

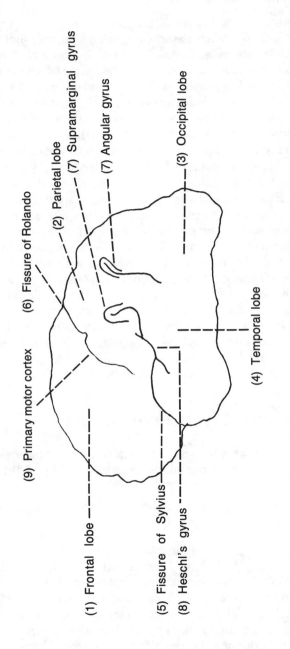

(9) Primary motor cortex   (6) Fissure of Rolando

(2) Parietal lobe

(7) Supramarginal gyrus

(7) Angular gyrus

(3) Occipital lobe

(4) Temporal lobe

(1) Frontal lobe

(5) Fissure of Sylvius

(8) Heschl's gyrus

Figure 9–2. Human cortex, facing left.

185

Convolutions and Fissures

The cortex of the human brain has a "wrinkled" appearance. The indentations are called **fissures** (or sulci) and the "bulges" are called **convolutions** (or gyri). Certain of these fissures and convolutions serve as important anatomical landmarks. The **fissure of Sylvius** (5), also known as the lateral sulcus, separates the frontal and temporal lobes. The **fissure of Rolando** (6), also called the central sulcus, separates the frontal and parietal lobes. The **supramarginal gyrus** and the **angular gyrus** (7) lie in the inferior part of the parietal lobe. And **Heschl's gyrus** (8), also known as the transverse temporal gyrus or the primary auditory cortex, receives all incoming auditory stimuli. One function of Heschl's gyrus is to separate different types of auditory stimuli (e.g., environmental noises such as buzzes, clicks, and whistles versus linguistic stimuli such as speech) and send them to the different parts of the cortex where they are interpreted.

The **primary motor cortex** (9) is a strip of cortex about two centimeters wide lying immediately anterior to the fissure of Rolando. Each discrete point in the primary motor cortex controls a discrete set of muscles. For example, stimulation of the superior part of the primary motor cortex will cause the leg muscles on the opposite side of the body to contract. Movements of the lips, tongue, and jaw are controlled by discrete areas located in the inferior part of the primary motor cortex, near where it meets the fissure of Sylvius. In general, the more fine-grained the movement, the larger the cortical area devoted to it. Thus, movement of the trunk has less cortex devoted to it than movement of the fingers does.

BACKGROUND OF NEUROLINGUISTICS

In this section we will discuss very briefly a few of the major figures who have contributed to our modern understanding of the neurology of language.

Gall

Modern investigations of the relation between brain and language can be traced back at least to a Viennese M.D. named Franz Joseph Gall (1758-1828). Gall was an anatomist and was well respected for his studies in this field. However, Gall was also the founder of **phrenology**, the "science" of inferring mental faculties and character from the conformation of the skull. His reasoning went something like this: Any striking behavior must be a manifestation of some discrete mental faculty; each mental faculty is subserved by a particular cortical organ, which varies directly in size with the keenness of the mental faculty; the increased size of the cortical organ, in turn, results in a cranial prominence. For example, take the case of someone with a striking ability to remember. Gall would assume that this behavior is a manifestation of the mental faculty of memory, which he thought was located in the cortical organ of the frontal lobe. Since this individual's memory is remarkable, we should expect the frontal lobe to be abnormally large. And this, in turn, will be evidenced by a cranial prominence leading to bulging eyes.

Phrenology, however, was received with justifiable skepticism by Gall's peers, who regarded it as nonsense. Consequently, even though Gall was reknowned for his anatomical studies, he was considered a rebel and an outcast for his phrenological studies. In fact, he was denied admission to the French Academy of Sciences in 1821. The major drawback to Gall's theory was that his evidence was solely anecdotal rather than experimental. That is, he based his theories on such evidence as paintings and busts of famous men who were known for particular personality traits. Moreover, he sought only evidence which would support his theories, ignoring or trying to explain away any counterevidence. For example, Robert Young, in his book *Mind, Brain and Adaptation in the Nineteenth Century*, reports that "when Descartes' skull was found to be remarkably small in the anterior and superior regions of the forehead, where the rational faculties were localized, Spurzheim [a student and colleague of Gall] replied that Descartes was not so great a thinker as he was held to be" (1979, p. 43).

On the other hand, Gall did make several contributions to the study of the neurology of language. First, he was the first modern **localizationist**; that is, he was the first to propose separate mental functions for distinct anatomical parts of the brain. Second, he articulated the first empirical approach to the localization of function; that is, he proposed a testable theory that could be refuted by uncovering examples of striking behaviors which did not correspond to enlarged areas of the brain (e.g., an individual with a striking ability to remember but without a large frontal lobe). Third, he associated language with the frontal lobe of the brain, a hypothesis that turned out later to be at least partially true. In fact, Gall is usually given credit for the first detailed description of aphasia resulting from a trauma to the brain.

Flourens

In contrast to Gall was Jean-Pierre-Marie Flourens (1794-1867). Flourens was awarded his M.D. at the age of 19 and gained fame as an experimental physiologist. Flourens differed from Gall in several respects. First, Flourens was an experimentalist, whereas Gall relied primarily on anecdotal evidence. In particular, Flourens developed the experimental method of **ablation**, a procedure whereby a particular part of the brain is surgically removed. After the operation, the analyst observes the organism's behavior and tries to infer the function of the part that was removed. Second, Flourens experimented solely on animals, especially birds, whereas Gall based his phrenological theories primarily on observations of humans. Third, Flourens was a **holist**, whereas Gall was a localizationist. That is, Flourens concluded from his experiments that even though low level muscle movements are localized in the brain, higher level mental functions are not. Unfortunately, Flourens' conclusion about mental functions is incorrect. It is, however, a logical consequence of trying to draw inferences about the human brain based on experiments with birds' brains.

Flourens' contributions can be summarized as follows. On the one hand, he developed the experimental procedure of ablation. This technique turned out to form the basis for later breakthroughs in the study of higher mental functions. In fact, it was Flourens' technique that was eventually used to establish the localization of cortical functions, which he opposed so vehemently. On the other hand, his major liability was drawing conclusions about higher mental functions of humans based on experiments with chickens. In particular, his holistic view of the brain (i.e., that separate mental functions are not subserved by different parts of the brain) is essentially incorrect. Instead, Gall's theory of localization of function turns out to come closer to the view scientists hold today.

As a general summary, we can say that even though Gall's methodology was deficient, his conclusions about cerebral localization were often accurate; likewise, it would be fair to say that even though Flourens' methodology was superior, his conclusions were essentially wrong. The two men's contributions can be contrasted as follows.

GALL	FLOURENS
Methodology (Anecdotal)—	Methodology (Experimental)—
Wrong	Right
Conclusions (Localization)—	Conclusions (Holism)—
Right	Wrong

Bouillaud

Jean Baptiste Bouillaud (1796-1881), a contemporary of Flourens and a student of Gall, advanced the theory of localization. Bouillaud was among the first to use disease to study localization of function, by correlating particular clinical symptoms with specific lesion sites in the brain. He followed Gall in arguing that language is controlled by the frontal lobe. More importantly, he emphasized that the power of language is distinct from the power of speech and furthermore that the two abilities are localized in different parts of the brain. Bouillaud, again quoted from Young, states: "It is important to distinguish the two causes which may be followed by loss of speech . . . ; one by destroying the organ for the memory of words [i.e., language], the other by the alteration of the nervous principle which presides over the movements of speech [i.e., speech]" (1970, pp. 138-139). In essence, Bouillaud was here laying the groundwork for distinguishing aphasia, a higher level deficit of language arising from cortical damage, from dysarthria, a lower level deficit of speech arising from brain stem damage.

In short, then, Bouillaud made two basic contributions to the study of language and brain: He was the first to use disease to study localization of function, and he set the stage for distinguishing between aphasia and dysarthria.

Broca

Localization of cortical function was finally demonstrated to the satisfaction of most neuroscientists by the French physician Pierre Paul Broca (1824-1884). Up until the time of Broca, followers of Gall and Bouillaud, on the one hand, and those of Flourens, on the other, were still hotly debating the localization issue. Broca, however, provided the evidence that convinced the majority of neuroscientists that the localizationist position was indeed correct.

Broca based his case primarily on two patients. First was Leborgne, a 51 year old male who had had brain seizures since his youth. At the age of 30, he lost his ability to produce language but not his ability to comprehend it. At the age of 40, Leborgne developed paralysis on the right side and became bedridden. (Recall that the left hemisphere controls the right side of the body.) Upon his death, an autopsy revealed extensive degeneration of the left hemisphere. Broca argued that the lesion had begun in the third convolution of the frontal lobe in the left hemisphere. In short, Broca correlated Leborgne's **expressive aphasia**—i.e., his inability to produce linguistic output—with (what began as) localized damage in the third frontal convolution, as illustrated schematically in Figure 9-3. Based on this evidence, in 1861 Broca reported his findings in a paper later translated into English as: "Remarks on the Seat of the Faculty of Articulate Language, followed by an Observation of *Aphemia*." (Broca used the term **aphemia** rather than **aphasia**, which was later introduced by Trousseau.) The case of Leborgne, however, was not completely conclusive since the patient's condition had degenerated slowly over the years and since he had numerous, diffuse brain lesions at his death.

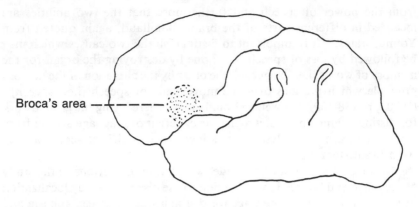

Figure 9–3.   Broca's area.

Broca offered additional evidence based on a second patient, Lelong, an 84 year old male who had had expressive aphasia for the past nine and a half years. The only words he could utter were *oui, non, trois, toujours,* and his name. Moreover, he was unable to write, although he knew how. His motor power, however, was intact: In other words, his inability to speak and write was not due to paralysis. After his death, an autopsy revealed localized damage to the third convolution of the frontal lobe in the left hemisphere, the same general area that Broca had argued was the site of Leborgne's original lesion. Later in 1861, Broca reported the case of Lelong.

Shortly thereafter, several other neurologists reported a total of ten cases of aphasia with damage to the third frontal convolution in the left hemisphere, essentially replicating Broca's findings. At the same time, a patient was reported with damage to the third frontal convolution in the right hemisphere, without any sort of language disturbance. Based on such cases, Broca contended a few years later that the left frontal lobe is specialized for language. The type of disorder described by Broca has come to be known alternatively as **Broca's aphasia, expressive aphasia** (because it affects linguistic output rather than comprehension), or **motor aphasia** (because the damage site is near the primary motor cortex).

In summary, Broca was the first to substantiate convincingly the localizationist theory of cortical function. Moreover, he was the first to propose the idea that the left hemisphere is specialized for language.

Wernicke

The next major step in our understanding of aphasia was put forward by the German Carl Wernicke (1848-1904). Wernicke was the first to differentiate the expressive aphasia described by Broca from **sensory aphasia**. Wernicke studied patients whose language disorders differed markedly from those described by Broca. In general terms, Broca's patients could comprehend speech but could not produce it; moreover, they displayed varying degrees of right-sided paralysis. In contrast, patients with sensory aphasia could not comprehend speech, but they could produce it (although it was characterized by errors); moreover, they exhibited a general absence of paralysis. Wernicke correlated this type of sensory disturbance with damage to the first convolution of the temporal lobe in the left hemisphere, as illustrated schematically in Figure 9-4.

Wernicke published his theories in 1874 as *Der aphasische Symptomenkomplex* (*The Aphasic Complex*). Consequently, the type of disorder described by Wernicke has come to be known alternatively as **Wernicke's aphasia, receptive aphasia** (because it affects linguistic comprehension rather than output), or **sensory aphasia** (because the damage site is near the sensory cortex).

In sum, whereas Broca localized language in the left hemisphere, Wernicke subdivided that hemisphere as subserving two different language functions: The frontal lobe controls expression, and the temporal lobe controls comprehension. Moreover, Wernicke's division of the left hemisphere into two different linguistic centers makes perfect sense anatomically. The expressive aphasia described by Broca results from damage near the motor cortex, which in turn controls outgoing motor movements, including the articulation of speech. The receptive aphasia described by Wernicke results from damage near the sensory cortex, in particular the primary auditory cortex (Heschl's gyrus), which processes incoming auditory stimuli, including speech.

Penfield and Roberts

More recently, research in the neurology of language has been advanced by Wilder Penfield and LaMar Roberts, two neurologists working at the Montreal Neurological Institute in the 1940's and 1950's. Penfield and Roberts were treating patients for epilepsy, a disorder characterized by abnormal electrical discharges in the brain. One method they used for treating this disease was to remove those areas of the brain that served as the sources for these discharges. However, they did not want to remove a part of the brain that subserved some necessary mental function such as language. In other words, they didn't want the cure for epilepsy to be worse than the disease itself.

In order to determine the function of different parts of the brain, Penfield and Roberts stimulated specific parts of the exposed cortex with a weak electrical current transmitted through silver probes. Since the cortex itself cannot feel pain, it was possible for them to remove part of the patient's skull under a local anesthetic and for the patient to remain conscious throughout the procedure. During stimulation they would have

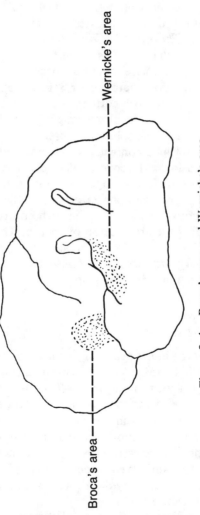

Figure 9–4. Broca's area and Wernicke's area.

the patient perform such tasks as naming an object in a picture. When they stimulated an area of the cortex subserving language, the patient would experience some sort of linguistic difficulty such as total arrest of speech, halting and slurred speech, repetitions, confusions of numbers while counting, or inability to name. It is impossible, however, to get a feel for their patients' responses without concrete examples. Penfield and Roberts state:

> An example is, 'This is a . . . I know. That is a . . . ' When the current was removed, the patient named the picture correctly. Another example is, 'Oh, I know what it is. That is what you put in your shoes.' After withdrawal of the stimulating electrodes, the patient immediately said 'foot.' Still another example is the inability to name a comb. When asked its use, he said, 'I comb my hair.' When asked again to name it, he couldn't until the electrode was removed. (1959, pp. 123–124)

It is interesting to note in passing that this last patient was apparently able to access the verb *comb* (as in *I comb my hair*), but not the noun *comb*.

Using this technique on numerous patients, Penfield and Roberts "mapped" the entire cortex. In 1959 they published the results of their studies as *Speech and Brain Mechanisms*. They were able to identify three discrete language centers in the brain. Their findings coincided, in general, with the earlier theories of Broca and Wernicke, except that they identified language centers in the cortex surrounding Wernicke's area and extending up to the supramarginal and angular gyri in the parietal lobe. In effect, they "expanded" Wernicke's area. In addition, they identified a third language area known as the **supplementary motor cortex**, which lies in the superior region of the frontal lobe anterior to the primary motor cortex. These areas are illustrated schematically in Figure 9-5. Moreover, they ranked these areas according to the degree of language dysfunction that damage to each area could be expected to cause. In descending order of importance, they are Wernicke's area, Broca's area, and the supplementary motor cortex.

Before leaving this section on the history of neurolinguistics, let me emphasize that we have touched only on a few of the major figures of the past 200 years. The scientists we have discussed, however, have made some of the most significant contributions to the study of language and the brain.

HEMISPHERICAL SPECIALIZATION

One of the most interesting findings to come out of the study of language and brain is that the left and right hemispheres of the brain are each specialized to carry out separate but complementary functions. A central

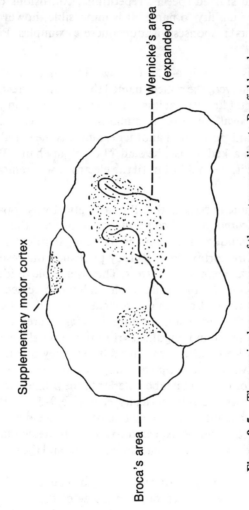

Figure 9-5. Three major language areas of the cortex according to Penfield and Roberts.

concept necessary to understanding the specific functions of each hemisphere is what is known as **dominance**.

Left Hemisphere Dominance for Language

Penfield and Roberts estimated that 98 percent of the population have their language centers in the left hemisphere. Thus, we might say that approximately 98 percent of the population is **left dominant** and approximately 2 percent is **right dominant**. (This is an oversimplification since a very small number of people have **bilateral dominance**, where the language function seems to be shared more or less equally by both hemispheres.) The term dominance as used here refers solely to the location of the primary language centers.

The evidence for left hemisphere dominance among humans comes from several sources.

Aphasia. It has been estimated that damage to the left hemisphere causes some form of aphasia in approximately 70 percent of all adults; damage to the right hemisphere causes an aphasic disturbance in only about 1 percent of the adult population.

Hemispherectomies. Adults undergoing a left hemispherectomy (surgical removal of the left hemisphere) generally suffer a permanent loss of their ability to process language; right hemispherectomies among adults are less likely to cause complete or permanent loss of the language function.

Planum Temporal. The planum temporal is a white fiber tract underneath both the left and right temporal lobes. Brain researchers such as Geschwind and Levitsky have found that this structure is larger in the left hemisphere in approximately 65 percent of adults. Moreover, other researchers such as Wada and Hamm have found that the planum temporal in fetuses is larger in the left hemisphere. Such findings may indicate that left hemisphere dominance in humans is biologically determined; that is, that the genetic program actually builds more neuronal structure into the left hemisphere to "enable" it to acquire language.

Subcortical System. The thalamus, part of the higher brain stem, is the lowest structure in the central nervous system to have a left and right hemisphere. Damage to the left side of the thalamus causes such linguistic dysfunctions as involuntary repetitions and naming difficulties; damage to the right side of the thalamus, however, generally does not.

Wada Test. In 1949 Juhn Wada reported on a new procedure for determining the brain dominance of an individual. In this procedure, the patient lies on his or her back in a comfortable position, and is instructed to count and move the fingers of both hands rapidly. At this point, sodium amytal, a sedative, is injected into either the left or right internal carotid artery in the neck. If the sodium amytal is injected into the left internal carotid, it will depress activity in the left hemisphere, and vice versa. This has the effect of temporarily paralyzing the opposite side of the body. If the affected hemisphere is non-dominant, then the counting stops and starts again within 30 seconds. The patient is able to speak, name, and read correctly, and remembers the paralysis. However, if the affected hemisphere is dominant, then the patient stops counting for one minute or longer, has difficulty in speaking, naming, and reading, and does not recall the paralysis. The results of this test indicate that the vast majority of humans are left dominant.

Dichotic Listening. In the 1960's, Doreen Kimura developed a technique called dichotic listening which also supports the claim that most humans are left dominant. In this procedure, a normal subject is fed two auditory signals simultaneously through headphones. Even though each ear has neural connections to both hemispheres, the most direct pathway is to the contralateral hemisphere. Thus, for all practical purposes, a signal fed to the right ear will be sent to the left hemisphere for processing, and vice versa. When the two stimuli are linguistic (i.e., words), the subject reports hearing the word that was presented to the right ear. Thus, for example, a subject presented with *boy* to the right ear and *girl* to the left ear would report having heard *boy* but not *girl*. Since the vast majority of subjects tend to have this **right ear advantage** for linguistic stimuli, these findings support the claim that most humans are left dominant.

Subsequent dichotic listening experiments have shown that most subjects have a right ear (i.e., left hemisphere) advantage for all types of linguistic stimuli: speech, nonsense syllables (e.g., /kɛb/, /lʌb/), synthetic speech, speech played backwards, CV syllables, and even Morse code. On the other hand, these same subjects have a **left ear advantage** (i.e., right hemisphere) for environmental sounds: nonspeech sounds, clicks, tones, buzzes, laughter, coughing, and so forth. In short, it seems that most humans process any auditory signal that is perceived as language or language-like in the left hemisphere; any other sort of auditory signal will be processed by the right hemisphere. Once again, this evidence suggests that the left hemisphere in most humans is specialized for language processing.

Split Brains. In the 1960's, another major breakthrough in the theory of left hemispherical dominance was made by Roger Sperry and his colleagues, most notably Michael Gazzaniga. Earlier work had shown that severe cases of epilepsy could be treated by surgically severing the corpus callosum, the white fiber tract connecting the two cerebral hemispheres.

The epileptic seizures originating in one hemisphere would travel to the other via the corpus callosum and increase the magnitude of the seizure. By severing the corpus callosum, the abnormal electrical discharges were confined to one hemisphere and, in fact, seizures dramatically decreased in both hemispheres. The effect of this operation is illustrated schematically in Figure 9–6. Thus, the normal brain can send information back and forth between hemispheres, but the split brain cannot.

It would seem that the effects of severing the corpus callosum would be devastating; remarkably, however, they are not. In fact, the overt behavior of a split-brain patient does not differ significantly from that of a normal subject. This is because under ordinary circumstances, both hemispheres receive sensory information simultaneously. That is, for example, when you look at an object, each eye sends information to both hemispheres simultaneously.

What is relevant to our purposes, however, is that Sperry and his colleagues discovered a way of sending visual information selectively to only one hemisphere. A normal brain, of course, would simply transmit this information to the other hemisphere via the corpus callosum, giving both halves of the brain access to the information. A split brain, however, cannot do this since the pathway for transmitting information has been severed. The effect, then, is to "trap" information in one hemisphere or the other. By covering one of the patient's eyes completely and blocking out the left or right visual field of the remaining eye, Sperry could control

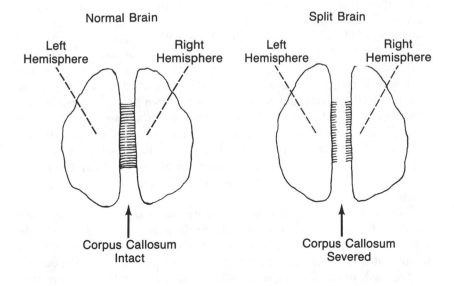

Figure 9–6. Normal brain and split brain.

which hemisphere received the information. This method depends on the fact that each eye has both a left and a right visual field; information from each visual field is transmitted to the contralateral hemisphere. Thus, if the left visual field were blocked, information (e.g., a written word) could be presented to the right visual field and thereby sent only to the left hemisphere. On the other hand, if the right visual field were blocked, information could be presented to the left visual field and thereby sent only to the right hemisphere. This procedure is presented schematically in Figure 9–7.

Now that we have some idea of how split-brain patients allow us to examine the processing capacity of each hemisphere independently of the other, let's take a look at some of the experiments that Sperry and his colleagues conducted. (In the following discussion, when I say that a stimulus was presented to either the left or right hemisphere, keep in mind that the stimulus was presented visually to one field of vision, as just described.) One experimental paradigm that Sperry used was to seat the patient at a desk, facing a screen. Hidden from view beneath the desk was a tray containing small objects. Sperry would then feed a word (flashed onto the screen) to one of the hemispheres. The patient would then be instructed to reach into the tray with the opposite hand (remember: contralateral control) and retrieve the appropriate object.

When Sperry presented a word such as *key* to the left hemisphere, the patient would retrieve a key from the hidden tray with his or her right hand; then, when asked to name the object, the patient would say *key*. However, when Sperry presented a word to the right hemisphere, the patient would be able to retrieve the object with the left hand, but *would not be able to name the object*. In fact, the patient had no conscious knowledge of what the left hand was doing. This suggests that the dominant hemisphere (the left, in all of Sperry's subjects) can process language both actively and passively; that is, it can both comprehend and produce linguistic stimuli. On the other hand, the non-dominant (i.e., right) hemisphere can process language passively but not actively. It can "recognize" a word such as *key* but cannot "produce" the word. In other words, in order for a human to be conscious of a linguistic stimulus, the dominant hemisphere must have access to information regarding that stimulus.

In another experiment, Sperry presented verbs such as *nod, wink*, and *smile* to the right hemisphere of split-brain patients. In each case, the subject was instructed to carry out the command presented on the screen. (Note that this would require a nonlinguistic response, just as the object-finding task in the first experiment did.) However, when the verb was presented to the right hemisphere, the patient not only failed to carry out the command, but also behaved as if he or she had seen nothing. Earlier

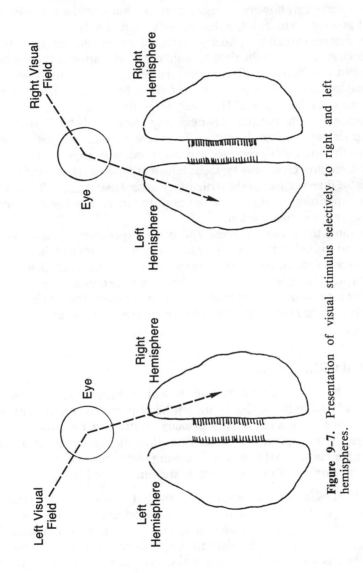

Figure 9-7. Presentation of visual stimulus selectively to right and left hemispheres.

199

we saw that the non-dominant hemisphere is able to process nouns at least passively (e.g., pick an object from a tray hidden from view). The results of this experiment, however, suggest that the non-dominant hemisphere cannot process verbs at all, either actively or passively.

In another experiment, Sperry presented incomplete sentences (e.g., *Mother loves* _____) to the right hemisphere of his patients. In each case, the patient was instructed to complete the sentence by pointing with the left hand to one of four words (e.g., *nail, baby, broom, stone*), which were fed to the same hemisphere. However, when the stimuli were fed to the right hemisphere, the patients only randomly pointed to *baby*. Even though this experiment requires the patient to choose a noun, the patient must integrate the noun into a sentence in order to make an appropriate choice. This task requires processing syntactic information, namely that the correct noun is the direct object of the structure *Mother loves* _____. The results of this experiment suggest that the non-dominant hemisphere cannot process syntactic information.

In sum, the results of these and other experiments performed by Sperry and his colleagues provide rather dramatic evidence that the left hemisphere is specialized for language in most humans. In particular, this research provides at least tentative evidence that the dominant hemisphere alone can process language actively. On the other hand, the non-dominant hemisphere appears to have some capacity for processing noun-like stimuli passively.

Left Brain-Right Brain

So far we have dealt almost exclusively with evidence that most human beings are left dominant; that is, the left hemisphere houses the language centers in the brain and exercises primary control for the processing of language. The implication underlying this discussion is that each hemisphere is specialized for carrying out certain specific yet complementary types of tasks, which are summarized below.

Left Hemisphere. As we have seen, the left hemisphere is specialized for language. This includes not only speaking and listening, but also reading and writing. In short, anything that is perceived as language-like is apparently processed by the left hemisphere. In addition, the left hemisphere is specialized for temporal order perception, the processing of any stimuli that arrive at different points in time. Suppose, for example, you were presented with a sequence of two tones, a buzz, and three more tones. If you were asked to determine where the buzz occurred in the series (i.e., third), your answer would require left hemisphere processing. Similarly, the left hemisphere seems to be specialized for arithmetical calculations, such as determining that $1 + 2 + 3 = 6$. Related to this is logical reasoning; for example, determining that if A is greater than B and B is greater than C, then A is greater than C.

Note that all of these left hemisphere functions involve step by step processing. That is, in order to process the sentence *Denny eats ketchup on fried chicken*, you need to know that *Denny* precedes *eats* and *eats* precedes *ketchup*. In order to determine when a buzz occurred amid a series of tones, you need to keep track of the tones. In order to determine that $1 + 2 + 3 = 6$, you need to know that $1 + 2 = 3$ and that $3 + 3 = 6$. In order to determine that A is greater than C, you need to know that A is greater than B and B is greater than C. All of these tasks require at least two or more sequential steps.

Right Hemisphere. In contrast to the left hemisphere, the right hemisphere is specialized for nonlinguistic auditory stimuli. This would include environmental sounds such as horns, whistles, laughter, the squeal of tires, waves breaking on the beach, musical instruments, melodies, and so on. In short, any sound that is perceived as nonlinguistic is apparently processed by the right hemisphere. Likewise, the right hemisphere is specialized for visuospatial processing. This would include depth perception; one's orientation in space; the perception of pictures, paintings, photographs, and patterns; recognition of faces; and even the ability to dress oneself. Similarly, the right hemisphere seems to be specialized for stereognosis, the ability to perceive the form and weight of an object by handling it or lifting it. In other words, the right hemisphere is specialized for tactile recognition (i.e., recognition of an object by touch). This would include the ability to tell that a box filled with feathers is lighter than an identical box filled with lead.

All of these right hemisphere functions involve holistic processing. That is, in order to process the sound of a horn or even a laugh, you do not need to divide it into meaningful parts. In order to recognize a familiar face, you presumably do not do it piece by piece but rather as an integrated unit. In order to tell that a box of feathers is lighter than a box of lead, you do not go through a series of mental calculations to determine their respective densities (i.e., mass per unit volume). Rather, all of these tasks require simultaneous integration of information.

By way of summary, it might not be too far afield to make the following generalization: The left hemisphere is specialized for analysis, or breaking a whole into its parts, while the right hemisphere is specialized for synthesis, or combining the parts to form a whole. Because the study of hemispherical specialization is a relatively new field of inquiry, much of what is now being hypothesized is still subject to debate and further investigation. However, what we have covered here is summarized in the following table.

LEFT HEMISPHERE	RIGHT HEMISPHERE
Language	Nonlinguistic auditory processing
Temporal order perception	Visuospatial processing
Calculation	Stereognosis
Analysis	Synthesis

Handedness

Before leaving this section on hemispherical specialization, it might be worthwhile to say something about the relationship between dominance and handedness. The reason that this topic is important is that Broca introduced a misconception regarding this relationship, which unfortunately seems widespread even today. Broca inferred from one of his patients that left-handed people are right dominant, just as most right-handed people are left dominant. In other words, he set up a more or less absolute correlation between dominance and handedness.

As we discussed earlier, Penfield and Roberts estimated that roughly 98 percent of the population is left dominant, while the remaining 2 percent is right dominant. At the same time, it has been estimated that about 95 percent of the population is right-handed and about 5 percent is left-handed. Since the match between these figures is not perfect, this raises the question of how handedness relates to dominance. In general, there seems to be a high correlation between right-handedness and left dominance. However, most evidence indicates that left-handers are divided: Approximately 40 percent are left dominant and 60 percent are right dominant. These very general correlations are illustrated in the following table.

HANDEDNESS	DOMINANCE	PERCENT OF POPULATION
Right	Left	95 percent
Left	Left	2 percent
Left	Right	3 percent

This chart, however, does not tell the whole story. Two other factors seem to affect the relationship between handedness and dominance. One is familial left-handedness: The more left-handed people in a family, the greater the likelihood of right dominance in those left-handers. (Familial left-handedness also increases the likelihood of bilateral dominance in right-handers.) The second factor is strength of handedness, the number of tasks one does with the same hand. For example, someone who throws and bats with the right hand has greater "strength of handedness" than someone else who throws with the right hand but bats with the left. Strength of handedness, in turn, correlates with contralateral dominance. Thus, someone who is strongly left-handed is more likely to be right dominant than is someone else who is "weakly" left-handed. The relation between these "handedness" factors and dominance can be illustrated graphically as follows.

LEFT DOMINANCE   BILATERAL DOMINANCE   RIGHT DOMINANCE
Strong right-handedness
        Weak right-handedness
            Weak right-handedness and familial left-handedness
                Weak left-handedness
                    Weak left-handedness and familial left-handedness
                        Strong left-handedness
                            Strong left-handedness and familial left-handedness

In short, the farther to the right that a particular individual falls on this chart, the more likely that person is to have bilateral or right hemisphere dominance.

DISORDERS

In this section, we will discuss four general types of brain disorders that can affect either language or speech: aphasia, agnosia, apraxia, and dysarthria. Let's begin by drawing some general distinctions among these four types of disorders. **Aphasia** is an acquired disorder of language due to cortical damage. It is important to note that aphasia is acquired; that is, only a person who has already developed a linguistic system can be stricken with aphasia. For example, a person with brain damage present at birth (or sustained immediately afterward) which prevents the acquisition of language would not properly be said to have aphasia. Moreover, aphasia is specifically a language disorder. Although brain damage may result in several different types of syndromes, only one that involves a language dysfunction is properly called an aphasia. Finally, aphasia is due to cortical damage, or to damage to the white fiber tracts immediately underlying language centers in the cortex. Thus, for example, a person sustaining damage to the brain stem which results in inarticulate speech would not properly be said to have aphasia.

    Agnosia is a loss of comprehension of sensations (visual, auditory, tactile, etc.) due to cortical damage. It is important to note that with this disorder, the sensory system is intact, yet the individual cannot comprehend or recognize what has been sensed. Thus, for example, a person with visual agnosia can see perfectly well but cannot recognize what is seen; a person with auditory agnosia can hear perfectly well but cannot recognize what is heard. In order to get a feel for this difference between sensing something

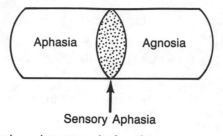

Sensory Aphasia

Aphasia = language dysfunction
Agnosia = loss of comprehension of sensation

Figure 9-8.   Relationship between aphasia and agnosia.

but not recognizing it, imagine that you are listening to someone speak a language you do not understand, say, Greek. You can hear this person perfectly well, yet you cannot understand what you hear. This situation, of course, would not constitute an agnosia, since there has been no cortical damage or loss of your ability to understand Greek. If, however, you had a stroke and could hear English but no longer understand it, this would be a form of agnosia.

As this example illustrates, aphasia and agnosia are not mutually exclusive. Thus, an acquired disorder of language due to cortical damage, which affects comprehension without disrupting the ability to sense, would technically be both an aphasia and an agnosia. In fact, such a syndrome describes an agnosia in general and a type of sensory aphasia in particular. The relationship between aphasia and agnosia is illustrated in Figure 9-8.

Apraxia is the loss of the ability to perform voluntary actions due to cortical damage, without the loss of motor power. It may be useful to think of apraxia as the mirror image of agnosia. Whereas agnosia affects comprehension, apraxia affects action. In both cases, however, the sensory-motor system for receiving stimuli and producing movement is intact. Thus, for example, a person who cannot smile on command, but later is perfectly able to do so spontaneously, has a form of apraxia. That is, the person is unable to perform a voluntary action, despite having the motor power to do so. As was the case with agnosia, aphasia and apraxia are not mutually exclusive. Thus, an acquired disorder of language due to cortical damage, which affects action without disrupting the motor power to act, would be both an aphasia and an apraxia. In fact, such a syndrome describes an apraxia in general and a type of expressive aphasia in particular. The relationship between aphasia and apraxia is illustrated in Figure 9-9.

Dysarthria is the loss of motor power to speak distinctly, resulting in slurred, inarticulate speech. Because dysarthria typically involves damage to the brain stem, it stands in contrast to aphasia, agnosia, and apraxia,

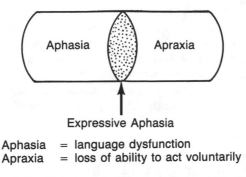

Aphasia = language dysfunction
Apraxia = loss of ability to act voluntarily

Figure 9-9.   Relationship between aphasia and apraxia.

which involve the cortex or the white fiber tracts immediately underlying it. Dysarthria cannot properly be said to be a true language disorder; instead, it is a problem in initiating and coordinating the motor movements of the various articulators to produce intelligible speech. I have included this brief mention of dysarthria solely to differentiate it from the other three higher order deficits.

Having distinguished among these various brain disorders, let's consider some specific types of aphasia, agnosia, and apraxia. It is important to keep in mind, however, that the terminology used to discuss brain disorders varies somewhat. As we saw earlier, Broca used the term **aphemia** for aphasia. Likewise, you will see **dysphasia** for aphasia, **anarthria** for dysarthria, and so on. With this in mind, let's take a look at some specific disorders.

Aphasia

Numerous types of aphasia have been proposed and discussed in the literature on the subject. Here, we will look at three of the most common types (Broca's, Wernicke's, and conduction), as well as three other types found in the literature (anomia, semantic aphasia, and word deafness).

Broca's Aphasia. This type of disorder, also known as **motor** or **expressive aphasia,** typically involves a lesion in the third frontal convolution of the dominant hemisphere. Note that this lesion is close to the motor cortex controlling the speech musculature. Symptoms usually include the following. First, motor function is normal; that is, the articulators are fully functioning. However, there is typically some paralysis on the side opposite the dominant hemisphere. Second, the patient's speech output is non-fluent; that is, it is hesitant, halting, labored, and lacks normal intonation. Third, the output is "telegraphic"; that is, it generally lacks grammatical morphemes, such as articles, prepositions, plural and possessive markers, tense markers on verbs, and so on. Thus, the more highly inflected the patient's language, the more severe the disturbance appears. For example, the output of a German-speaking patient with Broca's aphasia would be severely distorted, because German is highly inflected. Fourth, reading and writing usually exhibit the same deficiencies as speech. On the other hand, the patient's comprehension is usually fairly good. And the patient is usually self-monitoring; that is, aware of his or her mistakes and difficulties in speaking.

Let's now look at some examples of actual speech produced by patients with Broca's aphasia. In an unpublished article entitled "Classification of Language Disorders from the Psycholinguistic Point of View," Myrna Schwartz cites examples of such patients trying to describe a picture of a girl giving flowers to her teacher. Here is a sample of responses.

(a) *Girl is handing flowers to teacher.* Note the sporadic omission of grammatical morphemes. (Cf. *The girl is handing the flowers to her teacher.*)

(b) *The young . . . the girl . . . the little girl is . . . the flower.* Note the hesitant style. At each pause the patient seems to be giving up and starting over.

(c) *The girl is . . . is roses. The girl is rosing. The woman and the little girl was rosed.* Note here the use of *rose* as a verb.

Wernicke's Aphasia. This type of disorder, also known as **sensory** or **receptive aphasia**, typically involves a lesion in the first temporal convolution of the dominant hemisphere. Note that this lesion is close to the primary auditory cortex (Heschl's gyrus). Symptoms usually include the following. First, hearing is normal. Second, the patient's speech output is typically fluent, rather than hesitant or halting, and has a normal intonation contour. However, it generally consists of anywhere from 30 to 80 percent neologistic jargon. This term refers to "new words"— utterances that conform to the phonological structure of the patient's language, but are meaningless—for example, *bliven*, *glover*, and *devable*. Consequently, Wernicke's aphasia is sometimes called **neologistic jargon aphasia** (or simply jargon aphasia). In addition, the output is riddled with **phonemic paraphasia**, which includes repetition and reversal of phonemes. For example, *bowling shirt* might come out *bowling birt* or *showling birt*. (Phonemic paraphasia is sometimes called **literal paraphasia**, due to confusion in the older neurological literature between phonemes and letters of the alphabet. Patients were said to confuse "letters"; thus, "literal" paraphasia.) Third, the patient's comprehension is generally quite poor. Moreover, the patient is not self-monitoring; that is, the patient seems unaware that much of his or her output is error-ridden and incomprehensible.

On the other hand, the patient's syntax is relatively normal in the sense that, within a sentence, nouns appear where we would expect nouns, adjectives appear where we would expect adjectives, and so forth. For example, Jason Brown, in his book *Aphasia, Apraxia, and Agnosia,* cites a patient who responded to the question *What does 'swell-headed' mean?* with *She is selfice on purpiten* (1972, p. 65). Note that the syntactic structure of this sentence is perfectly normal: A subject (*she*) is followed by a verb (*is*) and a complement (*selfice on purpiten*). The problem is that the complement, where we would expect a lexical morpheme, is jargon.

Let's consider some more actual examples of the speech output produced by patients with Wernicke's aphasia. Brown cites another example from the patient just mentioned. In response to the question *What is your speech problem?*, the patient answered *Because no one gotta scotta gowan thwa, thirst, gell, gerst, derund, gystrol, that's all.* Note the phonemic repetition: *gotta scotta; thwa, thirst; gell, gerst;* and *gystrol, that's all.* Schwartz, in the article cited earlier, gives examples of aphasic patients describing a picture of a boy taking a cookie out of a cookie jar; the boy's mother and sister are standing in the picture. One patient's response is as follows.

> You mean like this boy? I mean noy, and this, uh, meoy. This is a kaynit, kahken. I don't say it. I'm not getting anything from it. I'm getting. I'm dime from it, but I'm getting from it. These were expreshez, agrashenz and with the type of mechanic is standing like this . . . . and then the . . . I don't know what she is goin other than . . . And this is deli, this one is the one and this one and this one and . . . I don't know.

Note that the output is fluent; it is not labored and there are few hesitations. Likewise, the syntax is relatively normal (*You mean like this boy?*; *I'm not getting anything from it*; *I don't know,* etc.). On the other hand, the output is so jargon-ridden that it is unintelligible.

Before leaving this section, let me try to clear up one point of potential confusion. We have drawn a distinction between Broca's aphasia, which is primarily a deficit in linguistic expression, and Wernicke's aphasia, which is primarily a deficit in linguistic comprehension. It is clear, however, that a major symptom of Wernicke's aphasia is the production of neologistic jargon, which appears to be a problem in expression. This is not a contradiction. The expression problem in Wernicke's aphasia is thought to be primarily a *result* of the fundamental deficit in comprehension.

Conduction Aphasia. This type of disorder typically involves the **arcuate fasciculus**, the association fibers connecting Broca's area and Wernicke's area and the adjacent cortex. In other words, conduction aphasia results from a disruption in the transfer of information between the language reception area and the language expression area. The primary symptom is the inability to repeat utterances. This makes sense anatomically, since linguistic input can be received (in Wernicke's area), but the information cannot be transmitted to the linguistic expression center (in Broca's area). Likewise, reading aloud is difficult for someone with conduction aphasia. On the other hand, output is generally fluent, in contrast to Broca's aphasia; but comprehension is typically normal or only mildly disturbed, in contrast to Wernicke's aphasia. Also, patients are generally self-monitoring. For example, Brown cites a patient who repeatedly interjected such comments as *Your baby could do better than I can* and *I can't do anything; what's wrong with me* (1972, p. 87).

Let's consider some of the actual speech of patients suffering from conduction aphasia. Brown describes a patient who responded to the question *Have you any headaches?* as follows: *Had one three to four week . . . days, Monday, Tuesday, Wednesday, Thursday, and Thursday it started to go away* (1972, pp. 87-88). Apparently, this patient is trying to access the word *Thursday* but cannot do so directly. Thus, she starts at the beginning of the week, goes through the days of the week, and is able to continue when she gets to Thursday. Note, however, that this pathological behavior is an exaggeration of normal behavior. If, for example, you are asked which letter of the alphabet precedes *L*, you might access *K* indirectly by reciting the alphabet up through *L*. Likewise, you might do something similar if asked to name the line of the Lord's Prayer that precedes *Give us this day our daily bread*. (Try it. What procedure do you use for coming up with the line?) Brown asked the same patient, *Can you give me the date (February 6)?* She replied, *It's the fu . . . 1-2-3-4-5, oh I don't know, there seems to me there must be something I could do but I don't know what it is* (1972, p. 88).

The major symptoms of Broca's, Wernicke's, and conduction aphasia can be summarized in tabular form as follows.

	BROCA'S	WERNICKE'S	CONDUCTION
LESION SITE	Third frontal convolution	First temporal convolution	Arcuate fasciculus
LANGUAGE OUTPUT	Non-fluent	Fluent	Fluent
COMPREHENSION	Unimpaired	Severely impaired	Unimpaired
SELF-MONITORING	Yes	No	Yes
PARALYSIS	Yes (contralateral)	No	Contralateral weakness
MAIN CHARACTERISTIC	Labored "telegraphic" output	Neologistic jargon	Severely impaired repetition

Anomia. This type of disorder has been associated with a lesion of the angular gyrus in the dominant hemisphere, along with diffuse lesions in the temporal lobe. The primary symptom involves the inability to name objects and general problems in accessing specific words. Consequently, the speech output appears empty, vague, and ridden with clichés. Patients tend to use an abundance of indefinite nouns, such as *gismo, thingamabob, whatchamacallit,* and *thing.* Their speech contains numerous circumlocutions, for example *what you drink out of* for *cup.* On the other hand, the output is fluent (unlike that in Broca's aphasia), comprehension is normal (unlike that in Wernicke's aphasia), and repetition is normal (unlike that in conduction aphasia).

Semantic Aphasia. This type of disorder has been associated with lesions in the temporal lobe of the dominant hemisphere. In fact, some specialists consider this disorder to be a mild form of Wernicke's aphasia. The primary symptom, **semantic paraphasia**, refers to the inappropriate use of words. For example, Brown cites the following utterance from a patient diagnosed as having semantic aphasia: *My son is just home from Ireland. He is a flying man* (1972, p. 32). Note the use of *flying man* for what appears to be *pilot.* Brown cites another example, this one written: *There are certain incidence which unfolded from my last living time in England Therefore I would rather not inform people of the last month of my Last England Life* (1972, p. 45). Once again, note *my last living time in England* and *my last England life* for something like *the last time I lived in England.*

Word Deafness. This type of disorder has been associated with the border of Heschl's gyrus and Wernicke's area in the temporal lobe of the dominant hemisphere. Patients with this disorder have normal hearing but cannot understand speech. Obviously, they have a severe comprehension problem and their ability to repeat is profoundly disrupted. On the other hand, their self-generated speech output is fluent and correct. Patients' comments on their disorder are especially revealing. Brown cites one patient who said *I can hear quite well but I don't understand; I can hear a fly flying past me* (1972, p. 127). Brown reports another patient as saying *Voice comes but no words. I can hear, sound comes, but words don't separate* (1972, p. 129).

Agnosia

Several different types of agnosia (disorders involving comprehension) have been noted and discussed in the literature. Here, however, we will briefly discuss only three: apperceptive visual agnosia, prosopagnosia, and autotopagnosia. Although these disorders do not affect language, they are of interest because, first, they exhibit certain parallels with linguistic disorders and, second, they provide additional evidence for the localization of various cognitive functions.

Apperceptive Visual Agnosia. This disorder typically involves bilateral lesions in the occipital lobe, which houses the visual centers in the cortex. The primary symptom of this disorder is the inability to recognize objects, even though vision itself is intact. (This disorder is similar to what is sometimes known as **cortical blindness**.) According to Brown, a patient with apperceptive visual agnosia can sometimes identify an object "upon touching it or perceiving it through another modality [e.g., smell]. . . . In recognition tasks, the patient will peer at or around an object. . . . or he will search for an object directly before him [as if nearsighted], at times identifying it when it falls in his peripheral field" (1972, pp. 204–205). Once again, the point to note is that the patient has no vision problem, but simply cannot recognize objects. It would be as if you were presented with a typewriter and you could see it, yet were unable to recognize it. However, upon receiving stimuli through some other modality (e.g., touching the keys or listening to someone type), you then were able to identify it.

Prosopagnosia. This disorder, which describes the inability to recognize faces, has been associated with lesions in the occipital lobe of the non-dominant hemisphere (usually the right). As with apperceptive visual agnosia, the patient's vision is perfectly normal, but in this case the symptoms are more specific—the primary dysfunction lies in the inability to recognize faces. Of one patient, Brown states:

> he was unable to recognize members of his family, the hospital staff or his own face in the mirror. . . . There was hesitancy in differentiating photographs of men and women, particularly if other cues, e.g., dress, hair length, were obscured. . . . He was generally able to guess the age of a face within a ten-year range, though performance was well below normal on this test. . . . Lincoln's face was excellently described from memory as 'tall, angular with a small beard, large nose and tasselled [sic] hair,' but he was uncertain about a standard portrait fitting this description quite perfectly. (1972, p. 226)

Note the correlation between the site of the lesion and the patient's symptoms: The right hemisphere controls visuospatial processing.

Autotopagnosia. This disorder, which describes the inability to recognize parts of the body, has been associated with lesions in the parietal lobes of both hemispheres. As with prosopagnosia, the disruption of comprehension is quite specific. Even though the peripheral sensory system is intact, the patient cannot identify body parts. Brown has this to say about autotopagnosia:

one case, asked to show his elbow, said 'My elbow, an elbow would be over there (pointing to the door).' A moment later, however, he was able to match the body part (elbow) to the correct name. Next asked to point to his forehead, he motioned in the air in front of him saying, 'It should be to the right of the door.' Asked what he was looking for, he replied, 'a forehead.' When asked what a forehead was, he said, 'I should know that,' and apologized for his poor performance. Patients may indicate through their response that they understand the command, as in De Renzi's case who, in connection with the word 'wrist,' said, 'there is the wristwatch,' or to 'ankle' spoke of his children breaking their ankles, though still unable to point correctly. (1972, p. 246)

It is worth emphasizing that autotopagnosia is almost certainly not a special case of sensory aphasia. Note that the last-mentioned patient apparently had no trouble in comprehending the *words* for wrist and ankle (he was able to use them appropriately, as in *wristwatch*); instead, his problem is recognizing the *objects* themselves.

Apraxia

Numerous types of apraxia (disorders of expression) have been discussed in the neurological literature. As was the case with agnosia, however, we will look briefly at only three: facial, ideational, and dressing apraxia.

Facial Apraxia. This disorder, which describes the inability to perform voluntary actions with the face, lips, and tongue, is generally due to lesions near Broca's area. (Recall that Broca's area is very close to that part of the primary motor cortex which controls the facial musculature.) Hughlings Jackson, in 1878, was the first to describe this disorder. He noted that patients with expressive aphasia were unable to carry out voluntary actions with their lips and tongues, yet they were able to do so spontaneously. For example, he noted a patient who was unable to stick out his tongue on command, but yet was able to do so spontaneously when licking his lips. Not surprisingly some form of facial apraxia has been found in 90 percent of patients with Broca's aphasia and 33 percent of patients with conduction aphasia. However, this disorder has also been noted in left-brain-damaged patients without aphasia. Thus, it is a separate disorder from Broca's aphasia.

Ideational Apraxia. This disorder, which describes the inability to use objects appropriately, has been associated with lesions in the left hemisphere where the parietal and occipital lobes meet. Brown describes a patient with ideational apraxia as follows:

when told to demonstrate how to brush his teeth, he did so promptly, but when given a toothbrush and asked to demonstrate its use, he first brushed his nails, then his pants, and only with much prompting did he finally use the toothbrush correctly. . . .

The patient is asked to call the operator on the telephone. He picks up the receiver and holds it properly to his ear, then with his right hand presses down on the tone button, saying, 'I don't know how to do it.' Encouraged, he continues to push on the button, then runs his fingers over the dial, stumbles into the second hole, and dials #2 repeatedly. (1972, p. 166)

The important point to note here is that it is the use of objects that causes the greatest problems for the patient. In the first example, he can use his finger to show how he brushes his teeth; he just can't use a toothbrush. Similarly, in the second example, the patient recognizes the phone (he puts the receiver to his ear), but has difficulty in carrying out the voluntary action of dialing it.

Dressing Apraxia. This disorder, which describes an inability to perform the voluntary actions involved in getting dressed, has been associated with lesions in the non-dominant hemisphere. Brown describes a patient, apparently the first case on record, "who did not know which was the inside or outside of his coat, put his clothes on upside down and his legs into the coat sleeves" (1972, p. 190). There is some sentiment that this disorder may actually be a type of agnosia, since some patients do not seem to comprehend the function of clothing. (A true apraxia would involve recognizing the clothes, yet being unable to perform the voluntary action of putting them on.) In either case, note the correlation between damage to the non-dominant (usually right) hemisphere and the deficit in visuospatial processing.

Before leaving this section on disorders, let me reiterate a few points. First, although I have presented each disorder as a discrete, self-contained syndrome, it is important to understand that such isolated, well-defined cases are relatively rare. Rather, cortical damage, even when it is very narrowly localized, may cause symptoms of two or more disorders to appear. We noted, for example, that facial apraxia occurs with 90 percent of the cases of Broca's aphasia. Likewise, anomia may occur in conjunction with other aphasic syndromes. And so on. Moreover, keep in mind that the best we can do at present is to make correlational and statistical statements. That is, damage to area A in the brain causes symptoms X, Y, and Z in B percent of the cases observed. Likewise, it is worth remembering that each syndrome (e.g., Broca's aphasia) is essentially a cover term for the correlation between specific cortical damage and a set of symptoms that typically coincide (e.g., non-fluency, near-normal comprehension, right-sided paralysis, and so on).

Second, all the disorders we have discussed (with the exception of dysarthria) are higher level, in the sense that they involve damage to specific areas of the cerebral cortex or the white fiber tracts underlying them. That is, these disorders involve either the interpretation of sensations (on the comprehension side) or conscious voluntary action (on the expression side).

Third, even though they are not specific to language, various agnosias and apraxias are relevant to the neurology of language for two reasons. First, language disorders involving comprehension and expression (Wernicke's and Broca's aphasia, respectively) parallel more general disorders involving comprehension and expression (agnosia and apraxia, respectively). Second, different types of agnosia and apraxia support the theories of both hemispherical specialization and localization of function, just as different types of aphasia do.

SUMMARY

Let's go over what we have covered in this chapter. We began with four observations about the neurology of language. However, we had no immediate explanation for these phenomena. Thus, we constructed a (partial) theory of neurolinguistics to account for our four original observations. This theory is based in part on the anatomy of the central nervous system—in particular, the left and right hemispheres and the frontal, temporal, occipital, and parietal lobes. In addition, this theory makes use of such concepts as localization of function, hemispherical dominance, hemispherical specialization and handedness. We have also seen that cortical damage can cause aphasia, an acquired disorder of language. Within this general category, different damage sites typically coincide with different complexes of symptoms, most notably Broca's aphasia, Wernicke's aphasia, and conduction aphasia. Finally, we have seen that damage to the cortex outside of the language centers can cause deficits in comprehension (agnosia) and expression (apraxia), and damage to the brain stem can cause a speech deficit (dysarthria).

As usual, I want to emphasize that there is a great deal more to the study of neurolinguistics than what we have been able to cover in this one short chapter. However, you have now been exposed to some of the basic ideas in the field; if you want to learn more, the readings at the end of the chapter will introduce you to additional information about the neurology of language. Meanwhile, the following exercises can be used to check your understanding of the principles we have covered.

EXERCISES

(1) When you go to sleep, you become unconscious, which suggests a decrease in cortical activity. However, you continue to breathe and your heart continues to beat. Does this mean that these functions are not controlled by the central nervous system? Explain.

(2) Assume you are left hemisphere dominant, you are not a musician, and you are listening to a musical composition by Bach. Which hemisphere is most likely to process this stimulus?

(3) Dr. Drool claims that word deafness is a form of apraxia. Is he right or wrong? Explain.

(4) Most patients cited in the neurolinguistics literature have incurred brain damage from strokes rather than from tumors or trauma. Why would stroke patients provide the most interesting evidence for the localization of linguistic function in the brain?

(5) An adult, right-handed stroke patient exhibits the following symptoms: normal (or near-normal) comprehension, fluent output, and the inability to repeat words and sentences.
(a) What type of aphasia is this most likely to be?
(b) Where is the lesion most likely to be?

(6) What type of aphasia is illustrated by the following utterance, from a patient cited by Brown (1972, pp. 64-65)?
"What my fytisset for, whattim tim saying got dok arne gimmen my suit, suit to Friday . . . . I ayre here what takes zwei the cuppen seffer effer sepped . . . ."

(7) The following account of an accident victim was published in the news within the last few years. What type of aphasia does the accident victim appear to have? List five symptoms mentioned in the passage that would support your answer.
BOSTON (AP)—A man whose brain was impaled by a 7-foot crowbar is home from the hospital, asking about neighborhood events and rousting slugabed teen-aged sons, his wife said Tuesday. . . .
Thompson's head was pierced by the metal crowbar when the station wagon he was driving struck a tree and the crowbar hurled forward from the back seat.
When rescuers reached Thompson after the May 1 accident, the crowbar was extended three feet from his forehead and three feet from the back of his head.

The ends of the 40-pound tool had to be sawed off before he could be removed from the car, but the rest of the crowbar remained in his head until he got to the hospital. The injury was on the left side of the brain, which controls speech.

Doctors say Thompson's vision and hearing were not impaired in the accident and he can understand everything that is said to him. . . . 'His speech is still halted and requires a good deal of effort, but we are very encouraged that he keeps doing better.'

Thompson is able to work, though his right leg is still weak. His right arm is paralyzed, but he is gradually learning to move it.

(8) A normal subject is presented with two auditory stimuli simultaneously, *see* in the left ear and *saw* in the right ear. The subject reports hearing *saw* but not *see*. Is this person left dominant, right dominant, bilaterally dominant, or non-dominant?

(9) Assume you are left-handed and have a history of left-handedness in your family. A team of neurologists performs the Wada test on your left and right hemispheres. In neither case do you have much trouble in speaking, reading, or naming. What is your cerebral dominance likely to be?

(10) Assume that a normal subject has the input to the right visual field blocked. A written command (e.g., *smile*) is presented to the left visual field. The subject smiles when presented with the stimulus. Explain how the subject is able to do this.

(11) True/False
   (a) The cerebrum is essentially made up of the two hemispheres of the brain.
   (b) Approximately 89 percent of all humans are left dominant.
   (c) Ataxia is a type of aphasia characterized by the inability to name objects.
   (d) Broca's aphasia is characterized by the absence of lexical morphemes.
   (e) Penfield and Roberts were the first to use disease as a means of studying localization of brain function.
   (f) Dysarthria is the loss of motor power to speak distinctly; it typically involves damage to the lower brain stem.
   (g) Flourens was essentially a holist even though he believed that certain higher level mental functions such as memory were localized in the brain.

(h) Right-handed people with a family history of left-handedness are more likely to be bilaterally dominant than other right-handed people.

(i) A patient with cortical blindness would be expected to have lesions in the parietal lobes.

ANSWERS TO EXERCISES

The following answers are, in some cases, not the only possible ones. Discussion of other possibilities is part of the exercises.

(1) No. Breathing and heart rate are controlled by the central nervous system, but they're controlled by the brain stem, not the cortex—the part of the brain that governs conscious mental activity.

(2) The right (i.e., the non-dominant) hemisphere. (Now imagine the same situation, but this time assume that you *are* a musician. Speculate on which hemisphere might process the music, and why.)

(3) Wrong. Word deafness is a deficit in comprehension, therefore, it would be more accurately classified as a type of agnosia.

(4) The damage from a stroke is more likely to be localized.

(5) (a) Conduction aphasia
    (b) Arcuate fasciculus of the left hemisphere

(6) Wernicke's aphasia

(7) Broca's aphasia is indicated by (1) damage to the left hemisphere; (2) unimpaired vision and hearing (this indicates that the injury was neither occipital nor temporal); (3) normal comprehension; (4) halted, labored speech; and (5) right-sided paralysis.

(8) Left dominant

(9) Bilateral

(10) The subject transfers the information from the right hemisphere through the corpus callosum to the left hemisphere, where the command can be interpreted.

(11) (a) T
     (b) F (98 percent)
     (c) F (anomia)
     (d) F (grammatical morphemes)
     (e) F (Bouillaud)
     (f) T

(g) F (lower level motor movements)
(h) T
(i) F (occipital)

SUPPLEMENTARY READINGS

1. Brown, J. (1972). *Aphasia, apraxia, and agnosia*. Springfield, IL: Charles Thomas.
2. Eccles, J. (1977). *The understanding of the brain*. New York: McGraw-Hill.
3. Luria, A. R. (1973). *The working brain*. New York: Basic Books.
4. Ornstein, R. (1973). Right and left thinking. *Psychology Today* (May), 87–92.
5. Penfield, W., and Roberts, L. (1959). *Speech and brain mechanisms*. Princeton, NJ: Princeton University Press.
6. Young, R. (1970). *Mind, brain and adaptation in the nineteenth century*. Oxford: Clarendon Press.

You are now prepared to read the relevant sections of all these works. Luria (3) provides a basic introduction to the brain sciences and it should be read first. Young (6) is a rich source of information concerning advances in cerebral localization during the nineteenth century. Penfield and Roberts (5) is a complete report of ten years of research on cerebral dominance and aphasia, using electrical stimulation of the cortex. Eccles (2), especially chapter 6 on "Brain, Speech, and Consciousness," contains a straightforward account of the "split-brain" experiments. Ornstein (4) is an elementary and lucid introduction to hemispherical specialization. Brown (1) provides a detailed source of clinical information on aphasia, agnosia, and apraxia.

Chapter 10

Conclusion

In Chapter 1, we discussed some examples of linguistic phenomena that specialists in allied fields might encounter and also outlined the general methodology that underlies theory construction in linguistics. In subsequent chapters, we continued this dual emphasis on data and theory. Each chapter began with some observations (data) that an adequate theory of linguistics should be able to explain and proceeded to construct a partial theory to account for these observations. In short, this book has continually emphasized the interdependence of data and theory that is at the heart of linguistics (as well as any other empirical field of inquiry). In this chapter I would like to elaborate a little on two contributions that linguistic theory can make to related disciplines. The more obvious one is that linguistic theory provides a way of explaining a vast array of phenomena that professionals in allied fields encounter on a daily basis. Somewhat less obvious is the fact that linguistic theory provides a model for explanation which professionals in neighboring fields may be able to transfer to their own disciplines. In short, linguistic theory can benefit allied fields on two levels: a practical level, by providing explanations for particular observations, and a theoretical level, by providing a model for analyzing data. I will take these up one at a time.

First, let's consider the practical contribution: explanation of data. By way of illustration, let us return briefly to the phenomena mentioned at the beginning of Chapter 1 and consider how the discussion in Chapters 2 through 9 might enable us to explain these phenomena. We started with the hypothetical case of a researcher in business communication who is trying to characterize how different management styles are reflected in the way that managers give directions to their employees. The researcher notes that one group of managers tends to give instructions like *Type this memo*, while another group gives instructions like *Could you type this memo?* Principles from pragmatics, in particular the distinction between direct and indirect speech acts, can be used to characterize these two different styles of giving directions. In this case, the researcher might note that the first group of managers tends toward direct speech acts, those in which the syntactic form (an imperative) matches the pragmatic function (an order). In contrast, the second group tends toward indirect speech acts, those in which the syntactic form (a *yes-no* interrogative) does not match the pragmatic function (an order).

We also looked at phenomena that might be encountered in the fields of education and composition. We saw that a kindergarten teacher might observe that students tend to give more correct responses to questions like *Which of these girls is taller?* than to questions like *Which of these girls is shorter?* The teacher might draw upon semantic theory and principles of language acquisition in order to explain this phenomenon, noting that children tend to acquire "unmarked" forms such as *tall* earlier than "marked" forms such as *short*. Note that *tall* carries fewer presuppositions than *short*. The question *How tall was the girl?* presupposes nothing about the girl's height—she might be 7 feet tall or only 4 feet tall. On the other hand, the question *How short was the girl?* presupposes that the girl is relatively short.

Principles from linguistic theory would also enable a composition instructor to understand the source of a syntactic structure like *I wanted to know what could I do* when encountered in a student's writing. The difference between this form and the standard form *I wanted to know what I could do* has a straightforward syntactic explanation. In standard English, *wh*-interrogatives in subordinate clauses do not undergo the rule of Subject-Verb Inversion (i.e., move the first auxiliary to the left of the subject). Some speakers, however, do apply this rule in indirect *wh*-interrogatives, leading to forms such as *I wanted to know what could I do*. (Note that the first auxiliary verb, *could*, has been moved to the left of the subject NP, *I*.) Furthermore, the instructor would note that such forms, because they are somewhat socially marked, may reflect negatively on the writer.

The last two phenomena mentioned in Chapter 1 were drawn from ESL and speech-language pathology. We pointed out that an ESL teacher might encounter a student who writes *I will taking physics next semester*. In trying to offer the student an explicit principle for constructing sentences of this type, the teacher can draw upon morphological and syntactic principles governing the relation between auxiliary verbs and the affix on the following verb form. The relevant rules here are (a) within a single clause the verb form following a modal (e.g., *will*) is always uninflected (e.g., *take*) and (b) the verb form preceding a present participle (e.g., *taking*) is always a form of *be*. The first principle alone would yield *I will take*; the second alone would yield *I am taking*; and the two together would yield *I will be taking*. Thus, any combination of principles that the student tries will result in an acceptable form.

Turning to speech-language pathology, we saw that a specialist in this field might encounter a child who says *tay* for *stay* but never *say* for *stay*. In order to evaluate and explain this form, the speech-language pathologist can draw upon principles from phonology and language acquisition. Here, for example, the omission of the /s/ in the /st/ cluster reflects the principle that single consonants are generally acquired before clusters. In fact, CV syllables are apparently universal, whereas CCV syllables are not. Moreover, the omission of the /s/ rather than the /t/ is explained by the tendency for stops (/t/) to be acquired before fricatives (/s/).

In short, language-related phenomena similar to those just described are encountered every day by researchers and teachers in the fields that neighbor linguistics. Linguistic theory, in turn, provides a system of categories and rules which can be used to analyze and explain such phenomena.

Now let's turn to the theoretical contribution that linguistic theory can make to specialists in allied fields: It may provide them with a model for analyzing the nonlinguistic (or quasilinguistic) phenomena within their fields. This, however, is not just speculation about a future state of affairs. During the last 25 years, a number of fields in the humanities and social sciences have looked to linguistic theory as a model for analyzing phenomena within their respective domains. Among these fields are those as diverse as folklore and anthropology, literary criticism, and rhetoric and composition.

Representative examples of this interest in linguistics among those outside the field are not hard to find. For instance, Robert Georges, a folklorist, states that "the theory and work of generative-transformational grammarians has direct implications for the study of traditional narrative [i.e., folktales]" (1970, p. 14). Similarly, Roger Fowler, a literary critic, states that "description *per se* is not the only way in which linguistics has been . . . employed in literary studies. . . . linguistic concepts have often been used . . . metaphorically to provide *models* of textual structure rather than *accounts* of the specific structures of sentences and texts" (1981, p. 19). Likewise, Ross Winterowd, a rhetorician, states that since the publication of Chomsky's *Syntactic Structures* in 1957, "composition teachers have been dazzled by the elegance of the notational system of the new grammar . . . , have been intrigued by the complexity and ingenuity of grammatical arguments; and . . . have allowed themselves to hope that from the new field would emerge *the* panacea for the ills of teaching composition" (1976, p. 197). The attraction that linguistic theory has had for specialists in other disciplines is summed up by the folklorist Lauri Honko, who states that "the only success-story in the humanities in the recent past [is] modern linguistic theor[y]'' (1979-1980, p. 6). Even though some of these high expectations have met with disappointment (see Newmeyer, 1983, Chapter 5, for discussion), there has nonetheless been a sustained interest in linguistic theory from practitioners in neighboring fields. Let's now take a look at some of the properties which the theory presented in this book has (or at least should have) and which may be applicable to other fields in the humanities and social sciences.

First, the theory should be **testable**; and therefore, it must necessarily be **explicit**. This criterion is necessary in order to make empirical (testable) claims about the structure of the phenomenon of interest; vague, inexplicit claims are impossible to test. Consider, for example, the following hypothetical statements.

(1)   We are living in the most corrupt era this country has ever seen.
(2)   More elected officials were indicted for felonies during the 1970's than during the entire first half of the 20th century.

The claim in statement (1) is simply too inexplicit to test. What indices is the writer using to define "corruption"? What length of time constitutes an "era"? The claim can be supported or denied only if these terms are made explicit. The claim in statement (2), on the other hand, is explicit enough to be tested. The subjects are well defined (elected officials), the criterion is well defined (felonies), and the time frames are well defined (1970 through 1979 and 1900 through 1949).

Consider how this principle applies to linguistic theory. You may recall from Chapter 1 that we tried to develop a theory of the distribution of antecedents for personal and reflexive pronouns: A personal pronoun cannot have an antecedent within its clause, and a reflexive pronoun must have an antecedent within its clause. Note that the statement of these two rules depends crucially on the concept of **clause**. Without a precise definition of this term, it is not possible to test our rules to see if they work (indeed, it would be impossible to hypothesize such rules in the first place). Even though we didn't define clause in Chapter 1, we could start with the following working definition: A clause is a syntactic structure consisting of one and only one main verb and its optional NP arguments (subject, object, indirect object, and so forth). Regardless of whether this definition is completely accurate, the point is that a precise definition of clause is absolutely essential for us to be able to test our theory.

The main point of this discussion is that demands of testability force linguists into stating their theories in precise, explicit terms. This, in turn, accounts for the widespread use of formal notation in linguistic theory. Even though nothing can be put into formal notation that cannot be put into words, the notation encourages the analyst to be precise and explicit.

Second, the theory should be **revealing**; that is, it should capture significant generalizations. This criterion is necessary because revelation is the primary reason for constructing a model in the first place; any analysis that is opaque or unrevealing is by definition useless. Failure to meet this criterion is similar to the freshman classification theme that sorts the seasons of the year into four and proceeds to point out that one follows the other in the order spring, summer, fall, and winter. Even though it is impossible to give a precise definition of what constitutes a revealing analysis, it is worth noting that we have relied on this concept, at least implicitly, throughout this book in choosing one analysis over another.

For example, in Chapter 4 we discussed the syntax of the following sentences.

(3)   Tiny Abner concealed the document.
(4)   Did Tiny Abner conceal the document?
(5)   What did Tiny Abner conceal?

Based on such sentences (among others), we constructed two theories concerning whether or not *conceal* takes an object. In our first theory, we proposed that if *conceal* appears in a declarative sentence (3) or a *yes-no* interrogative (4), it must have a direct object; however, if *conceal* appears in a *wh*-interrogative (5), it cannot have a direct object. This theory accounts for the data in (3–5), as well as all of the related data we discussed in Chapter 4. This theory, however, is not revealing. That is, it does not provide us with a clue as to why *conceal* sometimes is required to have an object and other times is prohibited from having one. Moreover, under this theory, it is completely unclear why one type of interrogative (*yes-no*) is required to have an object, while another type of interrogative (*wh*) may not have one.

On the other hand, our second theory proposed that in sentence (5), *what* originated in direct object position and was moved into sentence-initial position by a transformation. This theory, in contrast to our first, is revealing. That is, it does explain why *conceal* appears to have an object in some cases but not in others. In particular, this theory provides the following explanation: *conceal* has a direct object in all cases. If the object is not a *wh*-item (e.g., *the document*), it remains in object position. If, however, the object is a *wh*-item (e.g., *what*), it moves to sentence-initial position. Even though this theory does not explain why a language would have a rule of *wh*-Movement in the first place, it is nonetheless revealing in that it provides a straightforward and intuitively satisfying account of some rather perplexing data.

Third, the theory should be restricted to a characterization of **systematic** phenomena. This criterion is necessary because a theory is a model of a system that can't be observed directly, and only predictable, rule-governed phenomena can be modelled. Failure to meet this criterion results in a description in which the analyst "can't see the forest for the trees." In other words, the systematic properties of the phenomenon at hand are camouflaged by attention to unassociated detail. It would be like a theory of the game of baseball which, in addition to modelling systematic properties of the game such as the number of players, the number of innings, and the number of outs per inning, tried to account for idiosyncratic properties of the game such as depth of the outfield, the playing surface (grass versus astroturf), or the color of the players' uniforms or eyes.

It is just as difficult to give a precise definition of systematic phenomena as it was to define a revealing analysis earlier. One reason is that what may be systematic within one field may not be systematic in another. For example, the color of baseball players' eyes may be perfectly systematic within a theory of genetics, but it isn't systematic within a theory of baseball. Another difficulty is that the notion of systematic phenomena is somewhat dependent upon the point of view of the researcher. No researcher is going to study a phenomenon that he or she believes is not governed by principles which can be inferred through examination. The problem, of course, is that analysts sometimes disagree over what seems to be rule governed and principled versus what seems to be random and idiosyncratic.

Aside from such problems in defining the term, it is worth pointing out that we have relied on the concept of systematic phenomena throughout this book. For example, in our discussion of phonology in Chapter 6, we hypothesized that English has two systematic vowel lengths: relatively long and relatively short. This we characterized by means of the feature [±LONG]; and, through examining some relevant data, we postulated that a vowel is [+LONG] before a voiced consonant and [-LONG] before a voiceless consonant. At the same time, it is a well-documented fact that two speakers of English will pronounce the same vowel in the same phonological environment with different absolute lengths. Moreover, even the same speaker pronouncing the same word over and over will vary the vowel length. How then can we say that English has two degrees of vowel length? The answer is simple. We can do this by stipulating that the two degrees of vowel length are *systematic*. By using this term, we are essentially claiming that within the system of any speaker, there will be two types of vowels: relatively long and relatively short. Moreover, the relative length of the vowel is determined by the voicing characteristics of the following segment. The reason we don't try to model vowel lengths for individual speakers is that we assume that variation from speaker to speaker is idiosyncratic and for the most part unprincipled, at least within a theory of language. In short, by trying to account for all facets of some range of phenomena, the analyst risks confusing the systematic with the unsystematic and the relevant with the irrelevant.

At this point, it is appropriate to discuss how linguistic theory attempts to deal with the dichotomy between systematic and random phenomena. The theory articulated by Chomsky is what is termed a **competence** model. That is, it is a theory of the psychological system of unconscious knowlege that underlies our ability to produce and interpret utterances in a language. (You will recall that this is how we defined language in the first chapter.) In contrast to a competence model is a **performance** model; that is, a theory of the actual physical and psychological processes that a speaker might go through in producing and interpreting an utterance. Over 20 years ago, Chomsky made this distinction in a landmark book entitled *Aspects of the Theory of Syntax*:

> We thus make a fundamental distinction between *competence* (the speaker-hearer's knowlege of his language) and *performance* (the actual use of language in concrete situations). . . . linguistic theory is mentalistic, since it is concerned with discovering a mental reality [i.e., competence] underlying actual behavior [i.e., performance]. (1965, p. 4)

This is not to say that linguists have no interest in performance; certainly, performance data provides a way of studying competence. Instead, the point is that the central goal of linguistic theory, at least according to Chomsky, is to model the psychological system of unconscious knowlege that underlies behavior (competence) rather than the behavior itself (performance).

A good example of this distinction is provided by comparing two different interpretations of our rule of *wh*-Movement (move a *wh*-item to sentence-initial position). One interpretation of this rule would be to take it as a statement about performance. That is, when speakers of English produce an utterance such as *What did Tiny Abner conceal?*, they actually go through the following steps. First, they formulate a mental structure in which *what* is the direct object of *conceal* (did-Tiny Abner-conceal-what). Then they move *what* to sentence-initial position, thus creating another mental structure (what-did-Tiny Abner-conceal). Finally, they utter the sentence.

This, however, is not the way that *wh*-Movement is understood within linguistic theory. Instead, this rule is interpreted as part of competence. In postulating such a rule, the linguist is actually making a statement of the following sort: In order to make the judgments that speakers of English do in fact make about *wh*-interrogatives, they need to know that certain verbs (e.g., *conceal*) require a direct object. Moreover, they need to know that if the direct object is a non-*wh*-item (e.g., *document*), it is uttered in direct object position; however, if it is a *wh*-item (e.g., *what*), it is uttered in sentence-initial position. The linguist will try to explain this state of affairs by using the metaphor of movement; that is, the *wh*-item is "moved" from direct object position to sentence-initial position. In a competence model, the linguist is not claiming that speakers of English actually move *wh*-items from one position to another when they utter *wh*-interrogatives. Instead, "movement" is a convenient metaphor for describing the psychological system of unconscious knowledge which speakers possess, at least with respect to the distribution of *wh*-items and non-*wh*-items in English.

At this point it is appropriate to bring up a final concept closely associated with the study of competence, namely **generative grammar**. Simply put, a generative grammar is a theory of competence: a model of the psychological system of unconscious knowledge that underlies a speaker's ability to produce and interpret utterances in a language. Chomsky defines a generative grammar as follows:

> a generative grammar is not a model for a speaker or a hearer. It attempts to characterize in the most neutral possible terms the knowledge of the language [i.e., competence] that provides the basis for actual use of language by a speaker-hearer. . . . When we say that a sentence has a certain derivation with respect to a particular generative grammar, we say nothing about how the speaker or hearer might proceed . . . to construct such a derivation. These questions belong to . . . the theory of performance. No doubt, a reasonable model of language use will incorporate, as a basic component, the generative grammar that expresses the speaker-hearer's knowledge of the language; but this generative grammar does not, in itself, prescribe the character or functioning of a perceptual model or a model of speech production. (1965, p. 9)

A good way of trying to understand Chomsky's point is to think of a generative grammar as essentially a *definition* of competence: a set of criteria that linguistic structures must meet to be judged acceptable.

An analogy might make the point clearer. In *Transformational Syntax*, Andrew Radford compares a generative grammar to a municipal housing code, where the housing code is essentially a definition of house: that is, a set of criteria that housing structures must meet to be judged acceptable. Radford states:

> To interpret generative rules as well-formedness . . . conditions [i.e., as a definition of competence] . . . is to disclaim any implications about the processes and mechanisms by which sentence-structures might be formed. . . . Municipal regulations specify certain conditions that houses must meet: viz. they must be built out of certain materials, not others; they must contain so many windows of such-and-such a size, and so many doors; they must have a roof which conforms to

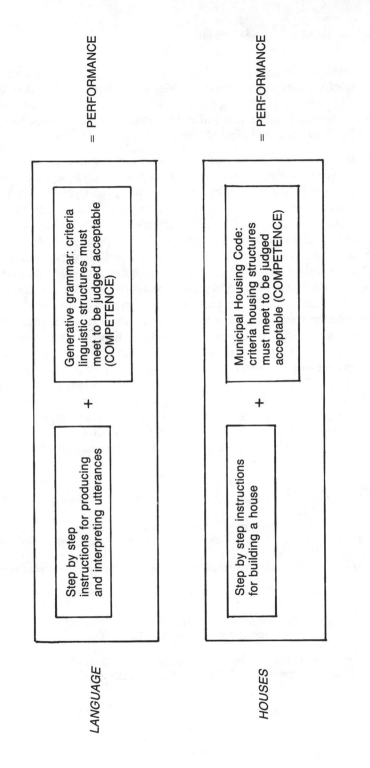

Figure 10-1. Relationship between competence and performance.

certain standards . . . and so on and so forth. Such regulations are in effect well-formedness conditions on houses. What they do not do is tell you HOW to go about building a house; for that you need a completely different set of instructions, such as might be found e.g. in *Teach Yourself Housebuilding*. (1981, pp. 90-91)

The analogy between a generative grammar and a municipal housing code is summarized in Figure 10-1. In short, to produce an acceptable sentence, a speaker needs *both* the step by step instructions specifying how to proceed *and* a generative grammar identifying the criteria linguistic structures must meet. Likewise, to construct an acceptable house, a builder needs *both* the step by step instructions specifying how to proceed *and* a municipal housing code identifying the criteria that housing structures must meet.

Let's review what we have covered in this chapter. We discussed two levels on which linguistic theory might benefit specialists in related fields. First, it is of practical use in that it provides explanations for phenomena that crop up every day in language-related disciplines. Second, it is of theoretical use in that it provides a model which professionals in allied fields may find helpful in analyzing nonlinguistic or quasilinguistic phenomena. In particular, linguistic theory attempts to be testable, revealing, and restricted to systematic phenomena. Specifically, it attempts to model linguistic competence (the psychological system of unconscious knowledge that underlies our ability to produce and interpret utterances in a language) by constructing a generative grammar (a set of criteria that linguistic structures must meet to be judged acceptable).

REFERENCES

Chomsky, N. (1965). *Aspects of the theory of syntax*. Cambridge, MA: MIT Press.
Fowler, R. (1981). *Literature as social discourse*. Bloomington, IN: Indiana University Press.
Georges, R. (1970). Structure in folktales: A generative-transformational approach. *The Conch, II*, #2 (September), 4-17.
Honko, L. (1979-1980). Methods in folk-narrative research. *Ethnologica Europaea, 11*, 6-27.
Newmeyer, F. (1983). *Grammatical theory*. Chicago: University of Chicago Press.
Radford, A. (1981). *Transformational syntax*. Cambridge, England: Cambridge University Press.
Winterowd, R. (1976). Linguistics and composition. In G. Tate (Ed.), *Teaching composition* (pp. 197-221). Fort Worth, TX: Texas Christian University Press.

Author Index

Subject Index